WHERE YOU WORK MATTERS

Student Affairs Administration at Different Types of Institutions

---

Joan B. Hirt

ACPA
College Student
Educators International

University Press of America,® Inc.
Lanham · Boulder · New York · Toronto · Oxford

DEDICATION

This book is dedicated to my parents, Ruth and Warren Hirt. They nurtured in me a love of learning that has sustained me throughout my career as an educator.

Contents

List of Tables

Preface

The path that led me to the student affairs profession was like that followed by hundreds of my colleagues. My undergraduate years at a liberal arts institution were rife with co-curricular experiences that enriched my collegiate life beyond measure. Upon graduation, I worked in the private sector for a few years but never fully embraced the corporate mentality. I wanted a career that would enable me to make some sort of social contribution. I longed to earn my livelihood doing something I found fulfilling. One day I realized my most rewarding college experiences were guided by campus administrators and that I could become such an administrator. I was thrilled there was a profession that would enable me to provide opportunities for college students like those that were provided for me.

Realizing that ambition, however, was more challenging than I had anticipated. My undergraduate institution enrolled fewer than 2,000 students. I had known most of my classmates personally. I had been on a first-name basis with most student affairs professionals on campus. The culture was nurturing and the institution provided many basic services. For example, I simply submitted a list of classes I wanted to take each semester and a week or so later my class scheduled appeared in my campus mailbox.

Imagine the culture shock, then, when in order to pursue my M.A.Ed. I found myself at a public research university that served more than 30,000 students. I knew no other students my first week on campus. Not only did I not know many administrators, I did not even recognize the titles many of those professionals held. There were services on the campus that had not existed at my undergraduate institution. Perhaps the most noticeable difference was the shift in responsibility. Whereas my undergraduate campus had taken care of many administrative tasks for me, my graduate institution expected me to take responsibility for those tasks. Rather than appearing magically in my campus mailbox, my class schedule was finalized only after I wended my way though multiple lines in the armory on campus to obtain signatures on the appropriate forms.

Upon completing the master's degree, my first professional position was at a comprehensive university that enrolled 7,000 students. The institution was part of a large state university system. Again, I needed to make fundamental adjustments in my perceptions. The focus on research at my graduate institution was replaced by a priority on teaching at the comprehensive school. The professionalism of the research university was exchanged for pragmatism at the comprehensive campus. Serving the best and brightest students was the mantra at the research university. Those at the comprehensive took great pride in serving students who might not otherwise have access to higher education.

At each turn in my professional path I encountered dramatically different institutional cultures and those cultures influenced my professional life. The work that I conducted, the relationships I had with others, and the rewards I reaped for my endeavors were different at each type of campus. So when I returned to a research university to complete my doctorate I moved from being a student affairs professional to studying the student affairs profession. I pursued that degree with the intent of becoming a faculty member in a graduate program in higher education and student affairs administration. I aspired to use what I learned from studying the profession to educate future professionals.

Indeed, it was a conversation among young professionals that led me to write this book. As I describe in Chapter One, I overheard a group of newly minted student affairs administrators talking about how different their work was from what they had experienced in their graduate program. They were employed at different types of institutions and found their lives to be quite unlike those they led at the research university where they had completed their master's degrees. As I pondered their comments, I realized that nothing in the student affairs literature addresses these differences. There are works that describe the different functional areas within the profession, and works that describe the skills that professionals need to succeed as a student affairs practitioner. Studies have been conducted on the characteristics of those in the profession and the career paths that successful professionals have followed.

When it comes to research on institutional type, however, the literature shifts fairly dramatically. The Carnegie system of classifying postsecondary institutions is the most widely cited framework in higher education. Studies have profiled the students that attend different Carnegie types of colleges and universities. There is also a wealth of literature on how faculty life varies by Carnegie type and an emerging body of work on academic administration at different kinds of campuses. The intersection between student affairs professional life and institutional type has not been explored, however. It is that gap in the literature that this book addresses.

Between 2002 and 2004 I conducted six studies that looked at the nature of professional life for student affairs professionals at different types of campuses. Overall, more than 1,100 student affairs professionals who worked at hundreds of two-year and four-year colleges and universities across the country provided the data I used to create the framework presented in this book. Distilling this mountain of data to explicate the nature of professional life at different institutional types was no easy task. What I attempt to do in the remaining chapters of this volume is to explain the findings from these studies.

In reviewing the results collectively, I found compelling consistencies across studies and powerful patterns among professionals from like institutions. After time, metaphors emerged to describe these professionals. In each chapter on an institutional type, I attempt to paint a general picture of what professional life is like for student affairs administrators at that type of postsecondary institution. The chapters are presented from a chronological perspective. That is, those institutional types founded first in the United States are addressed in earlier chapters of the book while those that emerged later in the country's history appear later in the volume.

I start in Chapter One by tracing the evolution of higher education in America as well as the history of the student affairs profession. I describe the studies that formed the basis for the book and offer some caveats about interpreting the work. The "standard bearers" who work at liberal arts institutions are described in Chapter Two. Professional life for the "interpreters" at religiously affiliated campuses is discussed in Chapter Three. The fourth chapter focuses on the "generalists" at comprehensive universities. In Chapter Five, I address the life of "specialists" found at research universities. The "guardians" at historically Black colleges and universities are described in the sixth chapter. The "producers" of the community colleges are the subjects of Chapter Seven. Finally, life for the "change agents" at Hispanic serving campuses is summarized in Chapter Eight.

In each chapter I start by elaborating a bit on the history of the institutional type. I discuss social and political factors that helped shape the type and how the type evolved over time to assume its current form. Next, I explore the nature of the campus. In this section I talk about the mission of the institutional type. I describe the roles that faculty assume given that mission. Finally, I profile the students who attend that particular type of institution. I do all this to provide readers with a context in which to understand the rest of each chapter. In the remaining sections, I talk about the nature of work, the nature of relationships, and the nature of rewards for student affairs professionals at the select type of institution. Throughout each chapter I use the words and stories of professional practitioners to illustrate the points I make.

In the concluding chapter I summarize how professional practice for student affairs administrators differs by institutional type. I suggest the types of skills and experiences that are needed to succeed in the different campus settings. This synopsis leads to a discussion of what graduate preparation programs might do to better educate students who aspire to work at various types of colleges and universities. Next, I identify steps that professionals at different types of campuses might take when recruiting and hiring student affairs administrators. Finally, I address professional development opportunities that campuses might undertake to enhance performance and maximize productivity among student affairs administrators.

It is also important to note that there is an obvious gap in this book: I do not address professional life at Tribal Colleges. Readers should know that this was not an oversight. I had planned to seek input from professionals at Tribal Colleges using the same protocol employed in the other studies. Unfortunately, repeated attempts over three years to collect data from professionals on these campuses were unsuccessful. It is my fervent hope to conduct such a study in the future to illuminate life for practitioners in this unique sector of higher education.

The book is targeted at several audiences. First, students in graduate preparation programs might benefit from understanding how professional practice varies based on institutional type. It may enable them to align their professional interests with an appropriate campus environment. In a parallel vein, faculty in preparation programs might use the book to develop courses and experiences that expose students to life at different types of colleges and universities.

Current practitioners should also gain insights from the book. Oftentimes administrators become so entrenched in their campus setting that they fail to see how skills and experiences can transcend institutional type. For example, it might surprise some administrators to learn that the relationships professionals at liberal arts campuses form with students are remarkably similar to the relationships with students that practitioners at community colleges develop. Those who aspire to teach undergraduates will find a greater opportunity to do so at religiously affiliated institutions. Professionals who hope to teach graduate students, however, would be better served to work at comprehensive universities. The rewards at research universities are more closely aligned with the rewards at community colleges than they are with the reward structures at any other type of institution. These and the other findings described in the book inform current practice in terms of hiring new staff and designing professional development opportunities for continuing staff. Moreover, they open new avenues for student affairs professionals. The book offers insights on the kinds of skills professionals gain on different kinds of campuses. They might use the information to market themselves to campuses they previously assumed were outside their realm of experience.

Finally, the book provides information to chief student affairs officers. The findings reveal the kinds of work, relationships and rewards that go beyond institutional type. Professional leaders should recognize the opportunities that the patterns in this book reveal. If they seek staff members with certain skills or experiences they need not limit their searches to professionals at like institutions. In fact, in some cases, purposefully expanding hiring endeavors might prove more productive and yield more effective results.

In short, this book plows new ground in the literature on the student affairs profession. Perhaps more important, it does so by employing the voices of those who work in the field. Countless student affairs professionals contributed to this work. I am deeply indebted to those who gave so willingly of their time and who offered such candid comments about their professional lives. The amount of data they provided was staggering. The richness of the information was astonishing. It is their stories that paint the portraits depicted in this book.

Acknowledgements

This book describes a framework for understanding student affairs administration at varied types of colleges and universities. The model is grounded in a series of six research projects that were conducted between 2002 and 2004. There are a number of organizations and individuals whose backing made those studies possible. First, grants from the National Association of Student Personnel Administrators (NASPA) and NASPA Region III supported one of the studies associated with the work. A second grant from NASPA Region III supported a second research project. I am most grateful for the contributions of these two professional associations.

Second, teams of graduate students at Virginia Tech were involved in all of the studies. Some were wise and assisted with only one of the projects, and I am deeply indebted to them for their assistance. This group includes Gary Kirk, Tess Mount, Sheila Nelson-Hensley, Jan Scheffler, Ron Esteban, Steve Schneiter, Kia Wood, Danielle Colbert, Jody Thompson, Evelyn Leathers, Lauren Pigott, Khalia Cousar, Ellen Plummer, Stacey Zis, Melanie Hayden, and Ian Austin. Others I was able to sufficiently delude into believing that working on more than one of the studies would expand their research skills repertoire. Included in this group are Lisa McGuire, Denise Collins, Catherine Amelink, Belinda Bennett, Terrell Strayhorn, and Trey Waller. My heartfelt thanks to all these individuals. Their support was invaluable.

Finally, the production of this book would not have been possible were it not for the support of my esteemed colleagues at Virginia Tech, Don Creamer and Steve Janosik. Their generous offer to assume my classes for a semester enabled me to jumpstart the project. I am deeply indebted to them both.

Chapter One

What Do We Really Know About Student Affairs Work

At a national conference of student affairs administrators a few years ago, I was waiting to meet some colleagues in the lobby of my hotel when a group of new professionals gathered nearby. Their comments suggested they had been enrolled as graduate students together and were reuniting for a dinner at the conference to catch up with one another. Their excitement at seeing former classmates was evident in the hugs and exclamations exchanged upon the arrival of each new member of the group. As they awaited their remaining colleagues, they started talking about their professional lives.

"You will not believe what I have to do in this job," commented one. "I had absolutely no idea how much time I would spend dealing with paperwork." "Paperwork is the least of my concerns," replied a colleague. "It's the pressure to figure out how to fund all the programs our office wants to sponsor that gets to me." "I'd be thrilled to spend some time dealing with budget matters," another chimed in, "but my days are completely booked with appointments with students. If only I could get a break to catch up on my paperwork."

After further musings about what they liked and disliked about their jobs, they turned their attention to their graduate school program. "I loved being a grad student," one sighed, "but what I learned in class and what I do in my job are two entirely different things." "I know exactly what you mean," a colleague added. "When I started on my job I had to learn so many different things that I wondered what purpose my master's degree served." "Oh, I know what purpose it served," responded another. "It proved we were capable of learning what we were going to have to do when we got a real job: Learn what being a

professional was really all about!" The others chuckled and nodded their heads
in agreement.

As the group sauntered off to enjoy their evening together, their comments
gave me pause. I have been a faculty member for the past 11 years in a program
that prepares student affairs professionals. Before that, however, I served as an
administrator on three different campuses: a small liberal arts college, a state
comprehensive university, and a large public research university. Each time I
assumed a new professional role, it was as if I had no previous experience or
academic preparation. I had to orient myself not only to the new tasks for which
I was responsible, but also to the people with whom I worked. Moreover, I
found the benefits I garnered from my work were markedly different at each of
the institutions. So the sentiments of this group of new professionals resonated
with me in a powerful way. I began to think about why working at different
types of institutions led to such varied experiences.

Higher Education in the United States

At first I considered the evolution of learning in the country. Education in
America boasts a robust history that spans nearly four centuries. As might be
expected, primary and secondary education intersected with and influenced the
evolution of higher education in certain contexts. In other ways, the two systems
seemed to develop relatively independently of one another. In general, however,
American education can be conceptualized in three broad periods (Urban &
Wagoner, 2000).

The first occurred in pre-colonial times when Native Americans and early
Spanish settlers initiated formalized education programs. The indigenous
peoples instructed their children in spiritual and cultural matters typically
through story telling and oral transmission. Other tribal members provided select
aspects of learning so that education was truly a community endeavor. Formal
educational settings can be traced back to the earliest Spanish settlers who
established missions responsible for religious and cultural instruction of the
native peoples. The first of these was erected in St. Augustine, Florida in 1565,
decades before the first British settlers founded a colony in Virginia (Urban &
Wagoner, 2000). So early instructional endeavors in the country pre-date what
many people assume to be the start of education in the New World, the arrival of
the British in the 17th century.

The second period in the evolution of American education covers over two
centuries and it was during this era that postsecondary education emerged. Most
historians date higher education in this country from the founding of Harvard in
1636. Indeed, for the next 225 years the colonial college was the dominant form
of higher learning (Brubacher & Rudy, 1997; Lucas, 1994; Rudolph, 1962).
Such institutions, however, did not closely resemble the image most people
conjure up when they hear the word "college." For instance, over the first 140
years in America only nine colleges were founded (Lucas). The primary purpose

of these institutions was to train clergy and prepare other colonial leaders (Brubacher & Rudy). The president of the institution was initially the only staff member, serving as the instructor, disciplinarian, librarian, and leader of the college. The curriculum focused primarily on Greek, Latin, logic, and ethics, and teaching consisted of rote memorization and recitation (Cremin, 1970; Lucas). Finally, to understand the impact of higher education in the pre-Revolutionary era, consider that fewer than 600 students attended Harvard during the entire 17th century and over 100 of those did not graduate. Enrollment at Yale stood at 338 in 1770 (Lucas). So the institution of higher education during this era was relatively limited and served primarily the interests of the country's elite (Rudolph, 1962). Learning was essentially a private matter that fell to those families that could afford the luxury of educating their children.

The period between the end of the Revolutionary War and the start of the Civil War marked an era of expansion, both in terms of the nation and in terms of the nation's educational system. As America's boundaries extended westward, its educational system developed as well, albeit episodically. Perhaps most important in this era was the shift from considering education as a private endeavor to viewing education as a public good. In the post-Revolutionary era, the nation's leaders were convinced that the new republic they hoped to form would be reliant on an educated citizenry. To that end, proposals to provide universal education were generated. Among the first was Thomas Jefferson's plan to introduce a system of schooling throughout the state of Virginia. Although his efforts failed to gain approval from the Virginia legislature, the seeds of publicly supported, universal education were planted. Throughout this period, elementary schooling expanded in the nation's urban centers and establishing schools became a priority as townships emerged (Urban & Wagoner, 2000).

In the higher education arena, the post-Revolutionary period was marked by growth. "Between 1782 and 1802, nineteen colleges were established, more than twice as many as had been chartered in the previous century and a half" (Lucas, 1994, p. 117). A number of factors influenced this expansion. The geographic extension of the country westward, the growth in population, and state rivalries, coupled with competition among the various religious denominations in the country all played roles (Kimball, 1986). Indeed, whereas there were nine colonial colleges at the time of the Revolutionary War, that number had mushroomed to 250 by the eve of the Civil War (Tewksbury, 1932) of which 182 still exist today (Rudolph, 1962).

Despite movement toward universal, publicly supported education in this era, it was the post-Civil War period that witnessed the realization of this objective. The period from 1870 to the present represents the third major period in the history of education in America. The shift from an agrarian to an industrial economy changed attitudes both toward elementary and secondary education and the way that education was delivered. Formalized systems of elementary schools accomplished two goals: They ensured a trained workforce for the rapidly expanding manufacturing sector of the country while simultaneously providing a degree of protection for children beyond that offered via child labor laws (Urban & Wagoner, 2000). The expansion of elementary schooling led to the development of secondary schools during this period. This evolution took time, however, and it was not until the middle of the 20th century that the system of primary, middle, and secondary schooling as we know it today was fully refined (Urban & Wagoner). It is rather remarkable to think that the educational system we take so for granted has existed in its present form for only 60 of the nation's nearly 300 years.

The emergence of primary and secondary schools impacted the country's higher education system in several ways. First, there was, at last, a tiered system of education in the nation in which lower levels of schooling fed into higher levels. Although this was the system Jefferson envisioned at the start of the 19th century (Urban & Wagoner, 2000), that vision was not realized until the middle of 20th century. Universal schooling at the lower levels also raised the consciousness of the nation. Higher levels of education came to be associated with upward economic and social mobility, so higher education came to be a pathway to personal and professional success (Lucas, 1994; Rudolph, 1962).

Beyond these intangible influences, universal primary and secondary education in America impacted postsecondary education in other more visible ways. Perhaps most obvious was the emergence of the normal schools. As K-12 schooling expanded, the need for teachers increased. Normal schools were founded to provide teacher training. Over time, many of these evolved into state teacher colleges. As demand for higher education grew, these state teacher colleges frequently became public comprehensive colleges and universities (Brubacher & Rudy, 1997; Lucas, 1994).

Four other major developments in the American system of higher education during the past 140 years also merit attention. The first relates to the shift in focus from teaching to research that permeated many institutions of higher learning in the decades after the Civil War. The influence of the German model of higher education that concentrated on the discovery versus the transmission of knowledge was adopted at a number of campuses. This led to the emergence of the research university and its tripartite mission of research, teaching, and service (Brubacher & Rudy, 1997; Lucas, 1994).

The second development relates to the appearance of colleges and universities for specialized populations including ethnic minorities. Although the first African Americans earned bachelor's degrees in 1826 from established colleges, it wasn't until after the Civil War that colleges and universities targeted to serve minorities proliferated. The establishment of the Freedmen's Bureau was the first federal effort to support education for African Americans. Indeed, some of today's leading institutions for Blacks were founded during this era (Brubacher & Rudy, 1997; Lucas, 1994). In the past century, Tribal Colleges have emerged to educate Native Americans. The most recent additions to the

American higher education scene are Hispanic-serving colleges. These institutions were not originally designed to serve Hispanics, but as the Hispanic population in this country has mushroomed in the past 30 years, the colleges and universities that educate large numbers of Hispanics have taken on a distinct identity.

The third development relates to the secularization of many of the liberal arts colleges. The colonial colleges were almost always associated with a religious denomination. Over the centuries these campuses expanded their curricular offerings but tended to retain their focus on classical education rather than adopting the practical and mechanical arts that became a mainstay at the public institutions. At the start of the 20th century, however, a major new program prompted the secularization of many of these colleges. In the early 1900s, the Carnegie Foundation established an endowment to fund pensions for all college and university professors who met certain criteria, including the requirement that they work at nondenominational institutions. This led many colleges to sever their church ties so that their faculty members could qualify for the retirement benefits. The end result was the emergence of secular private liberal arts colleges that grew to outnumber their religiously affiliated counterparts (Brubacher & Rudy, 1997; Rudolph, 1962).

Finally, the most recent institutional type in the American system of higher education, the community college, has emerged over the past century. In the post-World War II era, President Truman appointed a commission of leading citizens led by George Zook to critique the American system of higher education. A six-volume report published by the Zook Commission (as it came to be called) between 1947 and 1948 addressed the goals, methods, and resources of the educational system. The key proposal of the report related to the degree of educational opportunity afforded to all citizens. The commission recommended that a minimum of 14 years of education be made available to all Americans and estimated that nearly half of the population was capable of, and would benefit from, completing two years of postsecondary schooling. This led to the widespread emergence of community colleges across the country. An extension of the K-12 system, community colleges were designed to provide accessible, free or low-cost education to the public, including both technical training and preparing students to complete more advanced degrees (Brubacher & Rudy, 1997). The proliferation of community colleges between the 1950s and 1970s can be traced back to the Zook Commission.

Although this overview provides only a thumbnail sketch of the history of higher education in the U.S., it illustrates how many of the institutional types that embody the current postsecondary system evolved over the past 370 years. Indeed, it is the richness of institutional types as opposed to a national system of higher education that has been touted as the hallmark of American higher education. While these types have been assigned different labels, most notably by the Carnegie Classification of Institutions of Higher Education (Carnegie Foundation, 2001), for my purposes they can be referred to by more commonplace terminology: liberal arts institutions, religiously affiliated campuses, comprehensive universities, research universities, historically Black colleges and universities (HBCUs), community colleges, and Hispanic-serving institutions (HSIs).

As of 2000, the Carnegie Foundation identified 3,941 accredited, degree-granting two-year and four-year colleges and universities in the nation (Carnegie Foundation, 2001). Of these, 261 (6.6%) were research universities, 611 (15.5%) were comprehensive institutions, 606 (15.4%) were liberal arts campuses, 312 (7.9%) were religiously affiliated institutions, and 1,669 (42.3%) were community or two-year colleges. Although 28 (0.7%) of the 3,941 institutions were listed as Tribal Colleges and universities, numbers of other minority-serving institutions (i.e., HBCUs, HSIs) are more difficult to count, as they are not considered a distinct category in the Carnegie classification system. The remainder (454, 11.6%) was labeled "specialized institutions" and included medical schools and centers; schools of art, music and design; and other such organizations.

Given the array of colleges and universities in America today, then, I was not surprised to hear new professionals talk about the adjustments they had to make to their work settings. Their comments, though, also led me to examine how the student affairs profession evolved.

The Literature on the Profession

Thielen (2003) reported that during the two centuries between 1700 and 1900, college participation among traditional-aged (18- to 22-year-old) students was less than 5% but by 1970 that rate had grown to 50%. Higher education in the 20th century clearly became a mass activity rather than one reserved for the privileged. As higher education spread, the role of student service providers expanded concomitantly.

Services for students have been essential from the very start of higher education. Housing and dining services were just as necessary for students at colonial colleges as they are for contemporary students. As higher education broadened and became more complex over time, so did student affairs administration. A review of the historical development of the profession illustrates this trend. Indeed, the evolution of student affairs can be examined over three time periods.

The first era (1636-1850) covers both the colonial period as well as the early decades of the republic (Nuss, 2003). College presidents and faculty members were responsible for providing the spiritual and moral education of their students as well as their intellectual training. It is important to keep in mind that some college students in this era were only 13 and 14 years of age (Rudolph, 1962). They needed tutelage that far exceeded traditional classroom instruction and included out-of-class supervision and vocational guidance (Leonard, 1956). Institutions adopted a policy of *in loco parentis*. Translated literally, *in loco parentis* means "in the place of parents." Essentially, the policy gave college personnel the authority to act as parents to their students, to guide their growth both in the classroom and beyond. This notion of *in loco parentis* directed student–faculty interactions during the colonial period.

Shortly after the Revolutionary War, however, students took issue with the classical curriculum and spiritual rigidity of college campuses and initiated what came to be known as extracurricular activities. At first these took the form of literary and debating societies (Geiger, 2000). By the mid-19th century, college athletics and Greek letter associations had permeated campuses (Brubacher & Rudy, 1997).

It was not until after the Civil War, during the second era of student affairs administration evolution, that college personnel were appointed specifically to guide and monitor the non-classroom experiences of students. Several factors influenced this shift. First, the role of the president became much more complex, limiting the amount of time that could be devoted to students. Second, colleges started admitting female students and needed to employ women to monitor and chaperone these young charges. Finally, as faculty turned attention to the creation of knowledge, they spent less time on non-instructional activities (Leonard, 1956; Rudolph, 1962). As a result, officials were appointed to handle services like admissions, registration and records, and student health matters (Leonard; Rudolph). A shift from a classical to an elective curriculum led to the need for academic advisors. These early student service providers were not integral players on campuses, however. The focus on intellectual development of students left them operating in a state of benign neglect: Their presence was deemed necessary but unimportant (Williamson, 1961).

The status of student affairs professionals took on greater importance during the first half of the 20th century, however, particularly after World War I. That conflagration led to the development of personnel inventories and personal assessment techniques that were originally employed in the armed forces and subsequently adopted by college and university administrators (Brubacher & Rudy, 1997; Williamson, 1961). Many of the services for students that professionals provide today were established during this time frame, including career counseling and placement services and personal counseling. Likewise, the *Student Personnel Point of View* (American Council on Education, 1937) and the 1949 *Student Personnel Point of View Revised* (American Council on Education) were published during this era. These two documents form the profession's foundation.

Following World War II, student affairs administration came into its own. A variety of factors, including social movements and student unrest, led to the demise of *in loco parentis* and a shift in the relationship between students and institutions of higher education (Lucas, 1994; Nuss, 2003). At the same time, services for students expanded to include programs like orientation and leadership development as well as services for specific groups including women, minority, and disabled students.

This abbreviated summary of the history of student affairs, however, paints an overly simplistic picture and suggests a unified professional identity. As Fenske (1989) has noted, student affairs "has never had a single functional focus, has never been stable in its role over significant periods of time, and has never had a consensual integrative philosophy" (p. 27). This led me to explore what is known about the profession.

The body of work on student affairs can be conceptualized in several categories. The first examines the status of those who serve as student affairs administrators, including commentaries about the degree to which student affairs administration can be considered a profession. This question has been debated for decades with some scholars denying student affairs professional status (Bloland, 1992; Canon, 1982). These experts argued that certain criteria must be met before an occupational group can be considered a profession. They claimed that student affairs practice does not meet these criteria. Others maintained that student affairs administrators do merit the label "professionals." These scholars stressed that the theories and philosophy that guide practitioners confirm the occupation's compliance with the constructs of a profession (Stamatakos, 1981a, 1981b). This debate has surfaced periodically over the years and has not been fully resolved. As a result, it is a discussion that will likely continue episodically, suggesting that more will be added to this body of writing in the future.

A second category of literature describes the work of the profession and the roles that student affairs administrators have assumed over time (Rentz, 1996). Rentz and Saddlemire (1988), for instance, described in depth how various functions evolved, how they are organized, and the kinds of work administrators in these functional units do. They addressed disparate functions ranging from academic advising and admissions work to housing and student activities.

An extension of this school of thought has suggested two distinct types of student affairs professionals. There are those who work in functionally based programs like admissions, housing, or financial aid; services that are more historically entrenched in higher education institutions. Professionals in functional areas need a thorough understanding of the particular service they provide and an ability to provide that service to all students. The second group of professionals includes those who work with services for student groups (e.g., women, minorities, international students). These population-based services require professionals to have a thorough understanding of a group and to offer that group information about a variety of campus functions (e.g., admission, housing, financial aid, career services). Population-based services are relative newcomers to the student affairs profession; hence, they are typically less well supported by institutions (Hirt, 1992).

The literature is also rife with works on the skills and abilities needed to succeed as a student affairs administrator. Delworth and Hanson (1989) and Komives and Woodard (2003) identified a series of competencies including teaching, assessment and evaluation, and counseling and helping skills that are hallmarks of flourishing professionals. Others have discussed the talents that seem to be associated with student affairs leaders (Dalton & Gardner, 2002; Estanek, 1999; Thomas, 2002). Included in this collection are studies that focus on the role of leadership in the profession (Reisser, 2002) and those that compile and analyze the abilities of student affairs leaders (Lovell & Kosten, 2000).

Finally, there is a segment of literature that examines the characteristics of the student affairs labor pool (Turrentine & Conley, 2001). Of particular interest are works that have investigated attrition among student service professionals (Burns, 1982; N. J. Evans, 1988; Lorden, 1998). It would seem that there is a fair amount of concern about departure from the profession. Some estimates suggest that as many as 60% of new professionals leave the field within six years of assuming their first positions. There is work that suggests connections between characteristics of professionals and attrition rates (Blackhurst, Brandt, & Kalinowski, 1998). The new professionals I had witnessed talking about the challenges in their jobs were not discussing leaving the field, however. They were simply commenting on how their work lives differed from the expectations they had developed while training for the profession in graduate school.

What We Need to Learn About the Student Affairs Profession

It was at this point that the pieces of the puzzle began to fall into place for me. First, the evolution of higher education in this country has resulted in a complex system of institutional types. Second, there is ample literature about the people who comprise the student affairs profession and the abilities they need in order to succeed. Professionals practice at all types of institutions, however. What is the intersection between the practice of student affairs administrators and organizational setting?

Only recently has the influence of institutional type on professional practice been considered. Experts have noted the need to explore whether graduate programs are preparing future student affairs professionals to succeed in different types of environments (Lorden, 1998). Furthermore, they have exhorted professionals to understand the core mission of the institution at which they practice so that their actions contribute to achieving that mission (Kuk, 2002). In fact, Nuss (2003) argued that the commitment professionals make to support the academic mission of their institution is one of the enduring characteristics of the student affairs profession.

To a large extent, these issues are matters of professional socialization. Socialization to the profession occurs through the daily routines in which graduate students engage, the people with whom they work, the values endorsed in the campus environment, and the rewards they receive from their endeavors (Tierney, 1997). Professional socialization occurs when students adopt the norms of those who train them. Logically, then, the type of institution at which a graduate student trains influences the professional expectations that student takes into the work setting after graduation. A survey of 181 graduate preparation programs in higher education and student affairs reveals that 69% are housed at research universities (Hirt, 2001). The remainder is located at comprehensive institutions. These data suggest that graduate students are socialized to professional expectations that correspond to the values embraced at research universities and comprehensive institutions. Yet less than a quarter (22.1%) of all institutions at which student affairs professionals work are research (6.6%) or comprehensive (15.5%) schools (Carnegie Foundation, 2001).

If new professionals are socialized at research and comprehensive campuses but employed at liberal arts institutions, community colleges, religiously affiliated schools, HBCUs, or HSIs, they might expect to encounter a disconnect between the expectations they bring to the work setting and the realities they confront in that setting. This represents the conundrum my new colleagues were talking about and the gap in our understanding of professional practice in student affairs administration. There is a need for more information about the nature of professional life for those who work at different types of college and university campuses. To that end, I set out to explore this issue in greater depth.

The Studies

Over a two-year period of time, I conducted six studies related to the notion of professional work life and differences in that work life by institutional type. Five studies were national in scope, and one was regional. They involved professionals at seven different types of institutions. Since the conclusions I draw throughout the rest of this book are based largely on the results of these studies, a brief description of each is warranted.

The Calendar Study

The first of the studies sought to investigate how student affairs professionals spend their time. I worked with a research team, and we assumed that the tasks to which professionals devoted their time would help delineate the nature of their work. A sample of 112 professionals at a research university, two comprehensive universities, and two liberal arts colleges (one secular, one religiously affiliated) participated in the study.

Respondents provided the research team with copies of their daily calendars for a one-month period of time. They were given limited instructions in terms of a format for their calendars. We asked only that they note the starting and ending time of each activity. They deleted names from their daily schedules to ensure professional levels of confidentiality and simply reported the nature of each activity listed on their calendars. For example, if a participant was handling a student disciplinary matter, the name of the student was deleted but the participant noted that the time period was used to conduct a disciplinary hearing.

We asked participants to note all work activities for the month, including any evening or weekend engagements.

To compile the data we took several steps. First, we reviewed the entries and identified like activities. For example, items that referred to reading/replying to email, handling correspondence, and taking/returning phone calls were assigned to a category entitled "Communication." All activities that referred to preparing for a class, grading papers, or developing syllabus materials were assigned to a category entitled "Teaching." We identified eight such categories in the data.

Upon assigning all activities to categories, we then calculated the number and percentage of entries assigned to each category and the number and percentage of hours devoted to each category by each participant. We then summarized the data for individuals by institution and grouped the data by institutional type in order to explore differences in how student affairs professionals at different types of institutions spend their time.

The findings from the Calendar Study, then, were both thematic and quantitative. We calculated how much time professionals at different types of institutions spent in different types of activities. This process led to two outcomes. First, we could rank order the amount of time professionals at any given institutional type spent on the eight types of activities. For example, serving students consumed the greatest amount of time for those at liberal arts colleges, whereas strategic planning consumed the least amount of time. Second, we could look at any of the eight activities and compare the amount of time professionals at different types of institutions spent on that activity. We were able to discern, for example, whether those at liberal arts institutions spent more time on communication tasks than their colleagues at other types of campuses, or how the amount of time professionals at comprehensive institutions devoted to teaching activities compared to that of their counterparts at research or religiously affiliated institutions. Throughout the rest of this volume, conclusions about how much time professionals spend on different types of tasks are drawn in part from the findings of the Calendar Study.

The National Survey Study

The second study involved a national sample of student affairs administrators. A total of 541 professionals from two- and four-year institutions across the country completed the Nature of Professional Life Survey (NPLS) instrument consisting of 119 items in four categories: the nature of work, the nature of rewards, the nature of relationships, and the nature of the campus. The survey also included three open-ended questions asking participants to reflect on the culture of their institution.

The instrument was designed to yield interval data. We sorted respondents into six groups by the type of institution at which they worked (community college, liberal arts institution, religiously affiliated campus, comprehensive university, research university, minority serving institution). The findings enabled us to look at descriptive data from each category on the instrument for administrators from each type of campus. That is, we could calculate the degree to which professionals at community colleges reported they knew faculty or other academic administrators on their campuses, or the degree to which those at research universities were satisfied with the opportunities for advancement on their campus.

We could also calculate mean scores on items and run comparative statistics (ANOVAs) to examine significant differences among groups. For instance, we could compare whether there were statistically significant differences in the professional development opportunities offered to practitioners at liberal arts, comprehensive, or research institutions. In the subsequent chapters in this book, references to significant differences among administrators at different types of campuses are based on the findings from the National Survey Study.

The Community College Studies (Case Study and Follow-Up Study)

The Calendar Study did not include participants from community colleges, and the National Survey Study involved a somewhat limited sample of student affairs professionals at two-year campuses. Most of those were at large, urban, or multi-campus community colleges. To obtain a richer sense of student service providers at community colleges, I worked with another research team to conduct a case study of professional life at two rural community colleges.

Data were collected through a series of campus visits during which we observed student affairs professionals as they went about their daily routines. We also interviewed all the student service professionals on the campuses. These took the form of both individual and group interviews. The data were analyzed in multiple ways. Types of observations were identified and then frequencies of each type were calculated. The interviews were transcribed so that themes could be identified and interpreted.

The findings were collapsed into three categories: the nature of work, the nature of relationships, and the nature of rewards. It was interesting to note that these corresponded to three of the categories examined in the National Survey Study. The findings in this case, however, more clearly delineated life among professionals at rural community colleges.

To garner a sense of professional life for student affairs professionals at other types of community colleges, I worked with a research partner and conducted a Follow-Up study to collect data from community college administrators across the country. We used the same protocol as employed in the Association Study described below. Respondents provided quantitative data about the nature of their work, relationships, and rewards. A select group also participated in phone interviews during which they elaborated on their professional experiences. Overall, then, we had both quantitative and qualitative data from a national sample of practitioners at community colleges. Many of the conclusions drawn about community college professionals are based on the findings from these studies.

The Association Study

The fourth study involved a national sample of student affairs professionals from five types of institutions: community colleges, liberal arts colleges, religiously affiliated institutions, comprehensive colleges and universities, and research universities. Data were collected via focus groups conducted at the annual convention of a national student affairs professional association.

A total of 176 practitioners volunteered to participate in 1 of 24 focus group discussions. Each group consisted of professionals from a single institutional type. Overall, we conducted five focus groups with professionals from research universities, five focus groups with those from comprehensive institutions, five focus groups with representatives from liberal arts colleges, five more groups with practitioners at community colleges, and four focus groups with administrators from religiously affiliated campuses. The participants were fairly well distributed over four of the five institutional types. Thirty-five percent (35%) worked at research universities, 24% at liberal arts colleges, 18% at religiously affiliated campuses, and 14% at comprehensive universities. The community colleges were somewhat under-represented in the sample (8%) though this was not unexpected given the limited number of members from community colleges that belonged to this association. To address this concern, additional interviews with community college professionals were conducted after the conclusion of the conference (the Community College Follow-up Study described above).

Sessions lasted 90 minutes. Led by a team of two facilitators, participants were asked to complete three written exercises: one about the nature of their work, another about the nature of their relationships with other campus constituencies, and a third about the rewards they garnered for their work. After completing the exercises, respondents engaged in an extended dialogue about their responses and offered richer data about their professional lives.

The written exercises yielded quantitative data. In terms of the nature of work, respondents rated the degree to which their work reflected certain characteristics. For instance, they were asked to rate the degree to which their work was bureaucratized and how political their campus was. These data enabled us to assess the percentage of professionals from each institutional type that characterized their work in a certain way. For example, the findings revealed the percentage of professionals at religiously affiliated institutions that believed change at their campus occurred slowly versus the percentage of those at community colleges who felt the same way about change on campus.

In the exercise on relationships, respondents estimated the amount of time they spent with various constituency groups (students, faculty, student affairs colleagues, alumni, and community members, among other groups) and wrote descriptions of the positive and negative aspects of their relationships with those groups. We analyzed the data by calculating the mean percentage of time spent with each constituency and rank ordering those percentages for participants from each institutional type. Additionally, we grouped the words and phrases they used to describe their relationships with these constituencies into themes and examined the frequency with which participants from each institutional type mentioned those themes.

Finally, focus group members rank ordered a list of rewards. The list included both extrinsic rewards (e.g., salary, benefits, support for professional development) and intrinsic rewards (e.g., positive working relationships, autonomy, decision-making authority). To analyze the data, we calculated mean scores for each reward for professionals from each institutional type. We then ranked the rewards from those most valued to those least valued by practitioners at each type of campus.

All sessions were audio taped and those tapes were transcribed so that the discussion among participants after each exercise could also be analyzed. These narratives added tremendous richness and depth to the quantitative results from the written exercises. Overall, the quantitative data sketched a picture of professional life for student affairs administrators at each type of institution whereas the qualitative data generated from the discussions added texture and color to each sketch. Many of the conclusions drawn in subsequent chapters of this volume are based on findings from the Association Study.

The Historically Black Colleges and Universities Study

None of the previous studies examined what professional life for student affairs administrators at minority serving institutions was like. To that end, I worked with two other research teams. The first investigated administrative life at HBCUs.

A total of 71 student affairs professionals at HBCUs provided information about their work life. Data were collected using the same protocol that was employed in the Association and Community College Follow-Up Studies to ensure that we gathered similar information from all respondents at all types of institutions. In this case, however, we used two procedures to collect information. First, we attended a national conference of student affairs administrators who worked at HBCUs. While there, we conducted a focus group and collected written responses to the exercises on work, relationships, and rewards from other conferees. We also conducted abbreviated one-on-one interviews with those attending the conference to ask them about the nature of their professional life.

To add to the data collected at the national conference, we contacted professionals at over 25 other HBCUs. We asked them to complete the written exercises and, if they were willing, to participate in either a focus group or a one-on-one interview with a member of the research team. In some cases, members of the research team made site visits to campuses. In other instances, the instrument was administered in paper and pencil or online format and interviews were conducted by phone.

In all instances, focus groups and interviews were audio taped and transcribed. As a result, we could analyze the data from the instrument quantitatively and the comments from the transcripts qualitatively. That is, we could look at the same constructs (the nature of the campus, work, relationships, rewards) that were examined in all the other studies and could analyze the data from HBCU participants in the same manner as data from other studies were analyzed.

The Hispanic-Serving Institutions Study

The final study looked at professional life for student affairs administrators at Hispanic-serving institutions (HSIs) across the country. A total of 194 practitioners at 20 HSIs provided data to a final research team that I coordinated. We used the same protocol that was employed in the Association, Community College Follow-Up, and the HBCU studies. In this case, respondents completed the instrument in either paper and pencil or electronic format. At the end of the instrument, they were asked if they would be willing to participate in a phone interview with a member of the research team. Those interviews were audio taped and transcribed. The end result was a data set that mirrored the kind of information we had retrieved in the other studies but reflected the unique elements of life at a HSI.

Some Caveats

In sum, this book is based on data from over 1,100 student affairs professionals employed at hundreds of college and university campuses across the country. It is an initial attempt to explore the student affairs profession in different institutional contexts. I would be remiss, however, if I did not offer readers some cautionary words before going further. First, I have identified a conceptual framework through which to describe professional life. Specifically, I define professional life as the nature of the campus, along with the nature of work, relationships, and rewards on that campus. The beauty of conceptual frameworks is that they provide simplistic expressions of highly complex notions. In doing so, they rely on generalizations. Generalizations, in turn, represent the largest drawback to such frameworks. They encourage people to think in broad categories, and broad categories blur the individual differences and unique characteristics that can be found among the entities included in a category.

In this case, readers should be cautious about two sets of generalizations. First, I talk about institutional types in very broad categories. Although liberal arts colleges do share some common characteristics, each also has some unique attributes that distinguish it from its peers. There are 1,669 community colleges in the country. While I group them all together in this volume, common sense would dictate that there are multiple differences from one campus to the next. I urge readers to recognize the generalizations I employ in the book and interpret my comments in the appropriate context.

The second set of generalizations I employ relates to the metaphors describing professionals at these different institutional types. Not all those who work at research universities are "specialists," nor are comprehensive universities fully staffed by "generalists." These metaphors are designed to conjure up an overall impression of professional life at each type of institution. The terms represent labels that categorize individuals. The most sacred value of the student affairs profession is the inherent worth of the individual and the use of metaphors seems to fly in the face of this canon. Yet metaphors also enable people to interpret complex concepts in straightforward ways. In this sense, they serve a useful purpose and it was for this purpose that I employed the metaphorical approach taken in the book. I implore readers to interpret the book in that context.

Another caveat relates to the types of institutions not addressed in the book. I have attempted to talk about those colleges and universities that dominate in our system of higher education. There are many other sorts of institutions at which student affairs professionals work, however, including Tribal Colleges, women's institutions, graduate and professional schools, proprietary institutions, and hybrid institutions. Indeed, while conducting some of the studies whose results form the foundation for this volume, I received extensive correspondence from professionals who worked at these other institutional types. They all articulated the need for much more information about professional life at their types of campuses. To those professionals let me say that I wholeheartedly concur. There is a real need to explore professional life at a much broader cross section of institutional types. This book is merely a start but one that I hope will invite further work that more fully describes student affairs professional life.

It is also important to mention that I talk about work life at each institutional type from a collective perspective. I do not distinguish how professional life might vary given demographic characteristics like sex or race. It is likely that women or people of color experience life as student affairs professionals differently than do men or Whites. Addressing these differences, however, goes beyond the scope of this volume and I leave it to future scholars to explore those differences.

Finally, it is critical for readers to note that the findings described in the book are based on only six studies. Additionally, those studies focus on select elements of professional life, namely work, relationships, and rewards. There may be many other elements that influence professional life for student affairs administrators. The conclusions I draw should be interpreted in that light.

Conclusion

In conclusion, much more work needs to be conducted on student affairs professional practice at different types of colleges and universities. This book represents a start, however, and provides readers with a solid foundation upon which to build. By framing the book around metaphors, readers can begin to see what skills and abilities are utilized by student affairs administrators at different types of campuses. They can assess the relationships these professionals develop with others and the rewards they reap as a result of their efforts. Perhaps such understanding will enable new professionals to assess their own talents and interests so that they can pursue careers at the types of colleges and universities that best match those talents and interests.

For experienced professionals, I hope the book offers some confirmation of the value of your work and provides you a context in which to assess your future professional plans. It addresses ways in which positions can be marketed and identifies areas on which professional development programs might focus. This book offers a conceptual framework about professional life that is based on the lived experiences of student affairs administrators. I hope it offers practical and useful information to current practitioners and those who aspire to the profession.

Chapter Two

The Standard Bearers: Student Affairs Professionals at Liberal Arts Colleges

The liberal arts institution was the first type of college established in the U.S. and, in fact, was virtually the only form of higher education the country offered for over 200 years. It was at these institutions that the first student service officers served and where many of the functions that are managed by student affairs professionals today originated. It makes sense, then, to start with an examination of professional life for those who work at these institutions.

Liberal arts colleges are committed to promoting development among students in a broad sense; attending to students' intellectual, social, physical, psychological, emotional, and moral growth. This holistic approach to education is the standard of the student affairs profession: Practitioners believe in working closely with students to encourage development across a broad array of realms. So it is reasonable to refer to student affairs administrators at liberal arts institutions as "standard bearers." Those who work at such institutions believe that the small size and residential nature of these campuses enable them to work with students in individualized, multifaceted ways. Professionals get to know their students' backgrounds, interests, strengths, and vulnerabilities. They work closely enough with students to challenge and support them at appropriate levels. Moreover, administrators on liberal arts campuses work quite closely with one another, so they bring their collective forces to bear on the development of students. All this is perceived as providing the type of holistic educational experience that sets the highest standards in student affairs professional practice.

To better comprehend administrative life at liberal arts institutions, a more detailed understanding of how these campuses have evolved over time is helpful. I then provide a discussion of the nature of such campuses. This discussion examines the mission of liberal arts colleges, the role that faculty play on such campuses, and the types of students who attend these institutions. Given this context, the nature of work, relationships, and rewards for student affairs administrators illustrate how they can be considered the standard bearers of the profession.

Historical Evolution

Historians generally agree that the colonial colleges were modeled after the great English universities of Cambridge and Oxford (Brubacher & Rudy, 1997; Rudolph, 1962, Urban & Wagoner, 2000). There are two avenues that best illustrate this argument. The first relates to the curriculum. As noted in Chapter One, the early American colleges were founded to educate clergy and leaders of the emerging colonies. The religious denominations that dictated so much of life in the colonies were dependent on training future clergy in order to maintain their dominance. Beyond religious leaders, however, there was also a need for civic leaders. The goal of these early colleges was to provide the colony in which they resided with both civil and religious leaders who were steeped in the orthodoxy of the relevant denomination (Brubacher & Rudy).

To achieve that end, the curricula of the nine colonial colleges (those established between 1636 and 1770) focused primarily on the classical languages and literature, along with philosophy. Classes in Greek and Latin were supplemented with studies of ethics, politics, and mathematics, and what became known as the traditional liberal arts formed the foundation of the curriculum. It was assumed that classical learning was essential to the practice of theology, law, or medicine (Lucas, 1994), and such programs of study remained virtually unchanged for over 100 years (Urban & Wagoner, 2000).

Eventually, however, the knowledge unearthed in the 18th century Age of Enlightenment made its way to America, and colleges modified their curricula to reflect new bodies of information. In the years just prior to the Revolution, some of the colonial colleges started to offer courses in geography, navigation, and other practical and scientific studies (Lucas, 1994). Most, however, held fast to the classical curriculum and the debate over traditional versus applied course offerings was initiated.

This dispute took on greater dimensions in the years following the Revolution as higher education opportunities in the new nation expanded. During the first 20 years of the Republican era, 19 new colleges were founded. Over the next 40 years, institutions of higher learning were founded at an even more astounding rate. Some of this growth was fueled by denominational loyalties that prompted the establishment of liberal arts colleges throughout the new territories in the west. At the same time, rivalries among the states prompted the founding of publicly supported institutions. On the eve of the Civil War, then, the nation boasted 250 colleges (Lucas, 1994).

The debate over the curriculum prevailed during this period. As civic leaders called on higher education to train students in science and technology, some institutions introduced applied studies including mechanical and agricultural arts. Other academic leaders, however, were convinced that students were best served by studying the classics. The issue of electives further exacerbated the debate. As institutions offered a broader array of academic programs, many argued that students should be allowed to select which program of study to undertake. Critics, however, reasoned that educational experts were more qualified than students to determine academic requirements (Lucas, 1994).

The dispute culminated in a report issued by Yale in 1828 that called for developing the intellectual capacities of students' minds. Such development, the experts proclaimed, was promoted through courses in "mathematics, ancient and modern English literature, logic, rhetoric, oratory, written composition, and the physical sciences" (Lucas, 1994, p. 133). The Yale Report went on to suggest that academic courses should not include professional studies. Professional preparation was better accomplished through apprenticeships that were undertaken after completing a more traditional course of formal study, so the experts argued (Brubacher & Rudy, 1997; Lucas; Rudolph, 1962).

The tension between classical and professional studies has persisted among liberal arts institutions in the 140 years since the Civil War. Two factors played key roles in the controversy. The first was Charles Eliot who served as President of Harvard for 40 years (1869-1909). A chemist by training, Eliot was convinced that all disciplines were of equal worth and that students should have the right to select the program of study that best suited their talents and interests. His undying commitment to the elective system was enacted at Harvard over his tenure as president. This is not to suggest that there were not vocal opponents to the actions taken at Harvard. Leaders of denominational colleges as well as those at some of the colonial colleges criticized the secular approach advocated by Eliot and railed against his focus on science (Brubacher & Rudy, 1997).

The development of the curriculum was the second factor that fueled the debate. The advances in science, especially in Germany, coupled with the vocational and pre-professional programs emerging at land-grant institutions in the post-Morrill Act era led to specialization among faculty members. No longer was it acceptable for faculty members to be generalists. They needed to be experts in some discipline. Again, however, there were detractors, particularly from those at small liberal arts institutions who believed that a solid general education was more important than providing specialized training (Brubacher & Rudy, 1997).

The debate was further exacerbated by the ascension of women to higher education during this era. Women were admitted to a limited number of existing colleges, and a number of women's colleges emerged during this era. The curriculum for women was markedly different than that for men and focused on providing knowledge that would make women conversant in intellectual matters coupled with domestic skills that would render them successful homemakers. In general, the controversy between liberal arts and professional studies continued to be argued throughout the 20th century and is still a contentious issue today (Brubacher & Rudy, 1997).

The second avenue that connected American liberal arts colleges to the great British universities relates to what Rudolph (1962) called "the collegiate way." The term refers to the way in which students are viewed and the way in which colleges are perceived. American educators traditionally assumed that their students were immature, inexperienced adolescents in need of not only intellectual development but also social and moral guidance. In Europe, on the other hand, students were viewed as adults whose formal training prior to matriculation provided them with the life skills necessary to succeed in undergraduate study (Brubacher & Rudy, 1997; Rudolph, 1962).

To address the non-academic needs of students, then, American colleges from their inception provided housing, dining services, religious instruction, and other amenities to students. In light of certain circumstances, this is understandable. Bear in mind that there were college students in the colonial colleges as young as 11 years of age. Most were 13–14 years old when they matriculated. To a large extent, then, these amenities were essential for students. It is also important to consider the state of development in the country during much of its first 150 years. Students often traveled hundreds of miles to attend colleges and the lack of roads that were accessible year round along with the limited communication that college officials could have with families of students necessitated the provision of such services (Brubacher & Rudy, 1997; Rudolph, 1962). Nonetheless, American higher education has always adopted a view of students that differs from that taken in other countries and the liberal arts colleges embraced this perspective.

The second component of the collegiate way has to do with the image of a college. That is, colleges are more than simply students, faculty, and books. They involve residence halls, libraries, and recreational facilities, and are most often pictured on isolated hills and in flowering pastures near small towns in rural America. They are places where people come together as a community of scholars, where students are nurtured and individual development is fostered (Brubacher & Rudy, 1997; Rudolph, 1962). It is the liberal arts college that best illustrates the illusions associated with the collegiate way. Moreover, liberal arts colleges recognize that they represent this ideal of American higher education and capitalize on such public perceptions to attract students to their institutions.

The history of liberal arts colleges lays the groundwork that explains their current circumstances and it is to those circumstances that I now turn. What is the role of the liberal arts college in contemporary times? What roles do faculty members play in such institutions? What are the characteristics of students who attend liberal arts colleges? To understand the context in which student affairs practitioners ply their craft in liberal arts colleges, it is important to understand the nature of such campuses.

The Nature of the Liberal Arts College Campus

According to the Carnegie Foundation (2000), there were 606 baccalaureate institutions in the U.S. in 2000. This represents 15.4% of all postsecondary institutions in the country. These colleges educate 1,039,020 students, or just under 7% of the 15,079,149 students enrolled in American colleges and universities. As these data suggest, liberal arts institutions are typically small; 520 of the 606 enroll fewer than 2,500 students. These statistics sketch the outline of liberal arts colleges. To fully understand these institutions, however, it is important to understand their mission, their faculty, and their students.

Mission

The mission of liberal arts colleges and universities in the 21st century reflects a continuing focus on a traditional curriculum designed to promote holistic education and to graduate productive members of society. To illustrate this point, consider the following samples of mission statements from three different liberal arts schools:

> [Name of institution's] mission is to provide a demanding, expansive educational experience to a select group of diverse, talented, intellectually sophisticated students who are capable of challenging themselves, their peers, and their teachers in a setting that brings together living and learning. The purpose of the university is to develop wise, thoughtful, critical thinkers and perceptive leaders by encouraging young men and women to fulfill their potential through residence in a community that values all forms of intellectual rigor and respects the complexity of human understanding.

> The mission of [name of university] is to provide personalized education of distinction that leads to inquiring, ethical, and productive lives as global citizens. Founded in 1861, [name of university] is recognized for its liberal arts core, distinguished faculty, innovative programs and personalized attention to students. The university strives to develop in students the ability to think clearly, communicate effectively, explore issues from contrasting points view, value human and cultural diversity and make informed ethical judgments in an increasingly complex world.

> The College's primary mission is to provide students with a broad, deep, and life-enhancing education that fosters professional success, personal growth, and social responsibility. To this end, [name of college's] graduates should be equipped to pursue successful careers, satisfying personal lives, community service, and intellectually stimulating and physically active leisure.

These missions focus on "personalized education" that emphasizes "critical thinking" and "personal growth" and leads to "professional success" and "productive lives as global citizens" upon graduation.

This is not to suggest that the debate over traditional versus vocational programs has been resolved. Indeed, that dispute continues to capture attention. There are many who are committed to the value of a liberal education. They point to the historical roots of liberal arts colleges (Pfnister, 1984) and focus on the characteristics of such institutions. These campuses are almost exclusively undergraduate, serve primarily traditional-aged (18- to 22-year-old) students, and many are highly selective. They are residential and many boast large endowments to ensure their financial future (Delucchi, 1997). They confer baccalaureate degrees and require extensive general education courses consistent with a liberal education. The most popular majors are liberal arts and sciences and although the curriculum is designed to ensure that students are exposed to many disciplines, the academic program provides a common experience (Cejda & Duemer, 2001; Resneck Pierce, 2000).

In recent years, critics of liberal arts colleges have emerged. Arguments have been raised about mission drift among these institutions (Breneman, 1990, 1994; Delucchi, 1997). The enrollment-driven nature of such campuses has led others to suggest that liberal arts colleges have gone overboard and adopted an attitude of student as consumer at the expense of student as learner (Kluge, 2003).

These criticisms have been countered by voices that suggest how liberal arts colleges might reinvent themselves to ensure their future survival. Some proponents believe colleges have ignored their focus on responsible citizenship and that they need to rededicate themselves to this outcome for graduates (Lang, 1999). More frequently, they assume a more moderate position and suggest ways that liberal education can be integrated into and complementary to professional education (Hersh, 1999; Stober, 1995).

In the long run, though, traditionalism runs deep among those at liberal arts institutions. Most believe that "liberal arts colleges stand as a bastion of handcrafted education that best nurtures individual growth and the development of competence and confidence" (Hersh, 1999, p. 16). "Liberal education represents the last and best—but least understood and least appreciated—mechanism for achieving the fullest development of human potential" (M. Gregory, 2003, p. B16).

Concerns about the relevancy of liberal education are well founded if trends in types of degrees awarded are to be believed. The number of students at liberal arts institutions who earn degrees in liberal arts disciplines has declined precipitously. In the mid-1980s, 80% of graduates from liberal arts colleges studied traditional disciplines like sociology, literature, and political science. By the mid-1990s, that number had dropped to 57% (Pace & Connolly, 1999). To what degree do faculty members play a role in this trend?

Faculty

Faculty members at liberal arts institutions fulfill responsibilities that differ from their colleagues at other types of institutions. To start, consider their numbers. Although baccalaureate colleges comprise over 15% of all American institutions, they employ only 9% of all faculty members (Carnegie Foundation, 2000). And 63% of liberal arts faculty members are full-time employees, a higher ratio than at other types of postsecondary institutions.

As these data suggest, faculty members at liberal arts institutions spend a considerable amount of time in the classroom. In fact, professors at liberal arts colleges appreciate the teaching role they assume. Roughly 78% report that they value teaching, as opposed to only 60% of faculty members at research universities, for example, who value their instructional responsibilities (National Center for Education Statistics [NCES], 1999).

On average, teachers at liberal arts colleges spend more than 65% of their time teaching. Over half (54%) teach more than 10 credit hours per week and nearly a fifth (18.7%) teach more than 15 credit hours weekly. This translates to 3–4 courses per semester for most (54%) faculty and 5 or more classes per term for nearly 20% of professors who teach undergraduate classes (NCES, 1999).

The research responsibilities of professors at liberal arts colleges also take a somewhat different direction than the research conducted by faculty at other types of colleges and universities. While the evidence suggests that those who are better researchers are also better teachers, faculty at liberal arts schools engage undergraduates in their research endeavors and view that experience as training to prepare students for graduate level work (Michalak & Robert, 1981). In fact, the research that liberal arts faculty members conduct is typically achieved without the administrative infrastructure that supports research at other institutions. Studies at liberal arts campuses are individualistic, not entrepreneurial like those at research universities. Liberal arts faculty members view research as opportunities to teach students, to work with them outside of the classroom (Ruscio, 1987).

Although professors at liberal arts institutions have identified their niche with respect to teaching and research, this does not mean they do not have concerns about their institutions or the administrators that run them. Faculty members disagree about what the problems with liberal education are and who can solve those problems (Burhorn, 1980). For example, the liberal arts are tied to the notion of identifying and defining difference. As a result, promoting a sense of community can be problematic for faculty (Aleman & Salkever, 2002).

In general, though, faculty members at liberal arts campuses recognize that their roles are different than those of professors at other types of institutions, and they appreciate those differences. Issues like the size of the campus, the cohesiveness of the academic community, the collegiality among faculty, and the quality of academic life are all hallmarks of the culture at a liberal arts college. Teachers at these colleges feel they are an integral part of the academic endeavors at their institutions and the academic efforts of their students (Schnell, 1992).

Students

The students who enroll in liberal arts institutions also differ from their counterparts at other types of colleges and universities. To some degree, these differences are driven by students' perceptions of the value of a liberal arts education. Students and their parents rate the quality of higher education at private institutions as very high. Forty-one percent of parents believe that the quality of education is better at such institutions and 45% would prefer that their children go to a private institution. In fact, only the military earned a higher degree of public confidence than four-year private colleges and universities (NCES, 2001a).

These data do not necessarily mean that parents and students believe in the values associated with a liberal education, however. A college education primarily serves vocational purposes according to public opinion. Although 71% feel that it is very important that colleges prepare students for future jobs, only 65% believe that colleges should prepare future leaders or responsible citizens, hallmarks of a liberal education. Only 58% thought it very important that colleges assist students in developing values, another foundation of the liberal arts education (NCES, 2001a).

For the most part, however, those who attend liberal arts colleges do so because they seek the type of collegiate experience such institutions offer. They want small classes taught by faculty who develop close relationships with students. They seek an environment that demands their participation in a learning community and that prepares them to address important social problems once they graduate (Hersh, 1999).

Students at liberal arts colleges also benefit from the intersection between curricular and cocurricular life on campus. The intellectual, social, emotional, and ethical components of the collegiate experience are inextricably interwoven at liberal arts institutions. Growth in one area promotes development in others. This fusion appeals to students who like active involvement, extensive contact with faculty and staff, and an environment that nurtures mutual understanding and cooperation (Hersh, 1999). The liberal arts institution embodies exemplary educational practice, what students deem to be the collegiate experience, and for that reason they are drawn to such institutions (Chickering & Gamson, 1987). Student affairs professionals play a key role in providing that holistic collegiate experience.

The Nature of Student Affairs Work

The notion of holistic education entrenched in the liberal arts institution mirrors the focus on developing the whole student that is the standard of the student affairs profession. The work that student affairs professionals conduct at these institutions, however, is in some ways difficult to describe because it is elusive. As one administrator noted, "Typical of small campuses, many of us have our fingers in multiple pots and have more than one hat to wear. That can make the respecting of personal and professional boundaries difficult to honor at times."

Liberal arts administrators participated in three studies that yielded data about their professional lives. The Calendar Study yielded quantitative data about the amount of time practitioners at these institutions devoted to certain activities compared to their counterparts at other institutional types. The National Survey Study revealed quantitative findings that compared the nature of work, relationships, and rewards for those at liberal arts institutions to those at other types of campuses. The Association Study provided both quantitative and qualitative data about professional life at liberal arts colleges. Collectively, the findings suggest that the work of student affairs professionals at liberal arts colleges is complex and demanding. It is most readily described through three components: the work environment, the pace of the work, and the way in which work gets done. In each case, the findings from the studies are blended to describe work at liberal arts colleges as richly, yet as accurately, as possible.

The Work Environment

The consistencies among the findings across three studies suggest that there are certain hallmarks of student affairs work at liberal arts colleges. First and foremost, administrators on these campuses are service oriented and student centered, far more so than their counterparts at comprehensive or research universities. The following statements are typical:

> It derives from our mission. We want our students to be service oriented, so we just think that way all the time.

> Our missions (university; division and department) drive our actions and reactions in our professional positions. The University is student centered.

> The professional culture here is centered around the care of the individual student. Administrators who are successful here have great relationships with students and work to create a communal atmosphere.

In fact, 38% of their time is spent in activities best described as serving students. This percentage far exceeds the time spent serving students at other types of campuses. Liberal arts professionals handle extensive individual and group advising functions, spend time counseling students individually and in groups, and present programs to students as well as attend programs sponsored by students. Since the fundamental standard of the student affairs profession is promoting development among students, those at liberal arts colleges have earned the label "standard bearers" of the profession.

Second, professionals at liberal arts institutions work significantly more
independently than their counterparts elsewhere. Administrators spend less time
on managing others and report less centralized management of their own
activities:

> I think we have an environment where people are free to receive the training
> they need to have some autonomy to do things. . . . I just think we can give
> people that freedom versus [trying to] control everything too much.

> All members of this current staff have autonomy and are trusted and supported
> in the decisions we make.

To some degree, the limited amount of management is related to the
multiple roles that professionals at liberal arts colleges often play. It is not
unusual for staff to have both primary and ancillary job responsibilities. Hall
directors also serve as student activities coordinators or orientation
programmers. The upside to this is that the standard bearers are able to relate to
students in multifaceted ways, getting to know them in multiple arenas. The
downside is that time constraints can limit the communication among
professionals and between administrators and other elements on campus:

> The campus sees itself as a small place where everyone knows everyone. And,
> while it is small as colleges go . . . it requires better communication to keep
> everyone on board.

> The institution is really lacking in strong communication. For being such a
> small institution, people don't communicate like they should and it really
> makes people mad.

It seems that the small nature of the campus prompts people to believe that once
decisions are made, everyone will know about those decisions simply through
informal communication.

The intimate nature of these institutions might also lead to the assumption
that liberal arts environments are not particularly political. Although student
affairs administrators on these campuses report lower levels of campus politics
than their colleagues at other types of institutions, the campus can be politically
tinged:

> There [are] some issues that no matter how long you have been there, you
> [have] just got to have enough sense to know that you can't just go barge ahead
> and do this given the sensitivities around all kinds of things. There are
> processes and individuals with weight in the community whom you certainly
> want to consult with and bring along.

> I think that small colleges . . . are always institutions where because of the
> tightly coupled nature of the campus, the environmental impact of your
> decisions are always going to have way more impact.

The lesson here seems to be that professionals need to be sure that they do not become complacent in the small and personal campus. As standard bearers, it might be easy to assume that serving the needs of students holistically is an end in itself. It is not. Student affairs professionals need to ensure they are communicating with others and be vigilant about the political ramifications that their actions might generate. Communication may be challenging given the pace of the work environment at liberal arts colleges and universities.

The Pace of Work

When asked what one lesson they wished they had learned before starting to work at a liberal arts institution, one respondent summed it up concisely:

> [Professionals had] better understand the fast-paced environment of a small private . . . institution.

The personal and professional benefits derived from working closely with students are among the biggest draws of professional life at liberal arts colleges. Of 150 practitioners in the National Survey Study, nearly all mentioned how much they valued the opportunity to work so intimately with students. At the same time, however, the individualized nature of the services provided to students by the standard bearers can be enormously time consuming:

> Whenever I look at new professionals coming in, they all work 8:00 to 5:00. And every single thing that goes on in the evenings and on the weekend they're there. I think it takes a number of years to get that sorted out.

> The more one works, the more work you get. Do not over extend yourself or else [you] will be expected to work even longer hours, more days, etc., etc. . . . If you are always around, people will always expect it. It is more difficult to pull back and take on less than to set the boundaries of time spent at work and things one does after hours, over the weekend, etc.

An overwhelming majority of administrators in all the studies reported that they spent extensive amounts of time on work-related activities. Although professionals at all types of campuses report working beyond 40 hours per week on a regular basis, those at liberal arts institutions are particularly prone to work evening and weekend hours. Perhaps this is due to the close personal relationships they develop with students. What draws the standard bearers to work at liberal arts institutions is promoting holistic development among students. This desire may drive them to feel more obligated to attend events planned and implemented by those students, events that typically take place during non-business hours.

The number of hours professionals work, however, is not necessarily related to the degree of change they can accomplish. Student affairs professionals report a good degree of flexibility to try new programs and practices:

> Our trustees are very hands-off. They basically allow us to do what we are going to do and then report back to them. They take an interest and want to be supportive, but otherwise they don't mandate the course, which I think allows us to have more flexibility.

> We make decisions that we make on a daily basis because that's what we do. No permission necessary, it's just a collaboration within the institution.

The autonomy administrators have to make decisions, however, should not be confused with how quickly change can be introduced on campus. On that point, there is no contention. Many liberal arts institutions have been educating students for 150 years or longer. As a result, they are steeped in traditions that sometimes render them slow to adopt new ideas:

> Tradition, I think is a big thing in our college especially. I have been there for two years and a lot of times you hear "well, no you can't do it that way. The [name of college] way is. . . ." So things can change, we can do things differently, but it takes time. It takes the right people and really selling your ideas and going about it that way. But, tradition is a big thing that is always kind of thrown out there.

> And it's not "can we change quickly," we do sometimes. But in terms of intentional planned change, there is a lot of time spent plowing the ground. A lot of time spent putting the seeds in and then fertilizing it.

The need to be aware of the role that tradition plays should come as no surprise to professionals who work at these institutions. After all, liberal arts campuses pride themselves as setting the standard for the collegiate experience. As bearers of that standard, professionals may need to learn how to nurture the notion of change before trying to enact such.

One other point about the pace of work merits attention here. Although practitioners work long hours, and often work evenings and weekends, those with families report that the small, close nature of the campus enables them to include their families in many events. This is viewed as a real benefit:

> I find that my life can be more balanced at small schools because I can include my family in my work a lot more easily than I could when I was at a large land grant institution where having a three-year-old didn't quite work the same way it does on my campus where everybody knows my child and that's a cool thing. It works for me in terms of balance to be at a small place because my family is part of the community.

Many liberal arts campuses are located in small towns, in rural locations. The ability to incorporate family into the life of the campus seems to add meaning for many professionals with spouses/partners or families. This same setting can limit social contacts for those who do not have spouses/partners. They may find their social options more limited.

How Work Gets Done

The final element associated with the nature of work is to examine how work gets done. Frequently, those at liberal arts institutions are the only professional on campus with a certain expertise; many work in one-person operations. As a result, they are nearly always involved in decisions about their office, but they rarely have the opportunity to delegate tasks to others.

Like their colleagues at comprehensive, research, and Hispanic-serving institutions, liberal arts professionals also report that creativity is valued when addressing work tasks:

> What we see from the president on down is the notion to try different things and to know that if it fails you'll still be rewarded. Obviously there are still checks and balances along the way, it is not a free-for-all. But the fact is that people can go in and say, "Let's turn this upside down, inside out, do it a different way" and not fear failure. . . . It's nice to have that support.

> I'm trying to send a value of creativity in thinking about new life, new energy, new ways to use money in tight financial times. Although we're not cutting, we're still conserving. How to do things differently. In my world there is a value of creativity and I'm focused on it.

That creativity can have some drawbacks for those at liberal arts colleges, however, that are not evident at the other institutions where creativity is valued. Creativity often leads to new programs and services that come without new staff to manage them:

> People that go to work in [liberal arts] environments or stay in those environments have to be able to take on multiple responsibilities because we all do multiple things all the time. . . . I think it's just a part of it and when there is something new to [be] done or a new program, there's not money to add more staff so, someone currently there needs to pick up the responsibility.

> About staff wearing lots of hats, every year there is a body of things that just don't get done because you just can't get it all done. I spend a fair amount of time with my staff helping them feel okay about that and focusing on the positive parts of their job performance.

At first glance, the data on the issue of working independently versus working with others seem equivocal. In the National Survey Study, liberal arts professionals reported they were much less likely than their counterparts at other types of institutions to work with other student service professionals on most job tasks. In the Association Study, however, they reported working in team oriented settings and talked extensively about the teamwork that enabled them to get work done:

> I guess I see at my institution and my role in the institution as being very team oriented. We have five assistant directors and we spend quite a bit of time working collectively, so that we don't become . . . islands. I also think that our administration mirrors that for us. I think even our division of education and community services . . . is yet another team. I think that is fostered at our institution from my level right up through [the top].

Upon closer examination, however, the comments suggest that collaboration is tempered by a sense of accountability:

> The staff is absolutely amazing that I am working with. They are great people and I am amazed that we get along as well as we do personally and work style. But, there is definitely [a sense of] "this is your box, this is mine."

> Collaboration is good to a point . . . but . . . the bucks stop . . . with somebody. So you can listen all you want, but when I turn to you and say let me see the program, I don't want to hear [excuses]. [I] don't like it. I don't care. It's your program.

Overall, the findings suggest that the standard bearers at liberal arts colleges work collaboratively with colleagues, but that they are still held accountable for the work that falls within their area of expertise. The fact that so many staff work in one-person operations may help explain this ambiguity. On the other hand, perhaps this has to do with the kinds of relationships they have with others on campus.

The Nature of Relationships

The findings from all the studies that involved liberal arts professionals suggest that they work with several key constituencies, including student affairs colleagues, faculty, and parents of students. Far and away, however, the people with whom they work most closely are students. Overwhelmingly, they report that the opportunity to work with students and promote learning and development among students are what they most value about their work:

> I like to see them [students] come in with a unique set of challenges—issues they are dealing with—and watch them overcome them. . . . It is fun to watch them progress, especially over a four year period. I think that is unique for liberal arts that we have the ability to take an individual and watch them develop.

> You get to know students very well in a number of different contexts, but there is a certain amount of students that are just really a blessing, that for me reaffirm for me why I felt called into this profession. They sustain me in other relationships that are not a blessing and are not supportive.

> So, one of the wonderful things about places like ours is that we get to touch students in a lot of ways and they get to touch us in a lot of ways.

> I forget who the physicist is . . . who talked about particles being bundles of potentiality. That's all they were. In fact, particles might not even exist until they come into a relationship with something else. That is how I view students now. They are bundles of potentiality and it's the interaction with students at small liberal arts colleges [that makes our jobs meaningful]. We are just with them and we have all of these opportunities to touch them and interact with them that we wouldn't have at large schools.

Indeed, promoting holistic growth is why those at liberal arts institutions have been labeled standard bearers in this volume. To find that they value seeing students grow and mature is not surprising, though the fact that nearly all professionals in all three studies mentioned that fact certainly reinforces the nature of their relationships with students.

This is not to say, however, that there are not downsides to working with students. The overwhelming word used to describe what they disliked about working with students was the sense of entitlement that students at liberal arts colleges seem to have. There are other issues as well:

> The majority of our students come from very well-off families and backgrounds and have a strong sense of entitlement. Many expect that we will hold their hand through their four years.

> So again the way I see it, the way I work with students it's sometimes very difficult to suffer those bumps and bruises that they need to learn because they feel that they are paying so much money that they shouldn't have to wait or have something not go their way.

> I think that for me it's the disappointment. I have a history of taking chances on students, taking risks with students. When you take that risk and you give them every opportunity to succeed and do the right thing, etc. and they just don't for whatever reason—they don't want to, they don't care to or whatever. That becomes I think the biggest disappointment in the profession.

Professionals at liberal arts colleges also find themselves working with parents more frequently than their colleagues at all other types of campuses except HBCUs. Unlike their counterparts at HBCUs, however, for the standard bearers, interactions with parents are also grounded in a sense of entitlement:

> I think that some parents have a sense of entitlement there, a huge sense of entitlement and that causes a lot of problems especially with them stepping in

their child's place and not letting [the student] handle and take care of
problems. They feel they need to correct [any problem] and because they are
parents and paying to put their students there and they feel they deserve this
service, or "you need to work on this for us."

The fact of the matter is that we know the student very well, but it still makes
the student accountable for his or her conduct or choices that he or she makes.
The parents' response to that is . . . [disbelief] that we didn't involve them
earlier. "I can't believe that you wait until this point to call us. It's a small
place, you know what is going on . . . the sense of the caring and the
community." Sure, we know your kid and we know what has been going on
here, but that doesn't mean we are going to call you first thing. I think that is an
issue for us.

Beyond students and their parents, however, there are other key
constituencies with which student affairs professionals deal. Most notable
among these are faculty members. There seems to be a perception among
student affairs professionals in general that those who work at liberal arts
colleges are blessed to work with faculty members who understand and
appreciate holistic education. Many presume that faculty at these institutions
work closely with student affairs administrators to promote overall development
among students. This may be nothing more than a pervasive professional myth,
however. Although the standard bearers report that faculty at their campuses are
committed, stimulating, and supportive, this does not necessarily mean they are
partners in the work of student affairs professionals. They also report that
faculty are stubborn, somewhat elitist, and "don't get student affairs":

Faculty [are] normally cordial, but there seems to be a degree of distance
between faculty and staff because of the perceived educational differences.

[Faculty] know that counseling services does counseling but they don't see
those stages of development and understand why we do something and why
they might also want to do some different things. That's why I don't feel that
there is an understanding of what students are going through.

Student affairs professionals struggle to get respect for what it is we do. Faculty
don't quite get it and that makes our jobs more difficult. It is easy for a group of
faculty to criticize student behavior but they don't want to take part in trying to
modify that behavior or educate students to make better decisions. The faculty
are good at telling student affairs people what to do, but don't want to work in
collaboration with us.

More than their counterparts at other campuses, those at liberal arts colleges
believe that faculty members are interested in students and committed to helping
students grow but that professors do not necessarily take advantage of the
expertise that student affairs professionals bring to the table:

[Faculty are] glad we have a counseling center, they're glad we have residence life staff, you know people who address problems. And because it's the size and the nature of the institution they do know students' problems that are challenges and they know more about the holistic student so they are glad that there are those of us to help with that. But understand[ing] is different than collaboration.

They get us sort of, but [the idea] that we're all in it together you know we're not quite to that point.

Finally, it is important to note the camaraderie among student affairs administrators at liberal arts colleges. They describe their colleagues as collaborative and supportive. They provide one another validation, both personally and professionally:

I think that they [student affairs colleagues] are all the people that really understand what we do. We try to describe to the community what your work is—it is hard for them to understand or realize that people actually get paid for doing what we do. But, your student affairs colleagues do understand and see how you fit into the larger work [of the college].

Their energy. I mean they are revitalizing. Every time that you get down, you always know that somebody is going to do something to pick you right back up.

Again, however, the fact that student affairs staff work so closely with one another has some drawbacks. It takes time to nourish and maintain those relationships and given the amount of work that staff are expected to produce, time is of the essence for most professionals. Additionally, closeness means that people expect to know what is going on in each other's life, and drawing boundaries between the professional and the personal can be challenging:

[What I dislike about working with student affairs colleagues is] just the time involved in trying to keep those friendships and relationships going because it deters you from working with students - sometimes and that's frustrating.

[At] a smaller school, when people would ask me very nicely "where are you going to be on the weekend" or whatever [it was hard]. You are, very [much] an open book there. So, to have this kind of a lifestyle, your privacy issues, you are much more in the fish bowl.

Clearly, then relationships can be challenging for student affairs professionals at liberal arts colleges. They can also be rewarding, however. This prompts the question of what other rewards administrators at these colleges value.

The Nature of Rewards

The findings about rewards for professionals at all types of institutions reveal some very clear patterns. When asked to rank order a series of potential rewards, they overwhelmingly reported that intrinsic dividends far outweigh extrinsic benefits. This was true regardless of institutional setting.

Those at liberal arts colleges are no exception. They routinely ranked "meaningful work" as the most important reward:

> I really think that a lot of us really make up for [lack of fiscal support] in meaningful work and being able to be appreciated by that one student. Or you have a program that really goes well. That's worth getting up in the morning.

> The reason we are drawn to the profession is the nature of the work with students. I think for me that is why I am in the profession.

> The most important aspect is being able to come home at the end of the day and look in the mirror and be happy with what you see.

Beyond meaningful work, professionals at liberal arts institutions mirror their counterparts elsewhere when they rank other intrinsic benefits as important, including: a positive work environment, the ability to influence decisions, positive working relationships, and the degree of autonomy they are afforded on the job.

Equally as interesting is the fact that the rewards they rank as least important are all extrinsic in nature. These include benefits, opportunities for advancement, leave time, performance reviews, and office facilities and equipment. These rankings might be better understood in light of rewards available to practitioners. Professionals at liberal arts institutions report that extrinsic rewards are significantly less adequate than those reported by their colleagues at other types of institutions. Benefits like health, dental, prescription, and optical insurance are not available to many administrators at liberal arts colleges. They are significantly less likely to have adequate support staff or student workers. They are also less likely to be supported if they elect to take classes or to receive funds to support professional development activities. Finally, performance review procedures on their campuses are not good, nor are opportunities for career advancement. Terms like "lousy pay," "no upward mobility," and "long hours" were liberally sprinkled throughout their comments. Only those at HBCUs were as critical of their extrinsic rewards as professionals at liberal arts colleges.

Conclusions

What conclusions, then, can be drawn about professional life for the standard bearers at liberal arts colleges? Consider their work environment. First, they work in a service-oriented environment and they prefer that environment.

Providing services to students is firmly entrenched in the ethos of the student affairs profession. Indeed, it is what led to the creation of the profession. In this sense, those at liberal arts colleges are truly standard bearers.

They also are afforded a high degree of autonomy. To some extent, this may be a matter of necessity. Professionals routinely fulfill multiple roles. The student affairs ideology talks about dealing with students holistically and professionals who serve in multiple capacities on campus are well equipped to deal with not only the intellectual but also the emotional, psychological, physiological, and other capacities of students. Again, they uphold the fundamental standard of the profession.

At the center of their work is the student. Those at liberal arts campuses form close and lasting relationships with students and witness the changes that occur with those students over time. That aspect of their work seems to be what they find most meaningful. This primary focus on students resonates with the standards of professional student affairs work.

At odds with the notion of serving as student affairs standard bearers are relationships that professionals at liberal arts colleges have with faculty. The generally accepted notion that faculty and student affairs professionals at these colleges work hand-in-hand to maximize the overall educational experience of students seems to be a myth. Faculty members do care about students but do not necessarily understand what student affairs professionals do, nor appreciate their work.

Finally, the rewards for professionals at liberal arts institutions are intrinsic. They do not believe they are particularly well paid and their benefit packages are less extensive than those offered to administrators at other types of colleges and universities. They do not have the same degree of clerical or student worker support as their counterparts at other institutions either.

On the other hand, they derive enormous satisfaction from their work with students. They form close and lasting relationships with students and witness the differences they make in students' lives. They are convinced that what they do is important and an integral part of the liberal arts experience. Again, these are hallmarks of the student affairs profession and render the metaphor of the standard bearer appropriate.

Overall, the ability to engage in meaningful work, coupled with the positive work environment and working relationships they have with their colleagues are what draws them to work at this type of institution. The comments that professionals at liberal arts colleges offered when asked to describe the advantages and disadvantages of their work best summarize the nature of professional life at such schools:

> Advantage—a lot of experience, autonomy, and opportunity to grow professionally because you work on hundreds of things at once.
> Disadvantage—not enough pay/support for the amount of work that's expected and very little respect from the majority of the campus (faculty).

> Working with students to develop the "whole person" and learn the core values
> of being human is an advantage. Another advantage: our mission really drives
> our actions in all we do. A disadvantage are [sic] a few individuals who have
> been here forever and do not want to see change.

These comments reflect a perspective on student affairs practice that echoes
the fundamental values on which the profession was founded. In fact, some
comments address the role professionals play in perpetuating the liberal arts
tradition:

> Well, [student affairs work] is essential actually to the function of what a liberal
> arts education is. A liberal arts education is about being collaborative and not
> just studying engineering or just studying math or whatever. So, I think [what
> we do] very much ties to that.

> I think that compared to other environments, if someone does not feel that they
> are good in the liberal arts, they will self-select out. [You might] find several
> niches in a larger environment that will make you happy. . . . You can't get by
> with that on a small college campus because everyone has to [make a
> difference].

> I think we are projecting too a legacy. Somebody [did] that for us when we
> were in college. . . . So, I think your comment is—passing on what someone
> has done for us.

For student affairs professionals who work at liberal arts institutions,
making a difference in students' lives is what sustains them. They are convinced
that a liberal arts education ought to be transformative for students, and they
play a critical role in that transformation. They are convinced that the liberal arts
environment is most conducive to the holistic education at the heart of student
affairs administration. In that sense, they see themselves as standard bearers of
the profession.

Chapter Three

The Interpreters:
Professional Life at Religiously Affiliated
Institutions

It is certainly true that all the colonial colleges, as well as most of those established during the Republican era, were liberal arts institutions. This may not fully describe these institutions, however. It is perhaps more accurate to say that the vast majority were religiously affiliated colleges. For purposes of this discussion, I use the term "religiously affiliated" to describe colleges and institutions that have close ties to a denomination. Close ties may include a formalized relationship with a religious organization, extensive support from a specific church, or a denominational focus in the mission or curriculum of the institution. It also may include denominational influence in the governance structure of the institution. Typically this means a sectarian president, a strong denominational presence on the governing board, or both.

The work in which student affairs professionals engage at religiously affiliated institutions parallels the work of those affiliated with liberal arts institutions in some ways. That is, many of the programs and services at religiously affiliated colleges and universities mirror those at liberal arts colleges. The manner in which those programs and services are delivered, however, takes on a markedly different tone at denominational campuses. Staff exert both time and energy as "interpreters." Their role entails explicating the purpose of student affairs to institutional leaders and faculty, elucidating student affairs professional practice and the religious tenets of the campus, and translating the role of student affairs into a sectarian context. It also means interpreting their personal faith in light of their professional responsibilities and interpreting their professional responsibilities in light of their personal faith.

The ways in which religiously affiliated institutions have evolved over time in the U.S. provides some insight into the role the interpreters play on these campuses. The history of sectarian campuses describes the setting in which student affairs professionals conduct their work. Their relationships with others and the rewards they reap are also inextricably entrenched in the religious context of their institution. Their own words offer the most convincing evidence of how their roles differ from their colleagues at secular campuses.

Historical Evolution

Just as the colonies in America were founded to ensure religious freedom, the earliest centers of higher learning in the New World were created by religious leaders and were designed to perpetuate those religious interests. For example, in the 1600s, Congregationalists founded Harvard and Anglicans established William and Mary in order to ensure a sufficient supply of Congregational and Anglican clerics. Over time, some believed that the earliest colleges had strayed from the religious zealotry that should have guided them. This Great Awakening in the early 18th century led to the founding of additional colleges including Yale and Princeton. Although some campuses were established by groups of ministers from different denominations (e.g., Brown, Rutgers), in each such instance a single religion came to dominate the college in short order. In fact, all but one of the nine colonial colleges had ecumenical roots. The exception was the University of Pennsylvania, and even that institution had close ties to the Quakers of the Commonwealth (Brubacher & Rudy, 1997; O'Grady, 1969).

The post-Revolutionary period witnessed several developments with respect to the denominational hold on higher education in America. For one, the first public institutions were established in the decades after the war, led by the University of Georgia in 1785 and followed shortly thereafter by the University of Virginia (O'Grady, 1969; Rudolph, 1962). Second, whereas the Protestant denominations had monopolized higher education in the colonial period, Catholics joined the endeavor at the end of the century, starting with the founding of Georgetown University in the 1780s. Finally, the westward expansion of the country opened opportunities for both the Catholic and other Protestant churches to establish colleges and universities at a rapid pace. In Ohio alone, no fewer than eleven denominations founded colleges in the first half of the 18th century. The Lutherans founded Wittenberg and the Presbyterians opened Muskingham. Mount Union and Ohio Wesleyan were established by the Methodists. Otterbein was founded by the United Brethren. Other institutions were sponsored by Congregationalists, Episcopalians, Baptists, Swedenborgians, the Reformed Church, and Catholics (Lucas, 1994).

These trends suggest that higher education was flourishing in the Republican era and, if success is measured solely by the number of institutions, that might be an accurate perception. Most of these colleges, however, enrolled a very limited number of students. According to Lucas (1994), the average Ohio institution enrolled fewer than 100 students in the years just before the Civil War. At Lafayette, in Pennsylvania, there were more trustees on the board than there were students at the institution at one point during this era. The limited numbers of students seeking higher education in this period led to an issue of support. The colleges were reliant on tuition and donations. Given that some students were on scholarship and donations were sporadic, most campuses teetered on the brink of bankruptcy. To overcome such financial exigencies, they sought assistance from the state in the form of grants. Although they relied on grants, the institutions continued to be governed by denominations. Moreover, many were chartered by the state. These issues created a question of control: Were these institutions public or private entities (Lucas)?

This question was first addressed in a case involving Dartmouth College. Lucas (1994) offers a detailed summary of the case, but essentially the courts were asked to decide the degree to which the institution was public or private. In 1819, the U.S. Supreme Court ruled that Dartmouth was essentially a private entity. This decision set an important precedent: Whereas states might charter institutions of learning, they could exercise control over only those that were designated as public institutions when they were founded. The Dartmouth case established some initial parameters, but the relationship between the state and religiously affiliated colleges and universities continued to raise questions.

Religiously affiliated institutions faced a series of challenges over the course of the next 200 years. The first occurred in the post-Civil War era and resulted in forcing many religiously affiliated institutions to choose whether to retain their denominational ties or sacrifice those ties to meet other demands. The industrialization of America following the war enabled corporate leaders to amass mammoth personal fortunes. Among these was Andrew Carnegie, the steel magnate cum philanthropist. In 1905, he created the Carnegie Foundation for the Advancement of Teaching. Concerned about the deplorable salaries paid to faculty, he allocated $10,000,000 to establish a pension fund for college teachers. The intent was to provide pensions for those college instructors who met certain criteria. Those who had taught for at least 15 years and were at least 60 years old were eligible for pensions equal to 60% of their salaries, with provisions for their widows, as well (Brubacher & Rudy, 1997; Rudolph, 1962). There were, however, stipulations. Those at institutions with religious ties were not eligible for the pensions. Private college administrators, concerned about retaining faculty, were prompted to reconsider the institutional affiliations with religious organizations. Some opted to sever ties with their denominational sponsors whereas others reaffirmed those ties and sought alternative ways to provide financial security for their faculty (Brubacher & Rudy; Rudolph, 1962).

Gender issues posed another challenge for religiously affiliated institutions. Increasing interest in higher education on the part of women during the 19th century created a conundrum for these campuses. A select few elected to admit women. Most opted to establish separate institutions for women, with Catholics leading this movement. The disparities between educational opportunities for men and women persisted, however (Brubacher & Rudy, 1997; Rudolph, 1962).

Religiously affiliated institutions soldiered on during the 20th century until after World War II when another series of circumstances challenged their identity. Three distinct issues arose in this era. First, there was a need to expand curricular offerings in higher education to include the new technologies that appeared and rapidly expanded in the post-war years. Second, there was a need to expand capacity in higher education. At first, colleges and universities needed to absorb the millions of veterans who enrolled under the G.I. Bill. Within two decades, expansion was needed to accommodate the baby boom generation. Finally, there was a need to educate a broader array of students; broader in the sense of backgrounds, competencies, academic interests, and skills (A. W. Astin & Lee, 1972).

A final challenge to religious higher education in America emerged in the last quarter of the 20th century. Again, a set of circumstances coalesced. First, the end of the baby boom generation brought an end to the need for expanding capacity. In fact, there were predictions of dire decreases in college enrollments. Additionally, the demand by students for professional education increased. Religiously affiliated institutions, with their grounding in liberal arts, had to decide to what degree they were willing to accommodate such shifting curricular interests. These challenges influenced religiously affiliated colleges and universities in a number of ways, not the least of which was the nature of such campuses.

The Nature of the Religiously Affiliated College Campus

Religiously affiliated institutions have survived various threats to their existence over time, but their representation in the spectrum of higher education has diminished somewhat. In 1968, 712 or just under 31% of the 2,319 institutions of higher learning in the U.S. were denominational (A. W. Astin & Lee, 1972). Twenty years later, although the number of sectarian colleges had remained fairly stable, the total number of institutions in the country had increased. In 1988, there were just over 800 religiously affiliated institutions (Hunt & Carper, 1988). There were just over 3,400 colleges and universities at the time, however, so denominational campuses comprised less than 25% of the higher education sector.

The breadth of religious interests, however, remains extensive. At the turn of the 21st century, there are at least 23 religions sponsoring institutions of higher learning. These include relatively well-known Protestant organizations like Lutherans, Episcopalians, Baptists, and Methodists. Lesser-known sects are also active sponsors, including the Moravians and Disciples of Christ. Other religions are also active in the higher education arena; Catholicism and Judaism to name but two (Hunt & Carper, 1996).

Despite their diminished representation in the overall system of higher education, then, the array of denominations among religiously affiliated campuses suggest they retain a strong presence in the system of higher education. As such, they warrant attention in this volume. Their unique missions and faculty and student characteristics mean that student affairs work on these campuses takes on a different tone, one that involves interpretation.

Mission

In one sense, the broad spectrum of denominations represented among sectarian institutions suggests that their missions are disparate. Consider the following mission statements from four institutions representing four denominations:

[Name of college] offers students an exceptional opportunity to obtain an education of high quality built on the basis of solid academic programs, a strong commitment to values rooted in the Judeo-Christian tradition, and an environment that is truly both supportive and challenging. . . . [We strive] to prepare students intellectually, spiritually and morally to take their places in a rapidly changing global society and to have a positive impact on that society. Jesuit education prepares the whole person, developing knowledge, values, and responsibility for others. The Jesuit focus on ethics and values helps prepare [name of institution] students for the moral decisions they will have to make in their lives and careers.

[Name of college] is a selective national liberal arts college founded in 1847. [Its] affiliation with the Religious Society of Friends (Quakers) informs our emphasis on seeking the truth wherever it leads, respect for persons, learning from and with one another, conflict management and peacemaking, diversity, global education and on international experience.

[Name of college] is a Christian college of the liberal and applied arts and sciences. The College is committed to an embracing evangelical spirit rooted in the Anabaptist, Pietist and Wesleyan traditions of the Christian Church. Our mission is to educate men and women toward maturity of intellect, character and Christian faith in preparation for lives of service, leadership and reconciliation in church and society.

The mission of [name of] College is to glorify God by educating and ministering to a diverse community of students for the purpose of developing servant-leaders, transforming society for the kingdom of Christ. We accomplish this through biblically based programs and services marked by excellence and anchored by the historic, evangelical, and Reformed Christian faith. The curriculum is rooted in the liberal arts and sciences, vocationally focused and delivered through traditional and specialized programs.

Upon closer inspection, however, the common elements among these missions become clear. All four highlight their liberal arts foundation. In that sense, they are similar to the mission statements of liberal arts colleges described in Chapter Two. However, these institutions take the liberal arts tradition a step further. They talk about the religious and spiritual elements of the higher education experience. At non-denominational institutions there is an embargo on talk of moral and spiritual development whereas at religiously affiliated schools such talk is embraced.

In fact, the role that religion plays at these colleges and universities has been the source of extensive comment over the years as external pressures have raised questions about their spiritual focus. In the late 1950s and early 1960s, for instance, the future of church-related colleges and universities was at risk. Champions of sectarian education offered powerful arguments about the form of denominational education: "First, Christian higher education must be motivated by *the love of wisdom*; and, second, Christian higher education must be informed by the *wisdom of love*" (Putnam, 1964, p. 345). Perpetuation of denominational schools was imperative (Thompson, 1960) and required leadership at the institutional and governance levels that would work to assure the future of this form of higher learning (Rand, 1956).

A few years later, attention shifted to matters of continuity and control (O'Grady, 1969); in particular, control over curriculum. Proponents of religious education pointed out how the early religious seminaries produced graduates who went on to establish elementary and secondary religious schools that served as feeder institutions for religiously affiliated colleges (Naylor, 1977). As such, there was a seamless system of sectarian education that should ensure continuity.

At the same time, an economic recession and predictions of diminished enrollments raised questions about whether religiously affiliated schools should continue to receive funding from public sources. One expert suggested that "concern for religion will turn a liberal arts college into a 'quasi-religious' institution." In response, another countered, "Failure to take the religious question seriously will turn any liberal arts college into a 'quasi-educational' institution" (Averill, 1969, p. 86). Defenders of denominational institutions exhorted their colleagues that "their primary aim is to aid their students in developing a Christian philosophy of life" (Coleman, 1960, p. 316) regardless of the impact of such aims on potential enrollments.

In fact, however, students continued to pursue higher learning at religiously affiliated institutions throughout the 20th century. This has led experts to conclude that the future of religious higher education in the new millennium is bright (McMurtrie, 2000). Religion and spirituality are making a comeback (Wolfe, 2002). Indeed, spirituality plays an important role in sectarian higher education (Blumhofer, 2002; O'Keefe, 1997), and religiously affiliated colleges and universities represent a key element in a liberal democracy (Thiessen,

2001). Given past patterns, concerns over mission, control, curriculum, and the place of sectarian higher education are likely to resurface in the future. Therefore, the roles that faculty and students play at denominational campuses merit attention.

Faculty

The characteristics of those who teach at religiously affiliated colleges and universities have evolved over time. In the colonial era, nearly all instructors were members of the denomination that founded the institution. Keeping in mind that the role of institutions in that era was to train future clergy and that most teachers came from the ranks of the colleges' alumni, this may not be too surprising. During the Republican era, however, as more elective classes were introduced into the curriculum, faculty members who were qualified to teach these classes were needed. No longer were generalists who could teach many subjects of the classical curriculum sufficient. As a result, faculty members were hired who were laypersons or affiliated with other denominations (Burtchaell, 1998).

This trend was exacerbated in the post-Civil War period. The passage of the Morrill Acts in 1862 and 1890 led to the founding of universities that offered studies in agriculture, mining, and other technical fields. The specialized knowledge and skills required to teach in the expanded institution led to the hiring of experts by discipline and diminished the sectarian influence on the campuses of religiously affiliated institutions (Burtchaell, 1998).

As specialization among faculty in higher education has intensified over the past 100 years, fewer and fewer faculty members at sectarian campuses are members of the institutional denomination. This has changed the dynamics on campus and led to conflicts over issues related to research, governance, and academic freedom (Burtchaell, 1998). In terms of research, lay faculty members often have to fight to ensure their rights to conduct secular research (Shemky, 1967). This is particularly true when investigators attempt to explore issues that may contradict denominational dogma. For example, when faculty at religiously affiliated institutions study issues on which there is religious doctrine, like abortion, homosexuality, or stem cells, they may be subjected to greater campus scrutiny.

To some degree, this scrutiny is driven by the governance system on campus. Ecclesiastics lead most religiously affiliated institutions and the governing boards at such schools are typically dominated by members of the denomination. This often results in a conservative in-group that strives to maintain the status quo. Such an attitude flies in the face of conducting cutting edge research, an endeavor that most faculty members hold dear. In fact, some argue that conservative governance will prohibit sectarian colleges and universities from recruiting and retaining quality faculty members (Shemky, 1967). The problem is intensified by the inability of outside agencies to intervene. The National Labor Relations Board (NLRB) has no control over religiously affiliated campuses. Faculty members on these campuses complain that they have no role in the governance structure of the campus and they cannot unionize to garner a greater say in that governance system (Smallwood, 2002).

Despite these perceived restrictions, religion and spirituality are making a comeback among many scholars (Wolfe, 2002). Faculty members at religiously affiliated colleges and universities conduct research and let their faith inform their studies (McMurtrie, 2000). Indeed, those who work at sectarian institutions need to be committed to the notion of religious education. If they are not, they are likely to feel confined and constrained in the environment (Mooney, 1994). Whereas separation of church and state may have guided higher education in the past, accommodation of religion within higher education seems to be the contemporary thinking (Zirkle, 2001).

Students

This current perspective about religion and higher education is having an effect on students as well. Nearly one in four institutions of higher learning in America is religiously affiliated (Mooney, 1994), and Catholic campuses represent the largest percentage of denominational schools (Guthrie, 1992). Catholic institutions do not have a monopoly on sectarian higher education, however. Consider the case of Evangelical Christian colleges. Between 1990 and 1996, enrollment at public universities increased 4%, while at private institutions enrollments grew by 5%. Evangelical colleges, however, witnessed an astounding increase of 24%. There were an estimated 129,000 students at Evangelical colleges in 1996 (Reisberg, 1999).

There are a number of reasons for this increased interest in religiously affiliated postsecondary institutions. First, the growth in K-12 sectarian education in the 1980s is producing more graduates who wish to pursue higher education in a denominational setting. Second, stories of binge drinking, drug use, and extensive sexual activity at public colleges and universities have prompted many parents and students to look to religious campuses for a different type of educational environment. Additionally, the academic reputations of sectarian institutions have improved over the past two decades. Finally, denominational campuses have done a better job of marketing themselves to prospective students in recent years (Reisberg, 1999).

Students have responded to these efforts on the part of religiously affiliated campuses. At the end of the 20th century they are in a revival mode (Mooney, 1995). Similar to the "great awakening" that took place on college campuses in the mid-18th and mid-19th centuries, contemporary students are turning to religion more frequently. Unlike their counterparts in earlier eras, however, today's students have been exposed to non-Christian-Judeo philosophies. As a result, they seek spirituality and a personal relationship with God (Wolfe, 2002).

Sectarian colleges and universities do have an influence on students, then, and one that is welcomed by students. They positively influence the development of character among students (H. Astin & Antonio, 2000). Students appreciate the fact that many faculty members at religiously affiliated institutions are committed to the integration of faith and scholarship and strive to blend their beliefs into their classrooms (Mooney, 1994).

The roles of faculty and students at religiously affiliated schools seem to be linked. At issue is how student affairs professionals adapt their practice to the climate at denominational campuses. Based on their reports, they often find themselves serving as interpreters: translating their role to the campus setting, explaining their role to other key constituencies, and restating professional issues in terminology that reflects the sectarian influences of the campus.

The Nature of Student Affairs Work

The data on professionals at religiously affiliated institutions come from three studies. In the Calendar Study, practitioners provided information about how they spend their time, and data analysis unearthed how those time commitments differed from their counterparts at other types of institutions. Data analysis from the National Survey Study revealed statistically significant differences between those at religiously affiliated campuses and their colleagues at other types of institutions in terms of work, relationships, and rewards. There were also participants from religiously affiliated institutions in the Association Study. They provided quantitative data about work, relationships, and rewards that could be used to compare them with those at other forms of institutions. They also offered comments in that study and the National Survey Study that elucidated their professional lives.

In some ways, the work of the interpreters at religiously affiliated institutions seems similar to that of their colleagues at liberal arts colleges, particularly in terms of their work with students: (a) Support for and commitment to undergraduate students is very strong, and (b) From an idealistic perspective, the institution as a whole is very interested in creating the best possible experiences for its students.

In other arenas, however, those at denominational schools play a role that differs distinctly from colleagues at other types of institutions. These areas can best be described in terms of the work environment, their relationships with other groups on and off campus, and the rewards they believe are associated with the work they do.

The Work Environment

One way in which student affairs administrators at sectarian institutions interpret their roles differently than their colleagues at other types of campuses relates to how they spend their time. Although it might be expected that their time allocations would differ from those at research or comprehensive universities, the Calendar Study revealed that those at religiously affiliated campuses also spend their time in some very different ways than those at liberal arts colleges. For example, they spend only about half as much time (12%) on administrative tasks (e.g., planning programs, projects, and paperwork) than their liberal arts peers (23%). Somewhat more surprising, they also report spending much less time serving students (20% vs. 25%), which includes individual and group advising, presenting programs, and attending student programs. Perhaps this difference is due to the fact that they spend significantly more time teaching credit-bearing classes than their colleagues at liberal arts institutions (9% vs. <1%). Teaching is one of their interpretive duties: They translate course content into meaningful learning for students.

The notion of meaningful learning for students takes on a different interpretation, as well. It is perhaps best reflected in the missions of sectarian institutions. These missions require an awareness of the spiritual nature of their work:

> Balancing, the church's mission to today's ethics and values to today's youth is constantly, it's complex because society is changing more rapidly.

> There is a big emphasis at a number of our institutions on "how is your work [going]?" Not just on who you are personally and professionally, but also your faith, your faith and action. So it's a place where you can feel that you are on a spiritual journey, your work is a form of ministry and that you are doing not just good things, you are doing great things that are professional and confident and also help you grow spiritually. And I think there are some folks who work for us who feel very connected in that way and there is an emphasis on that. So there is . . . this notion of mission and mission congruity and then integration of self and faith in the work that we do. And one of the things being in a religiously affiliated college affirms is the opportunity to integrate that.

As these comments suggest, working at a religiously affiliated institution requires practitioners to interpret their work in the context of their faith and the missions of their campuses.

The spiritual nature of their work is also reflected in the ways they deal with students. In the Association Study, those at religiously affiliated colleges and universities reported that their work is more student-centered than their colleagues at any other type of institution. They attribute this emphasis to the denominational nature of the campus. The church with which their institution is affiliated influences their work with students:

> I think too in a [name of denomination] institution, or religiously affiliated [school], the backbone is there. It's the teachings of Christ: to go find your vocation. So you have got the foundation with a whole student centered, human centered taking care of the entire human [race]. [It] is easy to build a student center from that because everyone's focus is on God's children, to go out and find a vocation and help guide them in finding that vocation. So the faculty,

staff, [cleric] or otherwise . . . are there for the students—to help them with the
teachings of Christ and to learn and it's embedded in the Church's mission.

The message that's been given to me, and I've been giving it out I guess, has
been sort of to conform to what the college's image is and not get too far
astray. For instance . . . we're a [name of denomination] college. . . . We
wanted to do some spirituality stuff in student affairs and my director of student
activities is a little bit more on the evangelical side and I was called in to kind
of pull that back.

Student affairs practitioners at sectarian campuses have taken the fundamental
premise of the profession—the holistic development of the student—and
translated that into the religious context of their working environments.

Administrators at religious colleges also report their campuses are far less
bureaucratic than other types of campuses. Although they disparage
"bureaucracy that can hang students and staff up," they also note that there are
both advantages and disadvantages to limited bureaucracy:

I am trying to think of how to explain it. I have come from a public institution
into a private institution. The public institution that I came from was very
highly bureaucratic, which [was] extreme. This one seems to be at the opposite
extreme because we are so decentralized and sometimes I think there has got to
be balance in everything. So there is not a lot of red tape, but that causes
confusion sometimes because there are no rules.

On the other hand, in the Association Study they also rated their campuses
as more centrally managed than their colleagues at any other institutional type.
They report that the leaders on campus are highly powerful:

We also have the nine schools with the Deans reporting [to the President]. But
there is a central budgeting system, central purchasing system, basically one
university calendar. . . . So while we do have the nine there is still some central
stuff that is in place. Even though there is some autonomy I think its more
central[ized] than decentralized.

There are colleges at [name of university] and those Deans are very important.
So that decision making process is happening through the colleges and not so
much in central administration. So it's the colleges plus any number of VPs. So
decision-making, governance, just how the university operates is what we all
call fiefdoms.

Although leadership is powerful, the institutions seem to try to temper the
power of leaders to some extent, by empowering professionals and holding them
accountable for their respective areas of responsibility:

To me [the campus] is kind of organized, centralized. But there also is a
process for decision making in [which] we do try to empower folks to come up
with things.

> I would say we have our centralization aspect, but one of the things about
> [name of denomination] philosophy is a sense of the individual. . . . We do
> have central goals, but we also have individual responsibility.

If the notion of empowerment coupled with accountability sounds familiar, it
might be because those at liberal arts institutions also talked about the how the
autonomy they had in their jobs was mitigated by demands for accountability.

The parallels between those at liberal arts and religiously affiliated
institutions end when it comes to the political nature of their campuses. Those at
liberal arts institutions report a moderately political environment. At religious
schools, however, the climate is highly political. Across all denominations, the
church plays a key role in this climate. Consider comments from those at
Christian institutions:

> We are highly political, I mean off the charts political. Probably it relates to our
> religious affiliation and all its tolerance for activism. . . . [Name of university]
> is heavily a social science institution and it's right in [name of city]. People
> come there because they are already political, they want to be more political,
> and it's simply synonymous with our institution. The Methodist [agenda] is [a]
> social justice agenda that is highly visible and very aggressive.

> I am [at] a Baptist institution. You have to be very, very careful to understand
> who you are talking to and what their beliefs are religiously, not what they
> believe student affairs-wise or how we are running our division. And you have
> to monitor that, you have to keep yourself in check and there are times you may
> not say what you really feel because you know who is across the table.

> I can't get the funding for a project just because I attend a certain church, a
> certain Baptist church in the town and the person happens to be the Deacon so
> that is very political, in other words whether I get my money for the project I
> wanted.

Comments from those at Catholic institutions suggest that campus climates
are equally as political but that those politics are played out at different levels:

> I think within the religious community [of] the sponsoring institution there are
> frequently politics, and particularly when you are in a position to hire
> individuals from the religious community you supervise. You are a layperson
> and you are supervising a member of the religious community and there are
> politics involved in that, so within the community. And then within the broader
> religious communities at a Catholic institution is politics. So then you have got
> church politics on top of religious order politics, and I think it can get very
> complicated. And then your Board, the people on your Board and their
> affiliation with a particular church group [adds yet another level].

> Politics is everywhere, but I think what is unique about the religious affiliated,
> and I can only speak for Catholic tradition. But I am sure the Baptists will have
> theirs and you know the denominations of the Evangelical. . . . [But] the

religious orders, which they have their own politics, which is a whole, I mean
you need 10 more workshops on that alone. The Dominican versus the Jesuits
versus the Franciscans.

Even those who did not specify a particular religious denomination in their
comments agreed that there is a politically charged element at sectarian
institutions:

> I think that is another political aspect in church related institutions, Methodist
> to Roman Catholic. . . . It's just a matter of determining who the players are and
> identify[ing] the speaker of the house very quickly.

> The church is right across the street. [I look at it] pretty much everyday so I
> would say there is a lot of politics involved with what is going on with the
> governance of our school and how the church plays in that.

It is important to note that those at denominational colleges and universities are
not the only ones who work in a political environment. As will become evident
in succeeding chapters, life at comprehensive and research universities is
political. The nature of the politics at religiously affiliated institutions is
different, however. Politics at religiously affiliated campuses are more often
associated with the church, not the campus. This requires student affairs
professionals to be able to interpret their work within denominational politics. In
some ways, this difference is better understood in the context of the pace of
work at religiously affiliated schools.

The Pace of Work

Participants from religiously affiliated campuses in all studies uniformly
labeled the pace of work at their institutions in consistent ways. The first related
to the speed with which change takes place on such campuses, though perhaps
lack of speed would be a better descriptor. Their comments suggest that
religiously affiliated campuses are highly resistant to change:

> [Our campus is] not very progressive; not cutting edge. Changes don't occur
> very quickly or easily—not [just] major changes; but little changes that it
> shouldn't take too long to set into motion.

> Change comes exceedingly slowly.

> The environment is very collaborative which is a double-edged sword. You can
> often get assistance in the form of input and share resources with others; but it
> usually takes way too long to accomplish even the easiest of tasks that would
> make a huge difference in the program. A committee is often formed for many
> decisions which would more appropriately be made by a small working group
> or an individual.

The interpreters cite several explanations for this slow pace of change. The first relates to the people in positions of power on the campus:

> A high percentage of the professionals are alumni of the institution and do not want changes in administration. They are interested in their individual areas and seek power and money for their own projects regardless of the overall interest of the university.

> The President is a [name of college] graduate, many of the administrators in the cabinet are [name of college] graduates, so you combine slow to change with the politics and people are still trying to find their places.

These comments are supported by findings from the National Survey Study. Faculty and staff are significantly more likely to know the history and traditions of their institution at denominational schools and are significantly more likely to respect those traditions. The cultural norm is to maintain the status quo rather than introduce change into the culture:

> Change can and has happened but it's like pulling teeth.

> [The biggest disadvantage is] the guarding of tradition against new ideas at the institution.

> We do things this way because this is the way things have always been done. Longevity is rewarded more than professional development; growth; and learning.

> [I wish I had known before I started working here] how entrenched everyone was in doing things the same way. Folks are really threatened by change.

To some degree, these findings are not surprising. Religious orders, in general, are conservative organizations. Those who work at religious institutions, therefore, might expect them to be slow to change. Coupled with the resistance to change, however, the interpreters report that sectarian colleges and universities are more reactive than proactive, and more reactive than other types of campuses:

> We're so busy keeping up (or maybe catching up) with the high-profile events (things that are publicly seen) that we are unable to focus on the future and accomplish the tasks that are not as visible but certainly necessary (like proactive communications; evaluations; assessments; etc.).

> [My] institution is very crisis oriented/reactionary.

> There has been little time for long-term program development; and so decisions have been very often made on a reactive basis.

When change does occur at religious institutions, it seems to be in response to some sort of crisis. This reactive mode influences how work is accomplished on sectarian campuses.

How Work Gets Done

The ways in which professionals at religiously affiliated institutions conduct their work is also different in many ways than the way in which work is conducted at other institutional types. For example, creativity is valued over conformity at religious institutions:

> I think my institution also values creativity so I think there are a lot of creative thinkers and in the faculty and students I think that kind of is forward thinking and original ideas. I think all of that has been encouraged at my institution.

It is important to note, however, that those at denominational campuses reported lower scores in terms of how much creativity is valued than their counterparts at all other types of institutions. This was typified in what the above speaker went on to add:

> Some of them may not fly, but I think people appreciate the thought and the imagination that goes into the thinking and the learning environment.

In a parallel vein, the interpreters at religiously affiliated colleges and universities report that security is more valued than risk taking:

> So [it's not wise] to make high risk moves, especially if you know it's [a] very highly political environment you work in.

> And I would not say we are a high-risk organization, but I think we try to support that when we can. There are other schools not as risk taking.

When risk taking is valued, it seems to be tied to a change in personnel:

> We have a President who has been there, this is just his third year there. We have a new VP who was there, it's been a year, and between the two there was a lot of assessment in the entire division of student affairs. So I think a lot of that risk taking comes from a very recent short-term history.

> I think for me . . . it just happens to be this moment in time where our institution is at a very risk-taking mode. I am a new professional, and when I came into this institution, it was very directed towards me that we were evaluating every aspect of [my] position.

These comments suggest that professionals at sectarian institutions have to interpret their settings. The degree to which they can take risks is constrained by

the people with whom they work and the environment in which they conduct
that work.

The role of interpreter is most evident when those at sectarian schools
describe their multiple roles. The National Survey Study reveals that they are
significantly more likely than their peers at other institutions to have input into
decisions. This finding takes on greater meaning given that they are significantly
more likely to work with fewer other professionals and significantly less likely
to have adequate support staff. That is, they may be the only administrators in
their offices to make important decisions. They are also significantly less likely
to have adequate office equipment, including computers and supporting
software.

These quantitative findings paint a picture of student affairs administrators
at religiously affiliated colleges and universities who have to translate their
profession into their faith and their faith into their profession. The comments
they offer about the nature of their work reveal how it extends beyond
professional boundaries to incorporate faith:

> It's more of a mission than a job.

> [It's] a vocation.

> It's not an 8:00-5:00 job because it is a ministry.

This final comment is telling in another sense: Like their peers at liberal arts
colleges, those at sectarian institutions are significantly more likely to work
extensive evening and weekend hours than their colleagues at other types of
institutions. To some degree, this difference is due to their relationships with
students and other constituency groups on campus.

The Nature of Relationships

The role of interpreter that student affairs professionals at sectarian
campuses play in terms of their work is also evident in their relationships with
others. In general, they see themselves as interpreting their work to others on
campus:

> I think that is because I see myself responsible for getting the word out and
> making sure people do know what goes on and bringing them in to our team.

> At our institution, team oriented has more to do with being cross-divisional. In
> an effort to be student centered, we need to be team oriented so that the
> business side of the house is working with us towards the same objectives.
> Otherwise they will just be business and they probably will not be very student
> centered. . . . But it takes teamwork among ourselves. But more importantly, to
> be student centered and the way the institution runs, it takes teamwork
> including auxiliaries and the student accounts and the business operations to get

them to think about how students engage students. So it's a strategy at our institution.

Administrators see themselves as translating the work they do to other constituencies on campus. They strive to ensure that others understand their role and are on their "team" when it comes to serving students.

Their relationships with students also take on a different tone. It is significantly more likely that students know them. Given that there are significantly fewer professionals on sectarian campuses than on secular campuses, perhaps this is not surprising. The way in which those at religiously affiliated institutions describe their relationships with students, however, also reflects a unique language. They use words like "life giving" and "precious" and suggest that their role is to educate students and help them interpret issues:

> I used the word life giving because for me I don't get as much time as I would like [with them and they are] precious moments. And so it gives me energy in life, and I can't think of a negative word that would describe why I don't like being with [students]. Every moment that I spend with them is precious.

> The kind of interaction we have is, even if it's in an adversarial kind of opening, like if it's judicial or something like that, there is still something unusual about the conversation we have. . . . They see you, they see us as an employee and a professional to help them, not to you know, not for other reasons.

Even when they describe the downside of working with students, those at sectarian colleges temper their words and assume that some of the negative interactions they have with students are a result of their own situations, not those of students:

> You can never do enough for them. It relates to the entitlement I think. Which is why you are always having to say no. And in some ways you feel like you are putting up the roadblock because it's what I want, what's in it for me, and you just have to keep saying no.

> They make me very aware of how older I get. I am saying that seriously, it makes you aware you are aging. No matter how connected you might be with them, there is still that generational gap.

The second group that professionals at religious campuses talk about is parents. Here again, however, they view parents differently than their colleagues at other types of institutions. Those at liberal arts campuses talk about the sense of entitlement that parents have and the ways in which parents try to interfere on their children's behalf. At sectarian institutions, parents are viewed as partners in the educational endeavors. Administrators' roles are to help parents understand the role that they play in their students' lives:

I like the influence they [parents] have on the students. No one has a better
rapport with their child than they do. And if you can get them on the
bandwagon with you, trying to do as a college and work with their son or
daughter, it's that much easier because they have a bigger influence.

[The] university has put out to their students that care [for the] person is at the
heart of what we do. And whenever you don't want the talk, you know like
when students feel most offended, is when we don't live up to what we say. Or
when parents feel we are not living up to what we say so it's beyond just
entitlement it's when they feel like you are not personally [involved]. You are
not caring in this case for my son or daughter, you are not being congruent with
who I thought you were.

Partnering with parents is not unique to those at sectarian institutions. As noted
in Chapter Six, professionals at HBCUs also work closely with parents.
However, the denominational nature of the campus seems to be of particular
influence for the interpreters:

Sometimes parents have a greater interest in [the college] and sometimes they
try to hold the institution accountable for it's [sic] religious [status] to a greater
degree than the student wants.

To that same extent when you have suspended them from school, they will call
[and say] "aren't you a Catholic school? Aren't you Christian?"

Relations between faculty and student affairs professionals at religious
institutions, however, are not as clear. Those at sectarian colleges, compared to
those at liberal arts, comprehensive, or research institutions, are significantly
more likely to know faculty, and faculty are significantly more likely to know
them. Faculty relationships are still dichotomous, however, just as they are at
most other institutional settings. In some cases, practitioners see faculty as
partners in the academic endeavor:

One advantage of working at my institution is the dedication and commitment
of the faculty and staff in helping students be successful.

The faculty are very committed to the students and care about the students'
academic success.

There is a very strong work ethic and commitment to students and to the
institution. Faculty and staff work very hard and very long hours to provide the
challenges and supports students need to be successful in their lives.

In other cases, relations with faculty are more acrimonious:

They also have a monopoly on academic freedom that when they are tenured,
faculty in religiously affiliated institutions they can challenge and take up
issues with a bit more, a lot of immunity actually. So for example as a student

affairs professional I cannot take on a cause and champion like I could in a public institution to help students and advocate for them. However tenured faculty can.

I dislike when they become only focused on their discipline you know and the pushing of that discipline apart from the broader experience. And that is not often, but that occasionally will happen.

Finally, relationships with student affairs colleagues on sectarian campuses seem to be fairly positive overall. Professionals use words like "collaborative," "supportive," and "collegial" to describe their peers:

I think support and admiration. Again in the student services and student affairs division, I am very amazed and humbled by the dedication that other people put in at times, and it spurs me on. Whether its career services, the nurses, the personal counseling center, the residence life, all of that just I am really bolstered by the dedication that they have to their task.

Even when asked about negative aspects of their relationships with colleagues they are hard pressed to be overtly negative:

Cordial and collegial. Most all who work here share a true affection for the place and an understanding that there is a unique quality to the place. Certainly there is disagreement but it is most often respectful. There is a healthy respect for personal [differences].

Collaboration is a hallmark of student affairs professional practice at all the institutional types described in this volume. Those at denominational campuses, however, use words with religious connotations when speaking about their compatriots on campus. Terminology like "humbled," "dedication," and "blessed colleagues" is common. The sectarian nature of the campus permeates the language that those on such campuses employ.

The Nature of Rewards

The data about rewards that those at religious institutions value are remarkably consistent across studies. Like their counterparts at all other types of institutions, those at denominational colleges value intrinsic more than extrinsic rewards. Their most highly ranked rewards include: engaging in meaningful work, a positive work environment, positive working relationships, the ability to influence decisions, and autonomy.

Previously cited comments illustrate, to a great degree, how they feel about the work they do. One administrator put it succinctly and eloquently:

[What I appreciate most is] the extent to which the work is an expression of who I am and how I relate. If I am working at a place where there is not meaningful work, then why do it?

Evidently, to some degree this meaning is tied to issues of the spirit:

> Some people ask me what is, what is distinctive about a [name of religion]
> institution? My response is well it's the same as [name of religion] education in
> general and it's a contextual question. You are working in context that this
> education, this higher education is in service to something bigger than simply
> getting a degree or simply accumulating credits. That the only reason for there
> to be a [name of religion] university is that we are educating people to do
> something with their lives that are in keeping with some kind of a tradition or
> heritage. That is neat.

> I worked in advertising for three years. . . . I came back [to higher education]
> because the work didn't feed the soul.

The rankings revealed in the Association Study are supported by
quantitative data yielded in the National Survey Study. Those at sectarian
institutions are significantly more likely to believe they influence decisions, and
ranking that ability high on their list of rewards supports that finding. They are
also significantly less likely to work with other professionals in their immediate
office, thus reinforcing their degree of autonomy.

The rewards to which they attribute the least importance include: office
facilities and equipment, performance reviews, support staff, advancement
opportunities/leave time, and benefits. Again, the quantitative data support these
rankings. Professionals at religiously affiliated colleges and universities are
significantly less likely than professionals at other types of institutions to have
adequate equipment, including computer hardware and software. They are also
significantly less likely to receive regular performance reviews and have
adequate support staff.

Perhaps the most distinctive element of the reward structure at sectarian
campuses has to do with benefits and salaries. For instance, those at
denominational institutions are significantly less likely to have good (or any)
prescription coverage. Whereas professionals at all types of institutions
commented on the low levels of salary they earn, those at denominational
campuses talked about it more frequently than their colleagues at all other types
of schools except HBCUs. They also seemed to associate their low salaries with
the sectarian nature of their campuses:

> I kind of laughed when I saw salary. I thought, "I am at a religiously affiliated
> school, salary is not a reward, it is not why I am there," and I kind of laugh
> about that.

> The religious community takes vows of poverty and obedience. But as I remind
> them often, we live them.

In general, then, student affairs administrators at religious schools have translated the rewards they garner into the denominational nature of their work. They do not expect exceptional salaries or benefits but do expect work that "feeds the soul" and "humbles" them.

Conclusions

The nature of professional life for those who work at sectarian institutions seems markedly different than it is for those at secular campuses. Some of these differences relate to the work itself. Administrators at denominational institutions are far more likely to translate their work via a teaching role. This role involves formal instruction but extends beyond the classroom. These professionals work with students in ways that include a spiritual dimension. This is a dimension that student affairs administrators at other types of institutions do not address. In fact, many professionals at secular campuses feel compelled to exclude matters of religion or spirituality when working with students. Those at denominational campuses are driven to include such matters. They have blended the foundations of their faith with the principles of student affairs practice to create a unique perspective on professional life. This view enables them to interpret the work they do, particularly the work they do with students, in terms of that perspective.

They may be able to interpret their work in this way because of the environment in which they work. There are lower levels of bureaucracy at sectarian campuses, but that may be due to a higher level of central management and control. That is, most denominational schools are led by either clerics or laypersons who are deeply committed to the religious order. Under these circumstances, student affairs professionals are often called upon to take the secular knowledge they have of the profession and translate that into the denominational setting in which they work.

The religious affiliation of the leadership also results in campuses that are highly political. The normal politics found on secular campuses, like those among disciplines or between faculty and administrators, are evident on sectarian campuses. In addition to those tensions, however, are politics associated with the religious orders, between campus clerics and church leaders, and between sectarians at the campus and those at the board level. Professionals at denominational campuses need to be politically astute and highly diplomatic.

The religious nature of these campuses also renders them more conservative and resistant to change. In many cases, they are led by alumni who are steeped in the history and tradition of the institution. These leaders may prefer the status quo. The challenge for student affairs professionals is to interpret the reasons they wish to implement change into the context of those traditions.

As might be expected, resistance to change means that security is more valued than risk taking at sectarian institutions. Only when there is a change in administration at the highest levels is risk taking seen as viable. For many student affairs professionals, this is not an issue because they view what they do as much more than simply an occupation. For many, their work is a calling or a mission. This attitude informs not only how they conduct their work but also how they manage their relationships with others.

They see themselves as bringing different campus elements together to work on behalf of students. Since serving students is paramount, student affairs professionals are often the people who explain to other campus constituencies how their office or function relates to that goal. That is, they interpret for others how their work is tied to institutional objectives. Yet they describe their relationships with most other groups on campuses in very positive terms and in terms that reflect the sectarian nature of their environment (e.g., life giving, precious, humbling).

Finally, student affairs administrators at denominational schools are motivated by intrinsic rather than extrinsic rewards. Although this may be true of professionals at other types of institutions, there is less resentment about low pay and limited benefits among those on sectarian campuses. In fact, they find ways to laugh about it. This is yet another way in which the religious nature of the environment is manifested among professionals. Clerics have always received limited financial rewards for their work and accept this as part of the professional norm. Student affairs professionals adopted this norm and interpreted it to meet their own needs: They find their rewards in ways that "feed the soul."

Chapter Four

The Generalists:
Student Affairs Work at Comprehensive
Colleges and Universities

Liberal arts and religiously affiliated institutions dominated the higher education landscape throughout the colonial and Republican eras. After the Civil War, however, four other types of colleges and universities emerged. These four types are the focus of the next several chapters of this volume. Each represents a unique group of postsecondary institutions and each is closely tied to shifts in the social, economic, and political climates of the country over the past 150 years.

Comprehensive colleges and universities form the first of these four types. Although the Carnegie Foundation for the Advancement of Teaching no longer employs the nomenclature "comprehensive" to designate this group of institutions (Carnegie Foundation, 2001), I use the term because it captures much of the essence of such campuses. Institutions that I designate as comprehensive are those that focus primarily on undergraduate education and graduate education through the master's degree. Some offer a limited number of doctoral programs. The major thrust of these institutions, however, is undergraduate education and professional training.

The data from student affairs professionals at comprehensive schools suggests that they are the "generalists" of the profession. This idea plays out in several ways. For example, many professionals at these campuses describe their institutions as hybrids: They mix the traditional focus of liberal arts education with the research focus of a campus that offers graduate education. In a parallel sense, professionals at comprehensive institutions serve specific functions, but the nature of the campus enables them to work extensively in other functional areas thereby requiring them to view issues from a multitude of perspectives. Thus, the generalist nature of the campus and the generalist nature of life for professionals on comprehensive campuses are mutually reinforcing. A brief explanation of how comprehensive colleges and universities emerged in the hierarchy of American higher education institutions further illustrates this notion of professionals as generalists.

Historical Evolution

The first few institutions that would ultimately become comprehensive colleges and universities (e.g., teacher colleges, municipal colleges) were founded in the first half of the 19th century. Most, however, were established after the Civil War (A. M. Cohen, 1998). Comprehensive institutions have all evolved in the past 135 years but most have followed one of two paths to their current status. In a limited number of cases, liberal arts colleges have morphed into comprehensive campuses. The transition of such institutions was driven by changes predicted in the demographic characteristics of college students.

By the early 1980s, the last of the baby boomers (born between 1945 and 1961) completed their postsecondary education. This generation of students represented the largest pool of traditional-aged college students in American history. Since liberal arts colleges educate primarily traditional-aged students, enrollments in these colleges reached all-time records during the 1960s and 1970s (Breneman, 1990, 1994; Delucchi, 1997). As the baby boomers completed their baccalaureate degrees, the pundits predicted that the flood of traditional-aged students that had inundated the educational pipeline during the 1960s and 1970s would become a mere trickle in the 1980s. Since most liberal arts institutions are private, they rely on the revenues generated from tuition. Solvency for these institutions is directly linked to enrollments.

The risk of a diminished pool of traditional-aged applicants, therefore, threatened the survival of many liberal arts campuses. This concern prompted institutions to examine ways to ensure their future. Some added professional programs, like engineering or business, to their undergraduate curricula. To complement these undergraduate professional programs, many of these campuses also introduced graduate education in a limited number of fields. Hence, their status shifted from that of a liberal arts institution to that of a comprehensive college or university (Breneman, 1990, 1994).

The majority of comprehensive institutions, however, followed a different developmental path; one more closely linked to the evolution of K-12 education in the U.S. The current configuration of elementary (K-5), middle (grades 6-8), and secondary (grades 9-12) education in this country has been firmly entrenched for the past 60 years. It is easy to marginalize, therefore, the 300 years spent developing this system of universal education. This development took place in fits and spurts over those three centuries, and educational endeavors assumed different forms by region (Urban & Wagoner, 2000). The relationship between the K-12 system of education and the emergence of comprehensive colleges and universities, however, warrants a closer look at the regional development of basic education systems.

In the Chesapeake and southern colonies, education in the pre-Revolutionary era took five fairly distinctive forms. The first mirrored the European attitude that education was a private matter. Families educated their children based on their ability to home school them or hire tutors. The second form was associated with churches. In some areas, ministers established parsons' schools in which they taught students for a fee. In other cases, men of the cloth served as tutors to families. Primarily designed to supplement the ministers' incomes, these endeavors educated children from families that could afford them. A limited number of endowed schools were also established in more settled areas during this era. In these instances, a wealthy patron donated land and some source of funding so that schools could educate children in the local area. In rural regions where there were sufficient numbers of settlers, citizens built field schools and paid teachers to educate their children. Finally, the European apprenticeship system was transplanted to the colonies and trained children for employment, though it did not provide much in the way of literacy education (Butler, 1990; Urban & Wagoner, 2000).

In New England, education took on a somewhat different meaning in the colonial era. Two trends influenced this difference. The first related to literacy rates among the settlers of New England that were significantly higher than rates of other colonists. As a result, although education remained largely a responsibility of families, communities monitored families to ensure they were teaching their offspring. In Massachusetts, for example, a law was enacted that gave the state the right to intervene if families failed to educate their children. Second, the Puritans believed that the preservation of their religious beliefs rested on the ability of future generations to read and interpret the Bible. Hence, perpetuating literacy was essential. This led to laws mandating the establishment of schools in the New England colonies were enacted as early as 1635. Education in this region was a community endeavor from its earliest inception. It was, however, segmented. Women typically taught reading and rudimentary writing skills to students. Advanced writing skills, penmanship, bookkeeping, and arithmetic were taught by male teachers at publicly supported grammar schools. Those who aspired to attend college also studied classical languages (Butler, 1990; Urban & Wagoner, 2000).

In the middle colonies, the diversity of settlers led to a variety of approaches to education. In some locations, families assumed responsibility for educating their children. In other areas, communities assumed responsibility, and education was a public endeavor. In general, however, schooling in colonial America reflected the influences of the more powerful social institutions of family, community, and the church (Urban & Wagoner, 2000; Wall, 1990).

From the mid-17th to the mid-18th century, the ideas associated with the
Enlightenment had profound effects on America. The central premise of the
Enlightenment was that reason, not religion, guided knowledge. This, of course,
challenged the primacy of the church in regulating the social order. Indeed,
education was seen as a means to teach reason to America's youth. At the same
time, in the post-Revolution period, civic leaders recognized the need to educate
the citizenry about the fundamentals of the newly founded republic. To that end,
early efforts to systematize education were introduced in several states. Thomas
Jefferson's proposal for a state system of education in Virginia is perhaps the
most notable of these efforts. Despite calls for common schooling, however, the
states did not adopt organized systems and, at the end of the 18th century,
education remained largely a local endeavor (Urban & Wagoner, 2000).

In the decades preceding the Civil War, championed by educators like
Horace Mann, the notion of common schooling expanded, particularly in the
northeast and mid-west regions of the country. Although common schooling was
never adopted on a statewide basis in this era, these schools embraced practices
that have prevailed over time. Schooling was provided for free; funding was a
community not an individual responsibility. Education was open to all citizens,
not just the elite. Education promoted ethical and moral development but in a
secular rather than sectarian manner. Most germane to this volume, the
systematization of schooling at the elementary level led to the development of
post-elementary schools for those who wanted to pursue learning at higher
levels. There was also an assumption among proponents of common schools that
teachers should be trained to teach and to deal with children from a variety of
backgrounds (A. M. Cohen, 1998; Urban & Wagoner, 2000).

After the Civil War, however, schooling took on more formal structures.
Kindergarten education was introduced. Grade levels were designed to facilitate
the introduction of a standardized curriculum. Testing was introduced as a
means of assessing the quality of schooling. Schools were bureaucratized and
the first superintendents were appointed in this era. High schools proliferated
though not as systematically as elementary programs. By the turn of the
20thcentury, then, there was a rudimentary system of education in the U.S. from
kindergarten to high school. This system fed into the nation's colleges and
universities (A. M. Cohen, 1998; Urban & Wagoner, 2000).

It was in this era that the institutions that would become comprehensive
colleges and universities first emerged. As the notion of common schooling
expanded, so did the need for qualified teachers. Normal schools were founded
to meet this need. The first such schools typically offered two to three years of
training to students who had attended high school for two years (A. M. Cohen,
1998). Many of these students were women, and for the first time females had
viable alternatives for professional training at the postsecondary level.

During the Progressive era at the start of the 20th century, schooling in
America adopted the organizational bureaucratic structure that has persisted, in
large form, to today. As a result, teachers were professionalized and that led to

expanded teacher education programs. Normal schools expanded their
preparation programs to four years so that teachers earned bachelors degrees.
This expansion was accompanied by a change in status: Many normal schools
became state teachers colleges in the early part of the century (A. M. Cohen,
1998; Lucas, 1994; Urban & Wagoner, 2000).

The rapid industrialization in America during the Progressive era also led to
calls for more professional programs at the college level. The training of
business, agricultural, and other technical leaders led to expanded curricula at
state teachers colleges. Many institutions dropped the term "teachers" and
became state colleges (A. M. Cohen, 1998; Lucas, 1994; Rudolph, 1962; Urban
& Wagoner, 2000).

The post-World War II period had even more profound effects on higher
education. It was an era of explosive growth, both in terms of the number of
institutions and in student enrollments. Indeed, many refer to the period 1945-
1975 as the golden age of American higher education. It was during this period
that state colleges further expanded their curricular offerings and cemented their
roles as regional institutions. Many changed their titles from colleges to
universities to reflect that broader role. By 1975, these institutions, now known
as comprehensives, enrolled 25% of all college students and conferred 33% of
all bachelor's degrees and 30% of all master's degrees (A. M. Cohen, 1998).

Since the 1970s, curricular developments at comprehensive institutions
have mirrored changes in professional demands. For example, teacher education
now typically includes post-baccalaureate training. Credentials in the medical
field have expanded so that nurse practitioner and physician assistant programs
are also post-baccalaureate programs. The comprehensive colleges and
universities have continued to expand their programmatic offerings to meet the
demands for increased technical training. As they have expanded their graduate
education offerings, so also have they assumed a somewhat greater research
role. This change has increased their prominence in the higher education
hierarchy but, as the discussion below suggests, may also have diffused their
mission (A. M. Cohen, 1998; Urban & Wagoner, 2000).

The Nature of the Comprehensive University Campus

In 2000, the 611 comprehensive colleges and universities represented over
15% of the 3,941 public and private institutions of higher education in the
United States. Unlike the liberal arts colleges or religiously affiliated institutions
that are largely private, 45% of comprehensives are public, 54% are private not-
for-profit, and the remaining 1% are private for-profit organizations (Carnegie
Foundation, 2001).

Although they represent just 15% of all institutions, in 1998 comprehensive
colleges and universities enrolled over 3.2 million, or over 21% of the
15,079,149 students enrolled in postsecondary education in America. Most
comprehensives remain relatively small with an average enrollment of 5,288

(though there are a few that are huge and enroll more than 30,000 students). Their small size does not hinder their productivity, however. Comprehensive institutions confer a disproportionately high number of baccalaureate degrees: In 1997/98, they awarded 35.5% of all BAs and 32.5% of all BAs in the liberal arts. In that same year, they conferred 34.6% of all master's degrees in the country (Carnegie Foundation, 2001). This focus on teaching is illustrated in the mission of comprehensive campuses.

Mission

The mission of comprehensive institutions is reflected in the services that they have attempted to provide over the years. From their initial role as teacher training schools, they expanded to offer the BA degree in the liberal arts. As such, most became regional universities serving the geographic areas in which they were situated. In urban areas, they symbolized the path to upward mobility for millions of immigrants. In rural areas, they often provided the only access to higher learning. Finally, as they expanded their role in graduate education, a focus on professional training and credentialing and the concomitant research endeavors that accompany graduate education have been added to their role.

Mission statements for many of these schools reflect the multiple roles that they fulfill, as the following example illustrates:

[Name of university] is a large urban comprehensive university in the State University system. Its mission is high-quality education leading toward a broad range of baccalaureate and master's degrees spanning the liberal arts and sciences and many applied and professional fields. . . .

[Name of university] is committed to serving the people of [name of state]. To assure access and equity consistent with educational priorities, the University endeavors to serve students who can only attend in the evening as well as those who can attend during traditional day time hours, those who must attend part-time as well as those who attend full-time, and those from population groups whose rates of enrollment historically have been lower than average as well as those from groups that have had historically higher rates of education. . . .

The University's educational mission is to promote intellectual and personal development and to prepare students for lifelong learning as well as preparing them to succeed in a variety of professional endeavors and to function as informed, contributing members of the community. To these ends, the mission of the undergraduate curriculum is grounded in a strong general education program, emphasizing the acquisition of writing, critical thinking, and analytical skills and knowledge of cultural and artistic traditions, the analysis of human behavior and society in the past and present, and scientific modes of inquiry. The mission of all degree programs is to provide each student with the skills necessary to pursue knowledge and to integrate information from various sources, and also to provide depth in at least one area of specialization. The mission of the graduate programs is to prepare students to enter careers

requiring training beyond the baccalaureate, to advance in their jobs, or to
pursue advanced study. . . .

The University seeks to involve students in learning by offering most of
the curriculum in small sections taught by fully qualified, professionally active
faculty members, and by providing opportunities for undergraduate as well as
graduate students to work with faculty members in independent study and
research.

Notice how general the mission statement is. The campus offers liberal arts and
professional training, it serves day students, evening students, full-time students,
part-time students, those from groups that have always pursued higher education
and those from groups who have not. Another example further exemplifies the
broad mission of the comprehensive institution:

[Name of university] is a public comprehensive university, offering a wide
variety of degree programs at the baccalaureate, master's, and intermediate
levels as well as the Ed.D. in Educational Leadership. With a distinctively
residential campus and a faculty and staff characterized by high quality and
broad diversity of professional skills, [name of university] takes as its mission
the practice and propagation of scholarship. This is accomplished particularly
through instruction but also through the research, creative, and service activities
of the university community. [Name of university] is committed to excellence
in its undergraduate and graduate educational programs, while continuing to
serve as a center of cultural and professional activity within its state and region.

Founded in 1899 as [previous name of university], [current name of
university] evolved into a state teachers' college, later broadened its mission to
include the liberal arts, gained regional university status, and in 1971 became a
part of [the state university system]. From its beginning as a small local
institution, [name of university] has developed into a university with students
from every section of [name of state], as well as from other states and nations.
Throughout its growth, the university has maintained a strong sense of
community. It continues to provide educational leadership and service to the
state and region. . . .

[Name of university] is a comprehensive university, offering a broad range
of undergraduate programs and select graduate programs. Undergraduates
receive a well-rounded liberal education and the opportunity to pursue a special
field of inquiry in preparation for advanced study or a specific career. Graduate
students engage in advanced study and research while developing and
extending their academic or professional specializations. . . . With instruction
as its primary mission, the university is committed to excellence in teaching
and the fostering of scholarship.

This statement further illustrates how comprehensive campuses are broad
ranging. The school has a focus on teaching but notes the increasing roles of
research and service. It attracts students from all over the state but retains its
service to the local region. In sharp contrast to the short, concise mission
statements of the liberal arts and religiously affiliated colleges, comprehensive

institutions find it difficult to summarize their missions in any abbreviated format. A review of 27 such statements revealed that the briefest statement was four paragraphs long. In short, comprehensives offer a broad array of programs that require student affairs professionals who are generalists and are prepared to deal with that breadth.

The scope of these campuses has attracted a degree of criticism in recent years. Some argue that they offer a confusing array of options (Brownlee & Linnon, 1990) and suffer from a lack of a coherent identity (Kaplan, 1987). They need to cope with the competing demands that their research and teaching programs exert (Henderson & Kane, 1991). This has led some campuses to attempt to move toward becoming research universities (Arnone, 2003; Spangler, Grosz, Byrnes, Harlan, & Romero-Motlagh, 1991).

Most experts agree, however, that comprehensive colleges and universities excel in several arenas. First, they provide a solid liberal education at the undergraduate level. Moreover, the regional focus of such institutions offers higher education opportunities to populations that otherwise might not have access to postsecondary learning. They also offer advanced professional degrees, and many working adults can take advantage of the alternative delivery methods (e.g., evening and weekend options) frequently employed in such degree programs. Finally, they provide affordable educational opportunities (Brownlee & Linnon, 1991; Kaplan, 1987; Ogren, 2003; Spangler et al., 1991). Their future success lies in clearly articulating their mission to stakeholders and broadening their definition of scholarship so that they can achieve excellence in ways that distinguish them from other institutional types (Henderson & Kane, 1991; Spangler et al.). Obviously, this future is tied to the role that faculty members play at comprehensives.

Faculty

Although comprehensive colleges and universities comprise 15% of all not-for-profit institutions (Carnegie, 2001), they employ 21.5% of all full-time faculty members (NCES, 2001b). Their representation diminished slightly in the 1990s: In 1989 they represented 26% of all faculty (Youn, 1992). Campuses have dealt with the decrease in the number of full-time faculty by increasing the number of part-time faculty that they employ (Youn). More than a third of faculty members at public comprehensive schools are employed on a part-time basis and this ratio increases to 50% at private comprehensives (NCES, 2001b). This is a dramatic departure from faculty at liberal arts colleges, 63% of whom are full-time employees of their institutions. In some ways, the work life of faculty members at comprehensive institutions is similar to that of their counterparts at other types of colleges and universities.

Consider, for example their teaching responsibilities. Faculty members at comprehensive campuses devote 62% of their time to teaching activities. This is only slightly less than those at liberal arts institutions (65%) and community colleges (72%). It is, however, far more than the roughly 43% of time that faculty at research institutions spend in the classroom. In large part, this is explained by teaching loads that are much higher at comprehensive institutions than at research universities. Faculty members at comprehensive campuses typically teach four or more classes per semester as opposed to the two classes taught by most professors at research institutions (NCES, 2001b).

Teaching is the preferred activity among faculty at comprehensive colleges and universities (NCES, 2001b). In fact, those who teach at comprehensive institutions embrace instructionally related activities like systematic advising of students, prompt feedback to students, and egalitarian classroom atmospheres (Eimers, Braxton, & Bayer, 1998). They value interactions with students and believe in maintaining an ethical climate on campus that respects students (Schulte, Thompson, & Hayes, 2001). These instructional activities are associated with high levels of vitality among faculty (Chan & Burton, 1995) and are consistent with the comprehensive institution's focus on teaching.

Despite their interest in teaching, however, faculty at comprehensive schools are engaged in research activities. They spend approximately 10% of their time in research related projects but think they should be devoting at least half as much more time to these projects (NCES, 2001b). They recognize the importance of publishing their research and most (60%) believe that their research endeavors will lead to publications (Youn, 1992). The ways in which they have shifted their energies from teaching to research vary, however (Finnegan & Gamson, 1996). The drive to publish prompts some to seek graduate faculty status so that they can work with more advanced students and engage them in research (Deutcsh & Stanford, 1990). In other instances, faculty seek to reconceptualize their programs so that programs that target the development of research skills are distinguished from those that are designed to train professionals (Hickney, Cohen, & Reid-Williams, 1991).

The tension between teaching and research is also evident in other ways. For example, comprehensive institutions employ research university specifications when recruiting faculty (Youn & Gamson, 1994) in an effort to increase their prestige. The research culture is also dominant in the reward structure at comprehensive institutions. Although administrators say that teaching and service are valued activities, the data suggest that it is research that is rewarded in terms of salary increases (Fairweather, 1994). This finding has prompted calls to restructure the reward system (Van Tassell, 1999) and revise other institutional structures (Wangberg, 1987) at comprehensives to encourage faculty to increase their research productivity. Such changes would necessarily affect the students who enroll at these campuses.

Students

Comprehensive colleges and universities benefit students in a variety of ways. Sixty percent of such institutions enroll fewer than 5,000 students and only 13% enroll more than 10,000 students (NCES, 2001b). They are larger than typical liberal arts or religiously affiliated institutions but smaller than most research universities. Most students at comprehensives, therefore, learn in a small and intimate setting. They value the interactions this type of environment enables them to have with faculty (Schulte et al., 2001).

Relationships with faculty are perhaps more important given the types of individuals who are drawn to comprehensive colleges and universities. Historically, this segment of the higher education system has attracted students from under-represented populations. For instance, when many such institutions were normal schools or state teachers colleges they served women, a group for whom other higher education options were limited (Durbin & Kent, 1989). The urban comprehensive colleges and universities have educated generations of low income and immigrant populations, serving as a springboard for upward mobility (Ogren, 2003; Spangler et al., 1991). As Chapters Six and Eight will reveal, HBCUs and HSIs have provided the same sort of mobility for other groups of underserved undergraduate students. In addition to undergraduate opportunities, however, graduate education provided by comprehensive institutions has benefited older adults who need to work full time and can only pursue advanced degrees on a part-time basis (E. I. Cohen, 1991).

In the same vein, the outcomes for students at comprehensive institutions are positive. The comprehensives have always excelled at preparing teachers and other professionals (Neubert & Binkso, 1998). More recently, however, they have improved in other academic endeavors. Despite a belief by many faculty members that the quality of students at comprehensives has declined (Youn, 1992), entering characteristics of students are in fact stronger and persistence rates are higher (Oklahoma Higher Education, 1998). Indeed, an increasing number of alumni of comprehensive colleges are going on to earn doctorates (Academic Excellence, 2002; Spangler et al., 1991), one measure of the quality of education they receive as undergraduates.

So although there may be calls for comprehensive colleges and universities to rethink their priorities and identify a distinctive niche in the hierarchy of American higher education (Henderson & Kane, 1991; Kaplan, 1987), they seem to be fulfilling their multiple roles reasonably well as far as students are concerned. These institutions are truly comprehensive in nature and it is in this sort of environment that student affairs professionals operate. They need to succeed within the multiple functions of the institution and that requires them to excel in the role of generalists.

The Nature of Student Affairs Work

The conclusions drawn below are derived from data provided by professionals who work at comprehensive institutions and who participated in the Calendar Study, the National Survey Study, and the Association Study. Findings from the first of these studies exposed how student affairs providers at comprehensive institutions spent their time in ways that differed from their counterparts at other types of institutions. Statistically significant differences between those at comprehensives and those at other types of institutions in terms of work, relationships, and rewards were found in the National Survey Study. Finally, the quantitative data offered by participants in the Association Study revealed how they differed from their counterparts at other campuses. The observations they offered in the latter two studies reinforce what the literature suggests in several ways. First, their comments support the notion that comprehensive colleges and universities blend the liberal arts tradition with the scholarship of a research university:

> [The comprehensive institution] gives you the best of both words. [It] gives you all the quality of a smaller liberal arts type school with all the advantages of a research university.

> But there is much, much higher emphasis on teaching and faculty-student contact [at a comprehensive]. . . . Certainly the faculty are expected to do research and get grants, but it [research] is not the end-all and be-all that it is at a major research institution.

> Generally, you won't find research institutions that are very small. And you won't find liberal arts institutions that are very large. So [at a comprehensive] you have a breadth and depth that you might have at a liberal arts, but you certainly aren't a research institution.

Clearly, those at comprehensives recognize how their settings differ from liberal arts and research campuses. More than that, however, these comments set a tone that is repeated time and again by those who work at comprehensive institutions: They see issues from multiple perspectives and appreciate those different perspectives.

To start, those who work at comprehensives confirm that they serve students who might otherwise not pursue higher education:

> I think that the public comprehensive university is a primary tool for education for working class Americans who want a four-year experience.

Perhaps most convincing, however, are the comments they offer about the general nature of their work. The mix between providing a liberal arts education for undergraduates and professional training for graduate students is coupled with the fact that these institutions tend to enroll more students than liberal arts colleges but fewer than research institutions. This results in a demand on student affairs professionals to be generalists in the truest sense of the word:

> Because at the large universities—at least the one I came from—you have specialists that did just [one thing]. And then they'd go home. . . . And for young staff, this is an opportunity for them in fact to experience a broad array. . . . Our campuses are large enough that everything that occurs at the largest

university in America will occur on my campus. The incidence of it may be just
once or twice a year, but you have to have the same level of expertise to
respond and deal with it. So it's much more challenging; it's much more
invigorating. It's much more interesting, and I also think it's much more
rewarding. So I think it's a great place for younger staff to come, if they really
want to learn.

It's kind of the best of both worlds. . . . Like a larger institution, we have a
Greek Life Office and a Residence Life Office, and Student Affairs Office.
They're all separate, they're not splitting jobs three ways and things. So you
have access to different expertise, but those departments are all so small that an
entry level hall director or assistant director of Student Affairs can, if she or he
wants, get involved in some other area of campus out of interest. We had a hall
director once who did part-time work on his own in Development because he
wanted to get into Development in Alumni Affairs. And that was easy to do. So
I think it's that we have a diverse amount of professional opportunities, but
we're small enough that they have real access to them.

At my institution, if our young professionals so chose, they can be on college-
wide committees; they can be involved in all aspects of the community. From a
professional perspective they really have a generalist view of the totality.
They're involved. I have a lot of divisional committees and things like that. At
a major, large university they just would not have that experience.

Here again is evidence that they appreciate what large institutions have to offer
and recognize the advantages of small campuses, another example of their
ability to view their world from multiple perspectives. They understand that they
have opportunities to develop their skills as generalists, and they do so within
the work environment of the comprehensive university campus.

The Work Environment

Like those at liberal arts and religiously affiliated campuses, professionals
at comprehensive colleges and universities believe their campuses are student
centered, but this focus on students takes a somewhat different form. At the
former two types of institutions, serving students translates to providing
programs and advising in both individual and group settings. At comprehensive
institutions, serving students involves programming and advising but also
extends to other activities. For example, those at comprehensives teach
undergraduates but not as often as their colleagues at other types of institutions.
However, they teach graduate students at significantly higher rates, an
opportunity that administrators at the other types of campuses are typically not
provided.

Service to students at comprehensives often does not take the traditional
one-on-one format:

I often hear from my staff members that this isn't the career I signed on for 10 years ago. That they came into the profession thinking VERY student oriented. In areas like Admissions and Financial Aid and Student Records, and to some extent, Advising—we're into very technical kinds of expertise. The way we run our business now is not a one-on-one appointment with the student all the time. It's on-line student services, it's e-mailing. The way we interact with students is just very different. And so the expertise for—particularly for the Assistant Director and Director level—doesn't mean one-on-one student interaction.

I hear that with even younger staff who . . . sometimes I think our preparation programs with an emphasis on counseling in particular do a disservice because we're really looking for people who can make system change, systemic change. And to have the luxury of spending time one-on-one with a student is just not something that we have the luxury of doing very much.

The generalist nature of the work for student affairs professionals at comprehensive institutions generates a somewhat different work environment when it comes to working with students. It is important to note that many public comprehensive campuses are members of larger state systems of higher education. The focus on systemic change is endemic in such systems.

Other elements of the environment seem more ambivalent. For instance, the calendars of professionals at comprehensive institutions (obtained in the Calendar Study) suggest that they actually spend much less time handling management types of tasks. Their comments are inconclusive. They talk about having too much management on some occasions and too little management in other circumstances. Again, their appreciation of both sides of an argument is evident.

The ambivalence over the degree of management on comprehensive campuses seems to be associated with several other characteristics of the work environment: the degree of politics, bureaucracy, and centralization. Most professionals believe their campuses are highly political. Unlike their colleagues at research universities, who see politics as pervasive and problematic (see Chapter Five), those at comprehensives see politics as part of normal organizational dynamics, something to be expected:

I actually believe that most organizations, if not all, are really political. So I end up paying a lot of attention to the political processes on my campus, whether that's in the administration or with student government, or student organizations. And I try to teach my staff—I supervise a large, young staff—about being involved in the political process of the organization. Particularly in mentoring young women, I often hear, "I don't want to be a part of the politics. I'm just not going to do that in my career." And I immediately say, "that's not going to work." I mean every process is political. You have to embrace it and understand that it's just about relationships. So it's sort of a theme with me, why I always say that almost every process is political and I encourage every professional to understand the political process. So, politics is relationships and that's what our business is—building relationships and making them work.

> I really do think that in order to understand either behaviors or organizations or processes, you need to understand the political component, and not avoid the political thing.

In many cases, however, campus politics at comprehensives are tied into system politics. Since many public comprehensive institutions are members of state systems there are not only intra-institutional politics but also inter-institutional politics. It is not at all unusual, for example, for housing officers or financial aid staff at all campuses in a state system to transmit information on a regular basis about system-wide issues. This means they spend a lot of time communicating with one another. In fact when asked, professionals at comprehensives estimated that they spend about 5% of their time communicating with others. An analysis of their calendars, however, reveals that they actually spend 25% of their time in such activities. As one participant noted:

> I'm in a public institution within a system, so there's all kinds of politics in terms not only internal to the institution, but external to the institution—both with the community and with the system office.

Other elements of the work environment at comprehensives differ significantly from the environments at liberal arts or religiously affiliated campuses. For example, although bureaucracy is limited at the latter two types of campuses, it is rampant at comprehensives, as is centralization. The generalists report that "the bureaucratic impediments to change are significant" because there are "too many levels to get through to get answers." Many report that their "institution is far larger and more bureaucratic" and they "wish [they] had better skills to navigate that and get less frustrated by the demands from above." For those on campuses that are part of a larger system, bureaucracy takes on an added dimension: system-wide policies and procedures.

Ironically, the high degree of politics, bureaucracy, and centralization has a real upside for professionals at comprehensive institutions: They learn about strategic planning in the most elemental ways. An analysis of how they spend their time in the Calendar Study suggests that they devote 5% of their time to strategic planning activities. This is far more than their colleagues at any other type of institution. Strategic planning skills are essential if young professionals aspire to higher-level administrative positions so the opportunity to fine-tune those skills might be invaluable.

The Pace of Work

The generalist nature of professional life at comprehensives is also reflected in the pace at which work is conducted. When asked, those at comprehensive institutions differ from their colleagues at liberal arts and religiously affiliated campuses and feel that change occurs quickly on their campuses:

> You have to have the ability to change. You can't be a person who gets really agitated or irritated if that happens, or you would have a big ulcer.

However, they seem to temper their sentiments about the pace of change, recognizing the advantages and disadvantages that rapid change can cause:

> We have to be responsive, often quickly, because things are constantly happening and changing. On the other hand, I've been thinking a lot about [change] lately and working on with my staff—maybe not in a real overt way, maybe in sort of a covert way—that change just for change's sake is also not healthy. And you don't necessarily need to change everything every year—that change should be very thoughtful and planned for, and maybe one at a time— one thing at a time.

> If we're quick to change it can be very destabilizing to people who are looking for stability. And if you . . . take different positions all the time, approving policies of one sort one year and another [sort another year] people just can't predict and anticipate what you're expecting, what the standards of the institution [are], what the values of the culture are. So change, again, is good, but if everything is in flux all the time you've got total disorientation.

This same sense of seeing issues from multiple perspectives is evident in other aspects associated with the pace of work. For example, the National Survey Study revealed that turnover among staff is significantly higher at comprehensive campuses than at other types of institutions. This might lead one to conclude that there is a high degree of stress on these campuses. Yet professionals who work at comprehensive colleges and universities report a fairly balanced view of stress:

> Stress is expected and good.

> The . . . thing that's most stressful about the nature of our work is that if you're a person who needs a lot of control, you do not want to go into student affairs because you just don't have a lot of control on a daily basis. You cannot predict when a student is going to commit suicide, can't predict when there's going to be a tragedy on your campus, [that's] just the nature of the work.

> What doesn't kill you makes you stronger.

In a similar vein, decision making takes significantly longer at comprehensive institutions than at other types of campuses. As a result, professionals at comprehensives believe their campuses are more reactive than proactive. The same was true for those at religiously affiliated campuses. But at sectarian schools, reactivity was seen as negative. At comprehensives, being reactive is not viewed as all bad:

> We work very hard—we tend to be more reactive than we would like to be
> simply because of the nature of the waves and the occasional crest that we see
> coming our way.

Finally, the generalist nature of the work professionals at comprehensives do is also evident in their attitudes about the challenges they face. They were asked if they found the pace of their work to be positively or negatively challenging. Their responses suggest they find it to be both:

> I think, for me, a lot of the things I hear in my work life, it's a double-edged
> sword. In terms of the positively challenged, . . . it's sort of like I don't have a
> lot of control, and at the same time, I wouldn't want a job where I did. Because
> if every day was like every other day, I'd be bored to tears. And so, the flip side
> of it is that I like . . . a little bit of chaos . . . kind of keeps it fresh.

> You want waves on a college campus, I think you do. You want to avoid the
> tidal wave. Maybe that's where the stress [comes from]. . . . You see these
> waves building that may turn into a tidal wave. But if you didn't have the
> waves I'd be bored to death.

The pace of work for professionals, then, seems to reflect the generalist nature of professional life for these administrators. They see issues from multiple perspectives, perhaps because they work on campuses that have multifaceted missions and offer a broad array of programs. This generalist attitude is also evident in the ways in which work is accomplished at comprehensives.

How Work Gets Done

The data from the Calendar, National Survey and Association Studies suggest three consistent patterns across participants with respect to the ways in which work gets done. First, they are convinced that the culture at comprehensive institutions values creativity. Whereas those at research universities and community colleges report that creativity is valued in their work, professionals at comprehensive campuses rate the degree of creativity on their campuses far more highly than those at any other type of institution and their comments on the subject reflect their zeal:

> You get into a rut real fast if you don't value creativity. The opposite of that is
> that you just want conformity year to year to year, same old, same old, same
> old. And most of us would be real unhappy doing that.

> I think [it's] part of our field—it's part of the nature of who we are. We're
> highly evaluative and we don't evaluate and not react. So we evaluate, we look
> at how we can improve, how we can change. We like to look at as many
> options out there [as possible]. We're always looking for something new, a new
> approach.

The high degree of creativity, coupled with the ability to view issues from a variety of perspectives, results in a very heavy workload, however. Administrators at comprehensive colleges and universities are more likely than their colleagues at most other types of schools to find it difficult to say no when asked to take on more work. Like the blue-collar students they often serve, there seems to be a work ethic among those at comprehensives that renders them more prone to taking on excessive workloads:

> My job encompasses so much that I'm often not able to participate in opportunities to develop myself professionally.

> I wished I had learned to balance my life better and know that it's ok to say "no" to obligations and to participating in committees.

> [I wish I had learned] that the hours in which we work would be self-limited. That is, that there is an implied pressure to stay extra hours—sometimes up to 18 hours a day in my position—and that the talk of "taking time for yourself" is really valued very little in reality.

If they are going to work long hours, however, at least the professionals at comprehensive campuses work in environments that value collaboration over competition and are collegial in nature. Their comments almost universally suggest that they work well with others:

> [We are] cordial and collegial. Most all who work here share a true affection for the place and an understanding that there is a unique quality to the place. Certainly there is disagreement but it is most often respectful. There is a healthy respect for personal differences.

This congeniality among peers can be related to the generalist role they play. The nature of the campus—a hybrid of liberal arts and research—means that they need to work well with lots of other individuals in order to achieve their goals. To that end, they find it more productive to collaborate rather than to compete with others on campus. A review of the relationships they have with others on campus illuminates this point.

The Nature of Relationships

There are three constituencies on comprehensive campuses that seem to capture the essence of relationships that the generalists have with others in their work environments. The first of these, of course, is students. The data from the National Survey Study reveal that those at comprehensive institutions are significantly more likely to know students personally than their colleagues at other types of campuses. Likewise, they are significantly more likely to be known by large numbers of students. Some of this they attribute to the size of the campus. Like their colleagues at liberal arts and religiously affiliated schools, they believe that the smaller number of students at comprehensives enables them to get to know more students personally.

In another sense, however, their relationships with students seem to have to do with the types of students who attend comprehensives. Unlike their counterparts at liberal arts colleges, who witness a high degree of entitlement among their students, those at comprehensives report that "there is less of the entitlement kind of thing" and attribute that to the "the breadth of the students we have." They also wish they "had gained a better sense of the type of student who attends the institution" before they started working at a comprehensive so that they could have hit the ground running.

The nature of students at comprehensives also creates some challenges, however:

> [One] disadvantage [is the] technical focus of the students. Students want a formula and data for dealing with issues/problems. [They are] unable to deal effectively with issues with no definite solution.

> How [do you] do programming for today's students who are single parents working 40 hours and [whose] course requires them to complete clinicals (such as nurses; radiological technology; surgical technology)? When do these students have time to attend any extra-curricula activities?

As this last comment suggests, student affairs professionals are sensitive to the competing demands their students face, particularly academic demands. This in turn prompts them to work more closely with faculty and academic leaders. In fact, student affairs administrators at comprehensive institutions are significantly more likely to work with faculty than their counterparts at all other types of campuses except community colleges (see Chapter Seven). Their relationships with faculty also seem to be fairly cordial as they are significantly more likely to socialize with faculty members outside of work hours than professionals at most other types of institutions. They are also significantly more likely to work with academic deans on their campuses and to be known by those deans. For that matter, they are more likely to work with and be known by the president of their campus. This familiarity leads student affairs staff members to describe faculty in some positive ways:

> Inquisitive. As I said earlier, the faculty that I work with are always interested in what I'm doing, and I try to challenge them and bring out some of the student affairs aspects that could really help push the students to a new level.

> We've established really strong relationships in terms of they know their key people that they can call and get immediate help or assistance or answer to a question. I hear a lot "I knew that you would know what to do."

Well, a couple of reasons. One is that they're very intelligent and bright, and they don't settle for easy answers. You've got to be thoughtful when you're [dealing with] them. They often don't know much about what we're doing, so it's challenging to help them try to understand what we're doing.

This is not to say that their relationships with faculty are all positive. Professionals at comprehensives also describe faculty as being insensitive, narrow minded, and impatient. At times they feel faculty are demeaning and that efforts to work with them are one-sided. However, they seem more philosophical about working with faculty than their compatriots at other types of campuses. Again, the fact that comprehensives blend elements of the liberal arts environment with elements of the research environment enables student affairs professionals to appreciate both sides of the coin when it comes to faculty:

I'm sure you've heard the analogy, "it's like herding cats," sometimes trying to work with faculty. Sometimes it's hard to get everybody on the same page if you have a vision or a mission or an idea. Someone's always [questioning] and . . . challenging, which is a good thing too. But it's very hard to get a consensus with faculty. It's almost like an oxymoron as far as I'm concerned. And actually it's the beauty of being a faculty member. But on the other hand, when you're trying to get something done, move things forward, sometimes that independent quality can hang things up.

Perhaps some of the frustration they experience working with faculty is offset by the positive relationships they evidently have with their student affairs colleagues. Professionals at comprehensive campuses are significantly more likely to work extensively with their student affairs colleagues than those at other types of campuses, even more extensively than those at liberal arts and institutions. Likewise, they are significantly more likely to be known by other student affairs professionals on their campuses than their counterparts at, for example, research universities.

This may explain their comments that suggest a sense of genuine caring and respect among professionals:

Since I'm at an entry-level position, I'm always looking for opportunities to learn and to grow professionally. So I do tend to lean towards the higher administration such as our director and directors in other departments within student affairs for more educational opportunities. And they're always willing to take time out of their schedules to sit down and we talk all the time about journal articles, current trends, you know, whatnot, whether it be in an informal meeting or one-on-one.

And you also . . . share in the successes as well because you really are a family. And when Residence Life is successful at something, Financial Aid and Counseling and everybody else are right there with them. . . . There isn't any competition, even in success.

It's a team approach.

Professionally, we're all on the same page. And if you can help them achieve their professional goals, it's the joy. And that's the extension of you being an educator at this level.

In fact, even when asked what they disliked about their student affairs colleagues, professionals at comprehensive institutions couched their comments in terms of the conditions under which those colleagues work:

I put down tired. It's just because we do so much at all hours, day and night that if I had twice as many [staff], maybe we'd get it all done and people would be happy about it, but they're just running them hard.

I said sometimes beleaguered. The analogy I use on my kids is that sometimes student affairs is like Canada. The United States, the faculty, does not spend a lot of time [with or pay a lot of attention to] Canada, the student affairs staff.

I think I'm in the same boat. [Staff are] too easily intimidated in the institutional spectrum. I'm too worried about [how] they are perceived or not perceived. . . . [They need to learn to] speak for themselves [and] break down more barriers.

These comments are reminiscent of those offered by professionals at religiously affiliated campuses when asked about the downside of relations with student affairs colleagues. Some are hard-pressed to be negative.

In general, then, those at comprehensive colleges and universities seem to adopt a positive attitude toward other constituency groups on their campus. Perhaps this is due to the generalist nature of their work. Because their institutions blend elements of the liberal arts and research environments they learn to appreciate a variety of perspectives. This appreciation permeates their relations with others on campus. Given their seemingly amiable interactions with others it might be assumed that they are rewarded in ways that differ from their colleagues at other types of schools. This is not manifest in the data, however.

The Nature of Rewards

In the Association Study, those at comprehensive colleges and universities, like their counterparts at other institutional types, rank the intrinsic rewards they receive from their work much more highly than the extrinsic benefits of their jobs. From a list of seven intrinsic and eight extrinsic rewards, their five most highly prized rewards are all intrinsic in nature. First and foremost, they value the fact that they perform meaningful work:

Why go through all the stress and things that we have to unless it's meaningful work? We can find another profession.

If you have to work, there ought to be something that [is] significant—as much as you can control that.

Teddy Roosevelt said that the best prize life has to offer is the opportunity is to work hard at work worth doing. I kind of agree with him.

They also value the ability they have to influence decisions in their work environment (ranked second) and the degree of autonomy (ranked fourth) that their positions afford them:

I feel that I have an excellent supervisor who allows me autonomy in my work. Also, I am gaining invaluable experience as a manager.

I think, and again there's a whole range of ability to influence decisions. It's everything from one-on-one working with a student to some major policy decision in the institution. I think there's a range.

The fact that you're respected, that you can determine your own time-frame, you can figure out what your priorities are. None of us works in a vacuum, but there are levels of autonomy that you feel like you have enough support that you can determine how you need to spend your time and what you need to focus on. That's very reinforcing as an individual, as a human being. So that's why I think autonomy. . . . That's why I rated it so high.

Finally, administrators at comprehensive schools value the positive environment in which they work (ranked third) and the positive relationships they have with others on their campuses (ranked fifth):

I think that we all believe what we do is important, and we have to have that belief for us to be satisfied in what we're doing.

I think a lot of them are good relationships with co-workers, people working for a similar goal or similar vision in mind. I think those two are big things for me when I'm thinking of a positive working environment where you're all working toward the same end. Where there is recognition, there is praise.

It's a positive work environment to have good relationships with your co-workers. It's a reward in that over the years most of my friends are people I work with.

Conversely, four of the five rewards that professionals rated as least important to them are extrinsic in nature. Performance reviews, office facilities, leave time, and work schedules are not important to those who work at comprehensive colleges and universities:

I ranked [office facilities] as my last one because I spend so little time in my office. I just personally see me out on campus and in other locations more than I am in my own office. I just never thought of that. Maybe it's just me. It's a

personal thing I never really thought of that as being one of the rewards of my
[working] condition.

If the work hours are flexible and you have autonomy and you have a
supervisor that allows you to have a flexible schedule, sometimes you don't
even need leave time.

The only intrinsic reward that professionals at comprehensives ranked as
unimportant related to advancement opportunities. Evidently, the small size of
many of these campuses limits the advancement opportunities for staff
members.

People are so satisfied with administration and working conditions that there is
very little turnover and hence little mobility.

One major disadvantage I see is the inability to be promoted into higher
administrative positions. There aren't many positions beyond a coordinator or
director level.

The only disadvantage is that we are small and there is little chance of
advancing.

This is not to say that there are not extrinsic rewards for those who work at
comprehensive institutions. In fact, they are significantly more likely to have
support staff and student staff than professionals at liberal arts, sectarian,
HBCUs, or community college campuses. They are also more likely to receive
funding for professional development activities and to be rewarded for
entrepreneurial activities than their colleagues at those other sorts of campuses.
Like their counterparts at all other types of institutions, however, they simply
value the intrinsic rewards associated with their work more than the extrinsic
rewards of their jobs.

Conclusions

Throughout this chapter those who work at comprehensives have been
referred to as generalists. In large part, this stems from the nature of the
educational endeavors of these colleges and universities. The way they evolved
over time rendered them a hybrid between a liberal arts and a research
institution. They offer a liberal arts education to their undergraduates and
professional training to their graduate students. Although some suggest they lack
a coherent identity, those who work at comprehensives cherish the unique and
multifaceted nature of these institutions.

One of those unique characteristics relates to the types of students who
enroll at comprehensive institutions. Many undergraduates come from working
class families or other populations that have historically been underserved by
higher education. Graduate students on these campuses are often older, working

adults who would not be able to seek advance degrees were it not for the alternative ways comprehensives offer graduate education.

Student affairs professionals who work at comprehensive campuses do so because they are committed to these types of students. They are committed to serving those who might not otherwise have access to postsecondary educational opportunities. The different nature of their students, however, means that they need to understand the characteristics of a variety of different student groups: They need to be generalists in their knowledge of students.

The fact that their institutions are multifaceted compels professionals at these types of institutions to view their work environment in a multifarious manner. They see their campuses as political, bureaucratic, and centralized, but appreciate both the advantages and disadvantages of these characteristics. They believe their institutions can enact change quickly, but also recognize that change is not always beneficial. They work under stressful conditions, but know that stress can be put to positive uses. Their campuses value creativity, but that makes it difficult to say no when asked to take on new projects. The collaborative manner in which they work with others means that they share these additional responsibilities with their colleagues. Indeed, their relationships with other constituencies on campus are generally fairly amiable. Even when they describe the characteristics of others that they find less than attractive they are able to identify how such characteristics might serve that group well. Their ability to appreciate multiple sides of issues reinforces the image of professionals at comprehensive campuses as generalists.

Like student affairs administrators at liberal arts and religiously affiliated schools, those at comprehensive institutions value the intrinsic rewards associated with their work over the extrinsic benefits of their jobs. They are altruistic and passionate about the fact that what they do in their work makes a difference.

When considered collectively, it is easy to see how the term "generalist" describes student affairs professionals at comprehensive colleges and universities. The line that their institutions straddle between the liberal arts and the research mission requires that they view their professional endeavors from multiple perspectives. They meet the needs of multiple types of students. They work with faculty who are driven by both teaching and research demands. In order to succeed, they have to become generalists and those who work at these institutions relish the opportunity to do just that.

Chapter Five

The Specialists:
Professional Life at Research Universities

The comprehensive university was only one of several new forms of higher education that developed in the aftermath of the Civil War. A second type was the research university. Like its comprehensive counterparts, economic, political, and social dynamics over the past 135 years have shaped research institutions. Conversely, research institutions have helped shape the contemporary system of higher education in America.

Research universities are characterized by their complexity. They typically offer undergraduate education as well as graduate and professional programs. Most, particularly land grant campuses, engage in public service. The hallmark of these universities, however, is their focus on the generation of new knowledge. Extensive research is carried out by individual faculty members, graduate and professional students, teams of scholars, research institutes and centers, and other formal and informal organizational entities. The tripartite mission of these institutions—teaching, service, and research—render them intricate and complicated organizations. They are inhabited by specialists who strive to expand the boundaries of knowledge within their area of expertise.

The nature of professional life for student affairs administrators who work at research universities mirrors the culture of the campus. They describe themselves in ways that lead me to refer to them as "specialists." As the data reveal, their work is distinguished by depth in a select functional area rather than breadth across multiple areas like those at liberal arts, secular, and comprehensive institutions achieve. They collaborate fairly extensively with those within their functional area but do not necessarily work closely with their colleagues in other units. Indeed, the size and complexity of the institution often prohibit them from meeting and getting to know their colleagues around campus. A clearer understanding of research universities and how they have evolved over time provides a context within which to better understand the specialized professional life for student affairs staff at these schools.

Historical Evolution

Many practitioners are familiar with the role that the rise of research universities in the latter part of the 19th century played in the inception of the student affairs profession. In fact, two of the historic documents of the profession—*The Student Personnel Point of View* (American Council on Education, 1937) and *The Student Personnel Point of View (Revised)* (American Council on Education, 1949)— describe how the shift by faculty members from instruction to research after the Civil War diminished their focus on students. As a result, the need arose for professionals to fulfill the functions abandoned by faculty, and the student affairs profession was born. Since these documents are required reading in nearly all graduate preparation programs, most administrators link their professional identity to the proliferation of research universities post-1865.

The roots of the modern research institution, however, can be traced back to two related, yet contradictory issues that were addressed in the decades preceding the Civil War. The first was associated with the population higher education was designed to serve. Historically, liberal arts and sectarian institutions had served the privileged classes in America. Educators believed they were training the country's future leaders and assumed those leaders would come from the elite. In the first part of the 19th century, however, Andrew Jackson's presidency inspired new respect for the common person and the pragmatic skills need to succeed in occupations like agriculture and carpentry. Academic leaders were encouraged to expand higher education opportunities to serve an assortment of students. Some, however, expressed concern that the quality of higher education was being sacrificed to accommodate the quantity of institutions that were clamoring for a piece of the academic pie (Brubacher & Rudy, 1997; Lucas, 1994).

Concurrently, advances in science and technology spawned by the Enlightenment led to greater expansion of the curriculum in higher education. Courses in mathematics, sciences, economics, and agriculture, for example, were added to the curricular mix. The result was a smorgasbord of courses that some feared diluted all academic programs. One camp believed colleges should adhere to the classical curriculum that revolved around a series of required courses. Others embraced the new disciplines and supported the notion of an elective curriculum in which students would select their courses (A. M. Cohen, 1998; Lucas, 1994). As noted in Chapter One, in 1829 the debate culminated in the Yale Report, a carefully crafted argument calling for colleges to focus on classical education. The report was hailed by many as the answer to the curricular dilemma (Rudolph, 1962). The march of progress, however, was undeterred and by the 1850s many institutions were offering programs in chemistry, botany, zoology, and other scientific and technical arenas.

The shifting student population and the introduction of new academic programs coupled with two developments that occurred mid-century laid the groundwork for the diverse system of higher education that exists in the country today. The two mid-century events were the passage of the Morrill Acts (1862 and 1890) and the advent of graduate education with the founding of Johns Hopkins University in 1876. The Morrill Acts prompted many states to initiate public institutions of higher education. Until this time, most institutions had some ties to the state but were primarily private in nature. Only a handful of states like Georgia and Virginia had invested in publicly supported colleges prior to the Civil War and these state–college relationships were tenuous at best. The impetus behind the expansion of the public sector of higher education was directly linked to economics. The states sought to reconstruct their economies after the war. To do so, they needed to educate their citizens and capitalize on the industrialization that flourished in the post-war years. To achieve these ends, the state colleges and universities bolstered their practical academic programs (Brubacher & Rudy, 1997; Lucas, 1994; Rudolph, 1962).

Graduate and professional training also influenced the evolution of the higher education system. Throughout the 19th century, most Americans who sought post-college academic experiences traveled to Europe, and many sought the graduate education offered in German universities. They brought back with them notions about post-baccalaureate education, particularly the objective pursuit of knowledge through research endeavors. Johns Hopkins University was established as a graduate university focused on the pursuit of scientific discovery (Fincher, 1989; Lucas, 1994; Urban & Wagoner, 2000). From this point on, institutions of higher learning began to differentiate themselves. Some continued to focus on the classical curriculum: the liberal arts and religiously affiliated colleges. Others adopted the practical curriculum and research agenda; these campuses evolved into research universities.

During the period between 1876 and 1944 research universities addressed a number of issues: specialization among faculty, the professionalization of academic leadership, the emergence of administrators, corporate interests, and the influence of alumni (Rudolph, 1962; Urban & Wagoner, 2000). The emergence of specialized academic arenas is perhaps the most recognizable artifact of this era. Faculty members immersed themselves in their academic disciplines and research endeavors. Specialization within disciplines generated additional academic silos, and professional associations were established to create communities of scholars around disciplinary interests. The notion of graduate institutions like Johns Hopkins did not last long; most campuses recognized the need to provide undergraduate education. As faculty members' interest in research intensified, however, their interest in teaching undergraduates diminished. To some extent, undergraduate education was viewed as a training ground to identify those who might succeed in post-baccalaureate programs (Lucas, 1994; Rudolph, 1962).

The complexity that academic specialization generated required a new type of academic leadership in terms of both presidencies and governing boards. The clerics who had shepherded colleges and universities for the first 250 years in America were not trained to manage the multidimensional organizations into which research universities morphed in a relatively short period of time. Institutional presidents were selected from among the faculty, setting a precedent that persists to contemporary times at both public and private campuses. Likewise, members of governing boards needed worldly experience and an understanding of the evolving relationship between higher education and the corporate and government sectors (Lucas, 1994; Urban & Wagoner, 2000).

As faculty devoted more time to research and institutions became more complex, there was a need to manage campuses and that led to the rise of professional administrators at universities. The rapid industrialization of the country had led to the emergence of a managerial class in the private sector. Research universities adopted this managerial model and created academic administrators to supervise instructional and research endeavors, student affairs administrators to direct programs and services for students, and other administrators to manage the business functions of the institution like the physical plant and financial procedures (A. M. Cohen, 1998, Lucas, 1994).

The corporate influence on research universities is evident throughout this era. Industrial organizations were organized around specialized divisions (e.g., production, sales); academic disciplines on campus paralleled this structure (e.g., biology, history). Corporations were interested in transferring the products of research from campuses to markets, hence they developed close working relationships with institutions. Just as the corporate sector developed Boards of Directors, research universities created Boards of Trustees that were dominated by laypersons, many from the corporate sector. Although it is difficult to ascertain which organization influenced the other on any given issue, the interplay between research universities and the private sector during this time period is indisputable (A. M. Cohen, 1998; Urban & Wagoner, 2000).

This corporate influence even extended to the issue of alumni. Many of the scions of industry either graduated from these universities (though prior to their shift to research status) or sent their sons to the emerging research universities. Indeed, it was during this era that opportunities for women in higher education expanded as well, so daughters of corporate titans and those they employed could send their daughters to college. For the first time, women had access to the same curricular and collegiate experiences as men (A. M. Cohen, 1998).

In the latter part of the 19th century, many alumni cum industrialists "adopted" institutions and invested millions of dollars in developing them. Alumni served on governing boards, bringing resources and connections to government and industry with them. They were instrumental in establishing the entities that would go on to become university foundations. In general, they served as the lynchpins in the military-industrial-academic complex, the fiscal engines that drove the rapid economic expansion in the post-war nation (Urban & Wagoner, 2000).

This intense diversification among research universities was unabated for nearly 60 years. It was only in the 1920s and early 1930s that critics began to question both the purpose of higher education and the methods being used to deliver that education. Thorstein Veblen and Upton Sinclair are perhaps the most noted of these critics. Veblen was convinced that universities needed to eliminate undergraduate education and focus solely on the production of knowledge. Moreover, he argued that universities should abandon the business principles they had adopted, suggesting that such principles chained universities to vocational training and inhibited their pursuit of scholarship. Sinclair took the argument a step further, suggesting that research universities had abdicated their responsibilities to society by ignoring the important social issues of the time while perpetuating capitalist ideals. A. M. Cohen (1998) noted, these "criticisms are instructive because they reflect the magnitude of change in higher education and the speed with which it occurred. But the critics had little effect" (p. 173). The advent of the Great Depression and subsequent world war deflected attention from the deficits of research universities to the contributions they could make during times of national duress (Lucas, 1994).

The evolution of colleges and universities in the post-World War II period from 1945 to 1975 has been termed the era of mass higher education in America. The number of institutions increased from 1,768 in 1945 to 2,747 in 1975. During this same time, the number of faculty quadrupled and the number of students grew almost tenfold (A. M. Cohen, 1998). Research universities struggled to increase capacities to accommodate the explosive growth in enrollment while concomitantly expanding their research agendas. The rise of federal support for research formalized through government institutions (e.g., the National Science Foundation, the National Institutes of Health, the National Endowments for the Arts and Humanities) fueled a feeding frenzy among these institutions, leading to what many called the "golden age of higher education" (Brubacher & Rudy, 1997; A. M. Cohen, 1998; Urban & Wagoner, 2000).

It was not until the economic recession of the late 1970s and early 1980s that criticisms of research universities emerged once again. Detractors argued that excessive specialization among faculty had resulted in narrow visions of what issues should be studied and constrained the methods employed to investigate those issues. Additionally, critics lambasted the large research universities for the deterioration of undergraduate education and called on institutions to renew their commitment to that endeavor (A. M. Cohen, 1998). They castigated institutions for abandoning their traditional mission of civic education and exhorted universities to revitalize their commitment to public service (Checkoway, 2001).

These criticisms coupled with the diminished funding for higher education during a recession prompted responses from research universities. They restructured, reorganized, and retooled. They called on faculty to explore areas in which cross-disciplinary research might be developed. Collaboration became a buzzword, and research centers and institutes designed to bring together scholars from multiple fields flourished (A. M. Cohen, 1998; Geiger, 1990; Stahler & Tash, 1994). In an era of declining federal support for research, these organized research units typically aligned themselves with corporate interests resulting in innumerable questions about business–university relationships. The impact of these units has yet to be fully explored, but their influence on the way research is conducted is undeniable and they will likely be key players in research endeavors well into the 21st century (M. S. Anderson, 2001; Etzkowitz, Webster, & Healey, 1998; Slaughter & Leslie, 1997).

In this context, the specialization of student affairs professionals is more understandable. The size and scope of research universities require student affairs practitioners who can function in complex organizations. They operate in environments that respect and reward narrowly defined concentration areas, hence they have developed areas of expertise that reflect that culture. A more thorough discussion of the research university campus illustrates this notion.

The Nature of the Research University Campus

The 261 research universities represent one of the smallest sectors of the higher education system in America, second only to minority-serving institutions. The Carnegie classification system (Carnegie Foundation, 2001) identified two types of research universities: doctoral/research extensive and doctoral/research intensive. The former group confers a greater number of doctorates across a broader array of disciplines and garners more research funding than the latter group. For purposes of this discussion, however, those differences are negligible so I refer to all of them as research universities. Like their comprehensive institutional counterparts, most (64%) research universities are public institutions, though private institutions are well represented (36%).

Although they comprise only 6.6% of the 3,941 institutions of higher education, research universities enroll 4,318,521 students, or 24% of the college-going population. As these data suggest, most research universities are large. The average enrollment exceeds 16,000, 58% enroll somewhere between 10,000 and 29,999 students, and 11% serve more than 30,000 students (NCES, 2001a). It may not be surprising, then, that they confer 47% of all baccalaureate degrees in the U.S.; that they award nearly half (49.8%) of all the undergraduate degrees in liberal arts in the country is perhaps more unexpected (Carnegie Foundation, 2001). The fact that they produce such a disproportionately large number of graduates is even more interesting given the limited focus on instruction evident in the mission of most research universities.

Mission

The historic mission of research universities involved serving the public good (C. W. Anderson, 1993; Checkoway, 2001; Kennedy, 1997). Indeed, some argue that these institutions were key in nation building and paved the path to a civil society (Gamson, 1997; Hackney, 1986; Harkavy, 1997). Over time this mission expanded to include research. In fact, some have suggested that the focus at research universities shifted from that of service to that of scholarship over the course of the 20th century. This shift has been so dramatic, they argue, that faculty members' work is now designed to serve their disciplines and professional associations rather than society (Rice, 1996).

What is undisputed is the complexity of today's research universities. A review of mission statements from a selection of these campuses illustrates not only their focus on research and creative endeavors but also their tripartite mission:

> As a public land-grant institution, the University of [name of state] provides an accessible environment for discovery where distinguished undergraduate, graduate, and professional education are integrated with world-class basic and applied research and creative achievement. The University prepares students for a diverse and technological world while improving the quality of life for the people of [name of state], the nation, and the world. The University of [name of state] is among America's top research universities (based on NSF total research expenditure data) and is one of about 60 select institutions recognized by membership in the Association of American Universities.
>
> Geographically, the University includes the [name of city] campus, which is comprised of seven academic colleges, four professional colleges, and four colleges comprising the [name of state] Health Sciences Center (which also includes University Medical Center and University Physicians). It also reaches people throughout the state by encompassing the Science and Technology Park; the Cooperative Extension Service with locations throughout [name of state]; the [name of city] campus; and [name of university] South, a branch campus in [name of city].
>
> Compared to other top research universities, the University of [name of state] is unusually accessible to students of modest means and wide-ranging backgrounds. This is a place where every student is given the opportunity to reach high goals, and many students and faculty reach the very highest levels of excellence.

Notice in the first paragraph how "education" is "integrated into" research. Compare this emphasis to that of liberal arts and comprehensive campuses where research has been fitted into education. The focus on research is pervasive. The above research university's mission statement goes on for several additional pages that list what students can expect, including "access to world-class faculty and research facilities" and exposure to "leading-edge scholarship integrated into the curriculum throughout their educational experience." The university's vision also talks about how "researchers are valued for the important contributions they make to the advancement of learning, creative expression, scientific knowledge, and quality of life" and how "research is important to the University's ability to attract, retain, and educate students at all levels."

A second mission statement more concisely summarizes the three-fold mission of the research institution:

> The University of [name of state] is a public, land-grant research university, one of the most comprehensive in the United States and it encompasses virtually all academic and professional disciplines. It is the oldest and largest of [name of state]'s ten universities and is a member of the Association of

American Universities (AAU). Its faculty and staff are dedicated to the common pursuit of the university's threefold mission: education, research and service.

Teaching—undergraduate and graduate through the doctorate—is the fundamental purpose of the university. Research and scholarship are integral to the education process and to expanding humankind's understanding of the natural world, the mind and the senses. Service is the university's obligation to share the benefits of its knowledge for the public good.

These three interlocking elements span all of the university's academic disciplines and multidisciplinary centers and represent the university's obligation to lead and serve the needs of the nation, all of [name of state]'s citizens, and the public and private educational systems of [name of state] by pursuing and disseminating new knowledge while building upon the past.

The University of [name of state] is committed to providing knowledge, benefits and services with quality and effectiveness. It aspires to further state, national and international achievements in support of human values and improving the quality of life for the citizens of the state and the world.

To some degree, the mission statements from these two research universities are interchangeable. Both statements emphasize research, teaching, and service; both talk about their world-class standing; and both mention their membership in the prestigious American Association of Universities. Notice, too, the idea of competitiveness that is revealed in both statements: They are among the "top universities" and "compare" themselves to other institutions. They aspire to serve not just their states but their country and the world. Indeed, the parallels among research universities have been so strong since the start of the 20th century that there is little to distinguish them from one another beyond their status as a public or private institution (Geiger, 1985).

For some, the similarities among research universities are problematic. In the future, they argue, these campuses will need to differentiate themselves and determine what specific research niches they wish to fill. Maintaining stable sources of support will be essential, and existing resources may not be sufficient to support duplicative research agendas at multiple institutions (Massey, 1994; Saxon & Milne, 1985). If this is the case, the work of faculty will be impacted.

Faculty

Research universities employ a disproportionately large number of faculty members. Although they represent only 4% of four-year colleges and universities in the country, over 24% of all faculty members work at such institutions. This pattern takes on greater significance when the balance between full-time and part-time status is considered. The research universities employ 33% of all full-time faculty whereas only 21% of faculty on these campuses work on a part-time basis. This compares to comprehensive institutions where more than 33% of faculty members work part-time (NCES, 2001b). The number of faculty at research universities does not translate to more time in the classroom, however.

Faculty members at research institutions teach 66% of all undergraduate classes, but teaching assistants serve as instructors in far more undergraduate classes (14%) than at any other type of institution. In fact, faculty members devote only 43% of their time to instruction, significantly less than their counterparts at comprehensive or liberal arts institutions. This statistic is less surprising when the data on teaching loads are examined. Research university faculty members teach fewer students and fewer courses than those at other types of institutions. Between 35% and 40% of faculty members at research universities teach fewer than 4 credit hours per semester. That translates to one or two classes per academic term. For most faculty, the classes they do teach are small; they teach fewer than 50 students per term (NCES, 2001b). This is not to suggest that faculty members at research universities are not working. In fact, they work more hours than faculty at any other type of institution (Mingle, 1992).

The activity that consumes faculty time is research. To maintain employment, faculty members must earn tenure. Research productivity affects tenure decisions far more than teaching. There is a threshold for research that, if not met, cannot be overcome, even through exceptional teaching and service. Teaching is secondary to research in the tenure process, and service has almost no importance (Kasten, 1984). These values are difficult to adopt for most new faculty members (Reynolds, 1992). They strive to create classroom environments that facilitate learning. They enjoy interacting and providing feedback to students and believe in the value of proactive student advising (Eimers et al., 1998). Nevertheless, success for those at research institutions is associated with research activities and scholarly habits, and those who adopt these behaviors early in their careers are more likely to succeed (Hekelman, Zyzanski, & Flocke, 1995).

The tension between the competing demands that teaching, research, and service place on faculty at research universities takes a toll. They have reported declining morale in recent years (Kerlin & Dunlap, 1993). They are not convinced that their institutions can protect their interests and believe their quality of life has eroded (Johnsrud & Heck, 1998). Research universities need to increase salaries to address concerns about quality of life and faculty workload ("State Perspectives on Higher Education Faculty," 2000). Until then, however, it might be expected that attitudes of faculty will influence the experiences of students at research universities.

Students

As the above discussion suggests, life for students at research universities is different than it is for their colleagues at other types of institutions. Their campuses are typically quite large and organizationally complex. Navigating the campus, both physically and psychologically, can be a challenge. In terms of educational outcomes, however, differences between students who attend large research universities and those at smaller institutions are limited. Consider, for example, the issue of educational attainment. Students at large research universities are more likely to complete their degrees and more likely to go on to graduate school (Ethington & Smart, 1986; Smart, 1986). The overall effect of institutional size and type on educational achievement is minimal, however (Pascarella & Terenzini, 1991).

The same is true for occupational status among graduates of large universities. The breadth of academic programs and majors at research universities provides students with training in an array of potential occupations. It might be presumed that this gives them a powerful advantage over students who attend smaller comprehensive institutions or liberal arts colleges (Kamens, 1971). Again, however, this is true in only a limited sense; there is only a small positive effect on occupational status for students who attend large universities (Pascarella & Terenzini, 1991).

If they go on to graduate education in greater numbers and pursue higher status occupations than their colleagues at smaller campuses, it would be expected that students on large campuses like research universities would earn more than those at other types of institutions. In fact, this is the case (Smart, 1988), but the difference is relatively small and only affects income early in alumni's careers (Pascarella & Terenzini, 1991).

If large research universities have only a limited positive influence on educational achievement, occupational status, and earnings, it might be assumed that the experiences of students who attend these institutions parallel the experiences of students at other types of campuses. This is not the case, however, and much of the difference in experiences can be attributed to what Pascarella and Terenzini (1991) term "psychological size." Although large research universities offer a broad array of opportunities for students, there are simply more students attempting to take advantage of these programs and services. These numbers can limit students' social engagement on campus and negatively impact students' overall collegiate experience. Efforts to humanize the large research institution for students can ameliorate the negative influence of size, however. Since student affairs professionals are often the providers of these programs and services, the work that they do can have a potent affect on the success of students.

The Nature of Student Affairs Work

Professionals at research universities participated in the Calendar Study, and the findings reveal that they spend some of their time in ways that are quite different than those at liberal arts, sectarian, or comprehensive campuses. Results from the National Survey Study suggest that the nature of work, relationships, and rewards vary significantly in certain arenas between those at research universities and those at other types of institutions. In the Association Study, the quantitative data from those at research universities reveal some patterns that are similar to their colleagues at other forms of schools and some patterns that differ, particularly in the area of relationships. Their comments (offered in the National Survey and Association Studies) help explain both the similarities and the differences.

The conclusions I draw about those at research universities stem from the data they provided in these three studies. Those data are surprisingly consistent across studies. First, they affirm the nature of the research institution campus. The mission statements of research campuses talk about being top-tier and highly competitive. When asked about working at such campuses, comments from student affairs administrators at those campuses echo those sentiments:

> [We are] very prestigious with a strong reputation and respect locally and nationally. [We have a] strong academic reputation and outstanding students.

> We're an extraordinary public institution—the reputation is excellent. A certain amount of respect from the community, students, and alumni comes with that.

> [We are a] top 25 university with excellent students and faculty and staff. Alumni, students, and parents value our university's educational program. Students [come] from all over the world and the majority are from outside our geographical regional locus. Usually [we have] students from every state in the U.S. New administration [is] aggressively pursuing innovation and change within our institution.

This focus by professionals on competition is markedly different than the collaboration that was stressed by professionals at liberal arts, sectarian, and comprehensive institutions.

There are other distinctions as well. Recall how those at comprehensive campuses talked about working in a broad array of offices across campus. This description led to the metaphor of generalists. In contrast, the history at research universities reveals how faculty members are specialists whose academic endeavors are typically narrowly defined. Student affairs professionals who work at research institutions have mirrored this pattern. In their own words they talk about being specialists:

> [It's] very big, so sometimes I feel locked in my own area with little interaction with other student affairs areas. Sometimes I feel too specialized.

> We are such a large campus and I think that was my perception. On a large campus it's a lot more difficult because so many people are specialized. And so many people are set in their positions. You have to have a lot of movement above you in order to move up.

> Everyone is busy moving forward on their [sic] individual priorities. Less emphasis is given on campus wide goals and morale.

It is in this highly competitive, specialized culture that student affairs administrators at research universities work. This climate is dramatically different than the cultures of liberal arts, religiously affiliated, or comprehensive institutions and creates unique challenges and support systems for professionals.

The Work Environment

It is probably not surprising that in the National Survey Study, administrators at research campuses reported that teaching undergraduates is significantly less important on their campuses than it is at all other types of institutions. Conversely, teaching graduate students and conducting research were rated as significantly more important. The picture professionals paint of their environment is one that is politically charged, highly bureaucratic, and decentralized.

The specialization that pervades the research university environment generates a political climate for professionals:

> The university is a very political operation with competing factions and agendas among faculty; administration; and staff. There has been little unanimity of goals and programs; and almost no sense of shared resources. The territoriality . . . creates more competition than cooperation. Many initiatives are ego-driven rather than campus community focused.

> [I need to note] the degree to which politics and internal fighting rule at my institution which is a private, four year Carnegie Class I institution with major emphasis on cooperative education.

When asked what one lesson they wished they had learned before starting to work at a research university, nearly 50% reported a need to better understand campus politics and power. This is not to say that the political environment is necessarily negative. Rather, those who work on such campuses simply need to be aware of the degree of politics on campus:

> I think the more complex an organization is, the likelihood that it's going to be political just increases. There's no way to avoid that because what I find is different units that we interact with sort of go about their work differently. University Communications, Marketing and Advancement, Development, Research, Administration, Technology—all these units that are related to how we are effective, they all see the world differently than we see it. It's sort of an ongoing dance of well, you know, if you're going to deal with these folks, this is the approach you take. And that's part of how I would define political and I think it happens all the time. So I think it's pretty directly related to the complexity of the organization.

Recall that politics have been mentioned by those at sectarian and comprehensive institutions. At religious campuses, however, the politics of the church are most dominant. At comprehensives, politics play out on campuses to some degree, and in state systems to a larger degree. At research institutions, however, politics are more pervasive and guide both internal and external relations.

Like comprehensive institutions, research universities are highly bureaucratic environments. The size and complexity of these institutions require that professionals understand and appreciate the need for systems in organizations where there is "lots of bureaucracy, lots of experts, experience, [and] knowledge":

> Since we are so big the diversity of cultures at the professional level is vast. . . . I would say that we are often entrenched in the bureaucracy that is so integral in a large institution.

> There are so many policies and procedures that are either permanent memoranda or policy statements. There is a policy on everything!

Research university professionals seem to accept the need for hierarchy, noting that "bureaucracy and redundancy are inevitable at large institutions." Administrators who understand that will fare well on research campuses.

The specialization that permeates the research institution generates an environment that is highly decentralized, and student affairs administrators acknowledge that in their comments:

> [At] my institution . . . there is no articulated or available central mission and so each department within each of the divisions—there are 4 different divisions in Student Affairs at my institution—each division has their [sic] own mission statement. Each department has their [sic] own. We're pretty much thrown out there by ourselves to do our work individually. And unless we specifically outreach to do collaborative work it simply doesn't happen.

> Unfortunately, we are so decentralized that it makes simple projects extremely difficult sometimes, especially when another's area is affected.

Interestingly, a number of participants reported that their divisions had historically been highly decentralized but that they had moved to more centralized organizations in recent years:

> The culture in my institution has been decentralized, but as we start looking at the budget issues, the [policies] about emergency response, we're realizing that a decentralized model can't act quick[ly] enough in these situations. And so the whole institution is sort of like a battleship trying to turn, and it's taking us a lot of energy and effort. And I think that is where a lot of the conflict and stress resides, because we relied on the process where it's just out there and other units were [independent] and now I think that the president and the provost are saying "But, we need to have more control over this." And so that means that I have to do something different to provide that.

Nevertheless, the data in all studies are strikingly consistent: Research universities are decentralized organizations that are designed to allow individual units to change, adapt, and respond in ways that are unique. Decentralization promotes the specialized interests of units. In general, then, the political, bureaucratic, decentralized nature of the environment influences the pace at which work is conducted at these institutions.

The Pace of Work

Ask students affairs professionals at research universities about the pace at which their work is conducted and two overwhelmingly consistent themes emerge. The first has to do with the pace of change on their campuses. Responses suggest a real dichotomy. The daily work of administrators requires them to change rapidly and often. Major change, however, is harder to achieve and takes much longer:

> I mean we're very slow to change, mainly because oftentimes we have to go through three or four layers just to get to me, and then three or four levels back down to get to a lot of issues. And since we're looking at such a global picture, oftentimes we're tying to . . . we get opposing thoughts as to the same situation. So I think that the mold or the level at which you're in student affairs may affect your perceptions of response to change time.

> I think that's probably the conundrum for many of us, is being involved in institutions where on a global scale it's very slow, very slow to change, very slow to adapt to our students. But as the professional and being in that position, I can't sit [still for any length of time]. . . . It's like five or six different things [occur] sometimes within that time span.

> We're changing but some of the change is harder to change. . . . Whereas things are happening, there are always roadblocks and stumbling blocks that you're going really fast and all of a sudden you [come to] a screeching halt. We're in a paradoxical situation.

To a large extent, this seems to be explained by the culture of these campuses that are steeped in history and tradition. Like liberal arts and religious institutions, research universities are more resistant to change in general, let alone rapid change:

> "Traditions" and the belief that "we've always done it that way" permeate all facets of the campus. The professional culture is not open to change. Most parts of the campus operate as silos—as independent entities. This often results in duplication of effort and tasks as well as a waste of resources and capital.

> I've actually heard some of the higher administration say that they don't favor change. In other words, the institutional value is toward staying the same. The whole business of trying to promote tradition and history and all of that.

The second theme that emerges when professionals talk about the pace of work at research institutions focuses on the degree of balance between work and personal life. For many, there is a sense of imbalance:

> This means that I work for the university virtually all of my time. I work on campus; I work in the evenings; and I work the better part of most weekends either on Student Life matters or in preparation for my class.

> And at our institution, it's not . . . you just can't say no to something. And I also have a boss who is a workaholic, and so keeping up with both of those things is really hard. And I don't have the home expectations. I'm single; I don't have children. Yet I still feel that there's an enormous imbalance because the expectations that are being placed on me are very difficult for me to maintain or keep within an 8:00 to 5:00 realm.

> My husband and I chose not to have children because we looked at our professional careers in the future and knowing what we both wanted to do, didn't think that there would be adequate time to do both and chose not to have a family because of professional expectations.

This final comment contrasts sharply with the sentiments of those at liberal arts institutions who worked extensive evening and weekend hours but were able to incorporate their families into campus life.

Many research university administrators view this imbalance from a professional as well as a personal perspective and recognize that it is unhealthy and does not model appropriate behavior:

> I have been frustrated with the culture of our profession that rewards those who work 80-hours a week. What example does that set for our students and new professionals?

> The most effective professional relationships I have are with colleagues at my same level of professional experience who have the same beliefs I have about modeling healthy work behavior.

Indeed, there also seems to be a sense that professional/personal balance is something that can (and should) be learned:

> I'm a new professional. I've been in it for about 3 years this summer. And that might have a lot to do with it. I'm still kind of learning and spending a lot of time. But I also think it's the nature of our business. We're not putting together cars, we're growing people. So when things happen—tragedy or good things— they overflow and you don't . . . I personally don't stop thinking about them. Maybe years down the road after a long career in this business I'll better learn how to separate that.

And so it's kind of like a hazing process that we all go through. But we have to reach a new paradigm where we are actually thinking outside the box and blending ways in which we can have free time. And every day you're not going to go home at 5:00, but there should be some days that you are able to. And you have to find it within yourself to say, "this is my time."

The work pace at a large institution never slows. It's up to the individual to find a way to balance work and home life; the institution will never suggest one work less hours.

In fact, professionals talked about how they might achieve a better sense of balance over time. Administrators strongly recommended engaging one's partner or spouse in campus events and activities so that work and personal life could be blended. The same was recommended for those who had children. Bringing children to events on campus might provide not only quality time between parents and children but also enable children to see parents in the work context and provide them with a better understanding of what the parent did on a daily basis. Whereas those at liberal arts schools had already learned to integrate family and professional life, those at research universities seem to be just beginning to think about such opportunities. In general, there is a need to achieve a better professional/personal balance for research university professionals, and to achieve that might involve an assessment of how work is accomplished.

How Work Gets Done

According to the Association Study, professionals at research institutions believe their campuses value creativity far more than their colleagues at liberal arts and religiously affiliated campuses, though less than those at comprehensive colleges and universities. Like student affairs administrators at liberal arts colleges, they are often asked to take on more work and find it difficult to decline those requests. There are two defining characteristics associated with the way in which work is conducted at research universities, however, and the first relates to the degree of competition professionals experience. They report working with colleagues on many projects and programs, but the overwhelming sentiment suggested that work was often conducted in competitive ways:

[There is] lots of innovation and drive to be the "best" in the nation. Competition takes its toll on everyone; relationships and morale.

One must constantly market oneself or he/she can be lost in a large institution. One cannot afford to be humble. To obtain more funding one must promote existing programs and not wait to be recognized.

My institution is highly focused on image and perception which at times can be in conflict with the best interests of student learning and development.

> People do not really work together across departments—it seems like more of a competition to provide services for students.

In some ways, professionals should not be surprised by this sense of competition. The mission statements of research universities reflect the competitive nature of these campuses. They pride themselves on being on the cutting edge. They compete for research dollars from government and corporate entities and reward innovation. Yet the sense of competition is antithetical to the collaborative philosophy that many student affairs professionals embrace. Those who elect to work on these campuses must learn to deal with this ambiguity.

On a related note, those who work at research institutions believe that risk taking is valued. Again, this is consistent with the decentralization and sense of innovation that permeates research campuses and the comments from professionals echo that:

> Because we're decentralized . . . we can do lots and lots of things because people are willing to see what can be done. There's no preconceived notions; there's no "let's take plan B this year because we tried plan C last year." So we've been able to do a lot of experimental things.

> Risk-taking is valued because we have so many people; we have so many layers that if there are a few of us out there going nuts and trying new things, there are still enough other people are keeping life stable. And so, I think maybe that's sort [of], even almost . . . it's secure to go and take risks at our institution.

The nature of work at research universities, then, differs in some meaningful ways from work at other types of institutions. The constituencies with whom professionals work at research universities are the same as those at other campuses. Relationships with these constituencies, however, are different at research institutions.

The Nature of Relationships

First and foremost, student affairs administrators work with students. Professionals at research universities have relationships with students, however, that are different than those of their colleagues at other types of campuses. According to the National Survey Study, they are significantly less likely to know a lot of students on their campuses and significantly less likely to be known by large numbers of students. In fact, they spend less time serving students than their colleagues at all other institutional types. Although they believe the largest portion of their time is spent serving students, they grossly overestimate how much time they actually expend on students.

On one hand, they believe the students at their campuses are energetic, enthusiastic, and creative:

> They just come to the table with lots of input and enthusiasm and . . . want to do everything.

> Our students are exceptional and very motivated. They are great to work with.

On the other hand, they express concerns about the homogeneity of the students at their institutions. Many professionals described their students as "privileged," "elite," "wealthy." Students at research universities, like their counterparts at liberal arts colleges, seem to have a powerful sense of entitlement that professionals often must address:

> Every conversation I have with a parent or a student starts with, "Well I pay $35,000 a year. I SHOULD get my way. Who are YOU to tell me that I can't have my way." And the students approach pretty much everything like that. . . . And I think that just spans throughout the university with everything that we do. They feel the need that they should have everything that they want.

> It's very expensive. And I think that the students have also got a sense of entitlement now with technology and if they e-mail you at 2:00 in the morning they expect an answer back. We had a student who e-mailed my colleague a question and then a half-an-hour later he called. And I picked up the phone and he said, "Well I just sent Melissa an e-mail and she didn't e-mail me back." And I'm like, "She's been in a crisis situation for the last hour with another student, could you just be patient or could I help you?"

> One of the things we've noticed is that it's not necessarily the decision that they've been told no, but when something isn't dealt with in the way they think it should be dealt with, or in the time frame they think it should be dealt with. Some of our students now are going from the RA to the President of the institution via e-mail. . . . And then sometimes the Governor. But it's an immediate need for a response. And if it's not the exact response they want, then they're going to broadcast it to the world—and they can.

In general, then, professionals at research institutions believe they work with very talented and motivated students. They admire the energy and creativity that their students bring to the campus. The flip side, however, is the strong sense of entitlement that students often express. These sentiments mirror those held by professionals at liberal arts institutions.

Relationships with student affairs colleagues at research universities, however, are dramatically different that for those at all other types of school. Relationships mirror the specialized culture of the campus. Practitioners form close working relationships with colleagues who work in the same office or unit:

> [My colleagues are] collaborative, fun, and humorous. Because we always like feed off of one another most of the time. It's great to have somebody close by doing the same thing. It [helps to] have humor in the office and we have lots of that.

> I [describe my colleagues as] intelligent and helpful. I'm really on a very good staff. It's nice to not work with any knuckleheads.

> In my department; it is very supportive; student-focused; almost like family. I am very fortunate in my job.

Relationships with colleagues outside the office or unit, however, are characterized very differently. Administrators are significantly less likely to know many other student affairs professionals on their campuses and are significantly less likely to be known by other professionals and their comments illustrate this:

> Departments are fairly large; so interaction outside of units is not a regular occurrence.

> It is difficult to get to know other student affairs professionals outside of my functional area.

They talk about feeling "very isolated." They feel that "everyone works in their [sic] own worlds." They describe "functional silos that operate fairly independent of each other." Like faculty on their campuses, the fact that practitioners specialize in a certain area of student affairs administration leads to feelings of seclusion. It is perhaps not surprising then that professionals at research universities spend more time communicating with others than on any other activity. In fact, fully 25% of their time is spent in communication activities. The decentralized nature of the campus, coupled with the size, suggests that the specialists at research universities need to be excellent communicators.

Finally, it is important to look at relationships that professionals at research institutions have with the academic groups on campus. Interestingly, they tend to talk about faculty and academic administrators interchangeably. In terms of their working relationships, student affairs professionals at research universities are significantly less likely to know or work with faculty or academic administrators. It is also unlikely that faculty or academic administrators know student affairs practitioners. To some extent, this tendency may be explained by the specialization that permeates their work. In any event, it is evident in the way they describe their relations with these groups:

> [This is a] faculty-centered institution with an autocratic President. On the main, there are sharp divisions between student affairs personnel and faculty members.

> Faculty often do not know about student services and; therefore; either dismiss the importance of our work or unknowingly duplicate it.

The academic culture runs very deep and generally the faculty, staff, and advisors on the academic side of the house have little knowledge or desire to gain knowledge about our office's goals and purpose.

Their relations with faculty and academic leaders, however, are tempered by an overt admiration for these constituencies. Student affairs administrators at research universities describe faculty and academic leaders as "brilliant," "incredibly intellectual," and "award-winning." The positive terms they used to describe faculty are more effusive than terms used by professionals at other types of campuses. On the other hand, they report a greater degree of estrangement from faculty than their counterparts elsewhere. This seems to be an artifact of the culture of specialization that characterizes the work of both faculty and student affairs professionals at research institutions.

In general, then, relationships between student affairs professionals and many campus constituencies at research institutions seem to reflect different extremes: They can be extremely positive yet very troublesome. Administrators at these institutions, however, seem to thrive on such relationships. Perhaps they view the opportunity to work with a broad array of other groups as one of the rewards of the research university environment.

The Nature of Rewards

Rewards for those who work at research universities are primarily intrinsic in nature, just as they are for their colleagues at all other types of campuses. The most highly ranked reward was the ability to do meaningful work:

We know the value of what we do and although you may never see the end product in terms of how that student is affected or impacted by you, I think in your heart of hearts, you see the product. [You get the] sense of what the impact of what you're doing has on the whole, if you will.

An artist has a palette and they can see what they do. And I have to believe that somewhere down the road the work I'm doing is impacting somebody, and I have to feel good that I'm doing it.

Overtly, these comments seem to parallel the sentiments expressed by professionals at other types of institutions, but a closer examination reveals a powerful difference. At liberal arts and religiously affiliated colleges and universities, student affairs administrators talk about seeing growth in the students they serve. They watch students develop over years of contact with them. At research universities, professionals assume, rather than see, the impact they have on students. They "have to believe" they are promoting development among students even though they "may never see the end product." This is a potent difference in the rewards those who work at research institutions reap versus the rewards their colleagues at other types of campuses garner.

Professionals at research universities also prefer to conduct their work under certain conditions. Their second and third most valued rewards had to do with positive work environments and positive working relationships:

> I mean for me, if I work 10 hours a day and I sleep 8 hours a day, I'm spending more time with my coworkers than with anyone else. So that's why good relationships with my coworkers are important because I see them more than I see my wife. Except for the weekends—and sometimes then, too.

> In general; the people I work with both within my department and on various committees are collegial and work for the common purpose of educating students.

Administrators at research universities also value the power and personal freedom their work affords them. The ability to influence decisions (ranked fourth) and the autonomy they exercise in their positions (ranked fifth) were clearly articulated as benefits in their professional capacities. Again, the decentralized nature of the campus and the size of the institution promote these types of incentives.

The rewards those at research universities least value parallel those that their counterparts at other institutions value least, with one exception. Performance reviews, office facilities, leave time, and support staff are all extrinsic in nature and were ranked lowest by those at research universities:

> I dreaded doing performance reviews when I had to do them for people who worked for me, because I think that when they're done well, they're marginally helpful. But when they're done poorly, they're a detriment.

> I think performance reviews may be a little like office facilities. You don't think about it unless you don't have it.

> So office facilities are kind of viewed as reward. For instance, when you get the title "director" you go from having a metal desk to a wooden desk.

Only one intrinsic reward was ranked low by those at research universities: advancement opportunities. This may well be due to the fact that professionals at research universities are significantly more likely to have opportunities for upward mobility than their colleagues at other types of campuses. In fact, those at research universities routinely talked about the excellent salaries and benefits they receive. They were significantly more likely to believe they received good benefits, significantly more likely to have adequate support staff, and to receive support to take classes. They also had opportunities to pursue professional development events. In fact, those at research universities devoted more time to professional development activities than their colleagues at all other types of campuses.

In general, then, those at research institutions are experts who believe they are fairly well compensated for the specialized work they do, in both intrinsic and extrinsic ways. This perception is best illustrated by one respondent's comment:

> Our daddy used to say, "Do good and forget it." And when I got old enough to ask him what that meant without getting slapped, he went on to explain that if you are doing things for the reward it will give you, you will always be dissatisfied. You've got to find something in life to do that you think is important and go about doing it because it's important, because it's right.

Conclusions

Just as faculty at research universities are experts in narrowly defined arenas within their disciplines, so student affairs administrators are specialists within their functional areas. This notion of specialization runs throughout the data on this group of administrators. For example, their work environment is highly politicized and competitive. This is an element that student affairs professionals seem to not only understand but in some ways to embrace. The research university is also a highly bureaucratic and decentralized culture. Again, however, these are characteristics that student affairs administrators recognize and appreciate. In fact, it is these characteristics that create an environment in which specialization is prized.

The pace at research institutions is multifaceted. For individuals, the daily pace can be very hectic. Their work requires them to be highly flexible and able to change directions on very short notice. On the other hand, research universities are firmly entrenched in history and tradition. They are very slow to change and those who work on these campuses need to develop mechanisms to cope with the frustration this can generate.

Work is accomplished in ways that may seem contradictory to those outside the research university environment. Creativity is not valued, it is simply expected. Work at research institutions is often competitive. Risk taking is valued in that it might lead to outcomes that will better position a person or a unit. Those who work at research universities enjoy the sort of tension that accompanies working in a high-risk atmosphere.

To some degree, this attitude might be explained by the love-hate relationships they have with others on their campuses. For example, they work with highly talented, intelligent, energetic students. These same students, however, are predominantly privileged and elitist. They often exhibit a sense of entitlement that confounds professionals. Administrators believe faculty and academic administrators on their campuses are brilliant but irascible and at times petulant. Perhaps most important, they work very closely with student affairs colleagues within their offices, but the size and decentralized nature of the campus limits their ability to become acquainted with colleagues outside of their office. Specialization may promote the sense of competition on campus: It may be easier to compete with colleagues when you are less familiar with them.

Finally, the rewards for the specialists at research universities are both extrinsic and intrinsic. They earn relatively good salaries and benefits that are significantly better than they could earn at other types of institutions. They have ample opportunities for professional advancement and development. They may care less about rewards like office facilities and support staff because they are more likely to have access to those rewards than their counterparts at other types of colleges and universities.

Overall, these characteristics paint a portrait of a group of professionals who are specialists. They work in a culture that values adeptness. Others on their campus, particularly faculty, model what it is like to be an expert, and student affairs professionals adopt that model. In fact, they take pride in the expertise they develop within their functional area and enjoy the sense of competition that exists among units on campus. Student affairs administrators who work at research universities thrive in an environment that is complex yet vibrant, and they strive to be equally intricate and creative in their professional endeavors.

Chapter Six

The Guardians:
Professional Life at Historically Black
Colleges and Universities

The third type of institution that materialized after the Civil War reflects, in part, America's response to the emancipation of the country's slaves. Historically Black colleges and universities (HBCUs) were established to educate the millions of African Americans whose lives were altered irrevocably with the demise of slavery. Like the liberal arts colleges, religiously affiliated campuses, and comprehensive and research universities, HBCUs are a reflection of the country's social, political, and economic climate. Unlike their institutional counterparts, however, HBCUs were founded to serve a particular population rather than a curricular function (e.g., liberal arts, professional training).

In that sense, HBCUs span the institutional spectrum. Some are liberal arts colleges, and others are religiously affiliated. Many HBCUs are comprehensive institutions, and a few are research universities. As a group, they cannot be conceptualized within the traditional higher education hierarchy in America. Rather, their purpose is to educate students, primarily African American students. Indeed, some experts argue that there should be a distinct classification system for HBCUs. Given their focus on students, HBCUs should be classified based on the entry characteristics and outcome measures of those students (Coaxum, 2001).

It is this focus on students that has led me to characterize student affairs professionals on these campuses as "guardians." The ways in which they describe their work focus on their desire to protect students and promote their growth. They see themselves as surrogate families for their students. Their relationships with constituency groups resemble extended families; in fact, many are related to others on campus by blood or marriage. They choose to work at HBCUs because of their commitment to racial uplift. They see themselves as guardians of future generations of students. We refer to these institutions by the population they serve—Blacks—and those who work on HBCU campuses assume responsibility for the intellectual, social, spiritual, emotional, and vocational development of the students on their campuses. That is, they serve as guardians, figuratively if not literally for their students, as the data reveal. A review of how HBCUs emerged provides the context for this metaphor of guardianship.

Historical Evolution

In 1850, there were 4,000,000 Blacks in America, 500,000 of whom were free. Yet only 29 Blacks earned bachelor degrees in this country between 1619 and 1850 (Humphries, 1995). At the end of the Civil War, then, the need to educate Blacks was critical. This need was met through the efforts of three groups. The first two were religious organizations. The American Missionary Association established seven HBCUs and 13 normal schools between 1861 and 1870 (Browning & Willlams, 1978). This association comprised representatives from a variety of denominations including Unitarians, Presbyterians, and Congregationalists. These HBCU missionaries sought to enrich the minds of their students by teaching basic skills (reading, writing, math) but also hoped to save the souls of their pupils through religious indoctrination. The second group, Black churches, resisted the Puritanical objectives of some of these schools and founded their own institutions of learning (Garibaldi, 1984; Willie & Edmonds, 1978).

In either case, it is important to note that the vast majority of Blacks at the time were illiterate. As a result, most Black institutions started out as elementary schools. They offered secondary education as generations of students achieved sufficient levels of knowledge to warrant more advanced subjects. It was not until students had mastered these more fundamental levels of schooling that HBCUs could offer college level curricula. At the start, then, HBCUs combined all levels of education for Blacks (Allen & Jewell, 2002; Garibaldi, 1984).

These early institutions to educate newly liberated slaves were not established without opposition, however. Southern Whites, still convinced of the inferiority of Blacks, fought the notion of an educated Black population, arguing that schooling Blacks would be a disservice as it might lead them to expect that they were capable of achieving levels of success beyond their abilities (Lucas, 1994). Second, the religious groups lacked extended support from the North and battled the Army occupiers of the South over sites and supplies for the schools. Finally, there were disagreements among the denominations themselves over what pedagogical approach to take. Some took a parental approach and thought students ought to be introduced to subjects gradually and guided through those subjects slowly. Others were convinced that the former slaves needed to be treated as the adults they were and should be fully immersed in the educational experience from the start (J. D. Anderson, 1988; Browning & Williams, 1978).

In 1877, federal troops withdrew from the South, and that led to a backlash against much of the progress that had been made in terms of educating Blacks. The repressive society that emerged in the region disenfranchised Blacks. Policies limited education for Blacks and shifted the focus from teaching subject matters to vocational training programs. These efforts were sanctioned by the Supreme Court's decision in *Plessy v. Ferguson* (1896) that legitimized the establishment of separate but equal institutions for Blacks and Whites. *Plessy* served as a prelude to the third group that established HBCUs, the states (Browning & Williams, 1978; Bullock, 1967).

The Morrill Act of 1890 offered all states, including those in the South, the opportunity to establish public institutions of higher education that offered training in agriculture and mechanical arts. From the federal perspective, the policy was designed to promote agricultural productivity in the rural areas that were annexed as the country expanded westward. From the perspective of the Southern states, the Morrill Act justified the *de facto* efforts to create a new social order in which Whites were superior to Blacks. To this end, many states established public Black colleges. These institutions then competed for resources and support with the private Black colleges that had been founded before 1890 (Allen & Jewell, 2002; Browning & Williams, 1978).

As this discussion suggests, from the start the education of Blacks revolved around the debate over what form that education should take. From 1890 on, the historical evolution of HBCUs is so intertwined with the issue of the purpose of HBCUs that it is difficult to distinguish one from the other. In June of 1898, two years after the *Plessy* decision, a group of leaders from both the North and the South convened to plan a separate system of education for Blacks. There were about 35 public and private Black colleges at the time that fell into one of two curricular camps, each championed by a nationally recognized Black leader (Allen & Jewell, 2002; M. C. Brown, Donahoo, & Bertrand, 2001).

The first camp included those institutions that offered vocational education for Blacks. The Hampton Institute served as the prototype for the industrial education model and Booker T. Washington was the spokesman for this educational approach. Washington, a graduate of the Hampton Institute, was convinced that Blacks should be educated to take their place in the agricultural and industrial world that was rapidly evolving in America. The self-sufficiency that would result from such training would lead to a sense of dignity and self-worth among Blacks. Additionally, Washington believed that vocationally trained Blacks would share interests with laborers in the agricultural South and the industrializing North, hence promote racial reconciliation and harmony (J. D. Anderson, 1988; M. C. Brown et al., 2001; Browning & Williams, 1978).

The other side of the debate was promulgated by W. E. B. DuBois who was committed to the idea that a classical education, like that offered by the private liberal arts colleges, was the only road that would lead to enlightenment of the Black population. He posited that Black institutions of higher education should develop the most talented Blacks who would become professionals and leaders of the Black population. This "talented tenth" as DuBois called them, would address the problems of Blacks in the larger social context and ensure the continued development of the race. Moreover, he was convinced that vocational training for Blacks limited their aspirations and reinforced White stereotypes that Blacks were incapable of achieving higher levels of professional and personal success (J. D. Anderson, 1988; M. C. Brown et al., 2001; Browning & Williams, 1978).

Although DuBois was both ardent and eloquent in his arguments, government officials and business and civic leaders endorsed Washington's notions of Black education, and the vocational approach to schooling Blacks was incorporated into many institutions of learning throughout the South. These debates, however, revealed a lack of understanding about what Black colleges were actually accomplishing. Few HBCUs were accredited at the start of the 20th century, and it was difficult to discern whether a degree from one HBCU was the equivalent of a degree in the same field from another HBCU. In the early part of the century, issues of standardization in education were raised for both Black and White schools. Calls for curricular, structural, and certification standards were rife. In the case of Black schools, these calls were exacerbated by the overtly inferior system of Black education in the South (Willie & Edmonds, 1978).

To address these concerns, a series of seven studies was conducted between 1900 and 1954 to evaluate the quality of education in Black schools. The reports produced by these studies generated sufficient interest at the national level that Black schools were recognized and accredited at the state and national levels. The first two, by DuBois, identified those institutions whose curricula had developed to a sufficient degree that they could be called colleges and then stratified those colleges into tiers based on quality of curricula and number of students enrolled. The third, sponsored by an education foundation, offered a series of recommendations that included calls for increased financial support for HBCUs and equal salaries for Black and White teachers but also endorsed industrial education. The final four reports were government surveys that examined the scope of Black education in America and made recommendations to improve education for Blacks (J. D. Anderson, 1988; M. C. Brown et al., 2001; Browning & Williams, 1978).

In short, these reports revealed that both vocational and liberal arts curricula were being offered by HBCUs in the first half of the 20th century. Perhaps their most abiding contribution was the attention they brought to the Black educational system in the U.S. This attention led to both positive and negative consequences. On the positive side, the reports generated recognition by accrediting agencies that had heretofore ignored Black institutions. On the negative side, the reports uncovered the abysmal levels of support for Black education and the low levels of quality at these institutions (Browning & Williams, 1978). As Chambers (1972) noted, in 1916 HBCUs were viewed as no better than elementary schools and in 1928 they were portrayed as no better than high schools. Throughout this era, however, some Black educators shunned the idea of Black inferiority and persisted in their efforts to offer liberal arts education to Blacks. These institutions (e.g., Fisk, Spelman, Morehouse) garnered greater support, and a hierarchy of prestige among HBCUs began to develop. By 1942, even Southern Whites accepted the notion of liberal arts education for Blacks, and it was in this atmosphere of begrudging acceptance that the *Brown v. Board of Education* (1954) decision threw yet another curveball at the HBCUs.

The *Brown* decision proved to be a double-edged sword for HBCUs. There were some immediate benefits including increased funding for physical plant improvements and increased financial aid for growing enrollments. At the same time, however, two other trends had a negative impact on these institutions. First, the civil rights movement prompted historically White colleges and universities (HWCUs) to actively recruit Black students, offering them more educational options and forcing HBCUs to compete for the best and brightest Black students. Second, HBCUs were subject to the same desegregation regulations as their HWCU counterparts and were forced to open their doors to Whites and students from other races (J. D. Anderson, 1988; Browning & Williams, 1978). Although many HBCUs had always welcomed non-Black students, the post-*Brown* era required active promotion of diversity at HBCUs rather than passive acceptance of it.

In recent decades, public policy regarding HBCUs and higher education in general has taken two conflicting directions. There is a struggle to precisely define desegregation that is being played out primarily through legislative and judicial channels. Cases such as *Hopwood v. Texas* (1996) and the cases involving the University of Michigan (*Gratz v. Bollinger*, 2003; *Grutter v. Bollinger*, 2003) illustrate that the role of race in terms of access to education has yet to be resolved. At the same time, there are federal and state programs that extend funding to HBCUs in an effort to ameliorate past practices of discrimination (C. L. Jackson & Nunn, 2003).

The irony in all this history should not be overlooked. As M. C. Brown et al. (2001) noted, HBCUs were originally the product of a racist society, and the policy of "separate but equal" enabled HBCUs, and the students who attended them, to flourish. The *Brown* decision sought to dismantle the dual system of education in America and yet the HBCUs have suffered, in some respects, as a result of that and related decisions. It is in this climate of ongoing debate that HBCU campuses function today.

The Nature of the Historically Black College and University Campus

HBCUs are defined as institutions founded prior to 1964 for the primary purpose of educating descendents of former slaves (M. C. Brown et al., 2001). The number of HBCUs has varied over time. The 35 institutions that were in existence at the turn of the 20th century blossomed to 123 by 1964. By 1970, their number had shrunk to 105 (Gary, 1975). Coaxum (2001) reported a total of 104, but there seems to be more general agreement that there are currently 103 HBCUs (M. C. Brown et al., 2001; C. L. Jackson & Nunn, 2003). This number represents 2.6% of the 3,941 public and private institutions of higher education in the country (Carnegie Foundation, 2001). Of the 103, 38% are public four-year institutions, 44% are private four-year campuses, and the remainder includes public two-year (10%) and private two-year (8%) campuses. These colleges and universities are located in 19 Southern and border states as well as Michigan and the District of Columbia. Additionally, there are approximately 54 predominantly Black colleges and universities (PBCUs). These are institutions whose enrollments include over 50% Black students. Unlike their HBCU counterparts, PBCUs are scattered across the states (M. C. Brown et al., 2001).

Most HBCUs are small, enrolling fewer than 5,000 students (Nettles, Wagener, Millett, & Killenbeck, 1999). Collectively, they enroll 300,000 students (M. C. Brown & Davis, 2001) or 2% of the 15,079,149 college students in the country. Historically, HBCUs have been the primary enroller of Black college students, however (Allen, Epps, & Haniff, 1991, Garibaldi, 1984). Until 1991, they produced roughly 70% of all Black college graduates (Roebuck & Murty, 1993). Despite the fact that they represent only 2.6% of institutions, HBCUs enroll 17% of all Black college students and confer 28% of all bachelor's degrees (Kim, 2002), 15% of all master's degrees and 10% of all doctorates (Allen & Jewell, 2002) earned by Blacks in this country. Their commitment to educating Blacks is evident in the mission of HBCUs.

Mission

There are two perspectives relevant to the mission of HBCUs. First is their shared mission. As M. C. Brown et al. (2001) noted, "HBCUs were founded on and continue to be united by the distinct mission of positioning, preparing, and empowering African American students to succeed in what many perceive to be a hostile society" (p. 559). Others phrase it differently, suggesting that HBCUs are distinguished from predominantly White institutions in their commitment to preparing Black students for leadership roles and community service (M. C. Brown & Davis, 2001; Roebuck & Murty, 1993) and promoting racial pride in Black students (Harley, 2001). The overall message, however, is clear: HBCUs operate to serve Black students.

The second perspective on mission adopts the traditional approach: Mission is associated with institutional type. HBCUs, however, mirror the full spectrum of Carnegie institutional types and their individual institutional mission statements reflect this variation. Their mission statements are closely aligned with the missions of other colleges and universities in their institutional category. For example, consider how the following mission statement from a liberal arts HBCU mirrors very closely the missions of other liberal arts institutions with a focus on holistic education grounded in the liberal arts:

> [Name of] University is a private, historically black, faith based liberal arts institution. [Name of institution] has as its purpose the development of graduates who are broadly educated, culturally aware, concerned with improving the human condition and able to meet the competitive demands of a global and technologically advanced society. To achieve this purpose, the university strives to create and maintain an academic climate that is conducive to the pursuit of scholarship through programs of excellence anchored in the liberal arts.

Likewise, mission statements of HBCUs that are comprehensive institutions parallel the mission statements of other comprehensive universities. They talk about a broad, general mission with a primary focus on undergraduate instruction based in the liberal arts. Like their comprehensive counterparts, their secondary purpose is to offer professional programs at the graduate level. Additionally, they offer educational opportunities for the residents of their local communities:

> [Name of] State University is a public university whose primary mission is to offer high-quality educational programs at the baccalaureate level for a diverse student population. Master's level programs for professional study are also available from the university and through inter-institutional agreements. While the primary focus is on teaching and learning, the university encourages scholarship and creative activities by faculty and students, and engages in mutually beneficial relationships with the community in ways which complement its educational mission.
>
> The instructional program comprises three components—general education, specialized education and continuing education. General education provides for all students the academic foundations and cultural experiences essential to a liberal arts education. Specialized education provides students with the experiences necessary to master an academic discipline in preparation for employment and/or graduate and professional programs, including master's degree programs offered at [name of university]. The university is strategically positioned to provide unique opportunities for students through four centers of academic excellence in teacher education, information technology, health sciences and financial services. Continuing education offers individuals opportunities for personal or vocational enrichment through constant, periodic or occasional study.

Not surprisingly, the mission statements of HBCUs that are research universities are similar to those of other research universities, identifying the tripartite roles of teaching, research, and service. Unlike their PWI counterparts, though, their mission statements also highlight their focus on Black students:

> [Name of] University is a comprehensive, research-oriented, historically Black private university providing an educational experience of exceptional quality to students of high academic potential with particular emphasis upon the provision of educational opportunities to promising Black students. Further, the University is dedicated to attracting and sustaining a cadre of faculty who are, through their teaching and research, committed to the development of distinguished and compassionate graduates and to the quest for solutions to human and social problems in the United States and throughout the world.
> Vision
> [Name of] University is a comprehensive research university, unique and irreplaceable, defined by its core values, the excellence of all its activities in instruction, research and service, and by its enduring commitment to educating youth, African Americans and other people of color in particular, for leadership and service to our nation and the global community.

The breadth of institutional types represented among the HBCUs makes any sort of generalizations about their mission problematic. Perhaps the clearest way to summarize is simply to say that these institutions embrace missions that are similar to others in their classification but do so in the context of serving Black students. This commitment to serving Black students is also evident among faculty on HBCU campuses.

Faculty

The relationship between HBCUs and faculty can be viewed in a number of ways. First, HBCUs were the only institutions offering post-graduate education to Blacks for much of the 20th century. As a result, they produced most of the Black faculty in America for generations. Their role in educating current and future members of the professoriat continues. Forty percent of current full-time Black faculty members earned their bachelor's degree at an HBCU. In fact, 9 of the 10 undergraduate institutions that produce the most Black doctorates are HBCUs. The future of the Black professoriat is also tied to HBCUs: 27% of first year students at HBCUs report that they plan to earn a Ph.D. as opposed to the national average of 17% (Perna, 2001).

It is not surprising, then, that whereas only 5% of full-time faculty nationally are Black, at four-year HBCUs 58% are Black (Johnson & Harvey, 2002) and at two-year HBCUs 72% are Black. In fact, 37% of all Black faculty members in the country are working at the 2.6% of institutions that are HBCUs (Perna, 2001). These numbers have not changed significantly in 20 years (Billingsley, 1982). Representation varies dramatically, however, by discipline. In 2000, Blacks earned 6% of all Ph.D.s conferred in the country, but most of these were in education and the social sciences. Only 86 Blacks earned doctorates in the physical sciences and only 14 earned Ph.D.s in math (D. H. Jackson, 2002).

A second point of view on faculty at HBCUs adopts a work life perspective: What are teaching, research, and service responsibilities like at these institutions, and how do those roles impact future trends among Black faculty? Consider, for example, teaching loads. The average teaching load at HBCUs is four classes per semester (Johnson & Harvey, 2002). Professors at HBCUs, however, are like their colleagues at other institutional types. They enjoy teaching and the opportunities it provides to interact with students and impact their lives. However, there are downsides to working at an HBCU that faculty members also acknowledge. They typically teach twice as many classes as their colleagues at research universities, and they have concerns about the facilities at HBCUs and the time that teaching takes away from research activities and personal study. They are also dissatisfied with levels of student motivation and recognition that good teaching garners at HBCUs (Diener, 1985).

This same sense of ambivalence is evident in research endeavors among faculty at HBCUs. Although there is some evidence that working at a HBCU is not related to research productivity (Perna, 2001), faculty at these institutions are less satisfied with the opportunities to conduct research (Diener, 1985) and the work setting in general on their campuses (Perna). Administrators at HBCUs, however, recognize that the future of their campuses may depend on greater research productivity so are building research centers on their campuses and establishing partnerships with research universities (L. M. Brown, 1999). They see collaboration as a way to attract and retain more faculty as well as more research dollars. Attracting more research dollars is seen a key to the future of HBCUs. In 1998, Johns Hopkins University alone received more federal research funds than all the 103 HBCUs combined. Among HBCUs, six institutions captured more government grants for research than all other HBCUs combined (Harley, 2001).

What, then, draws faculty to HBCUs? It is certainly not salaries; full professors at HBCUs earn an average of $56,400 compared to $72,700 at all institutions. For all ranks, the difference is even greater (20%): $45,300 for those at HBCUs versus $56,300 at all institutions (A. L. Evans, Evans, & Evans, 2002). Moreover, faculty members express frustration with salaries and benefits at HBCUs (Diener, 1985). Their satisfaction, it seems, comes from the service they are convinced they are providing. Study after study documents the sense of commitment that faculty at HBCUs have towards the students they serve. They enjoy a unique sense of purpose—the uplifting of Blacks—that they garner by working at HBCUs. They view their work as a higher calling, not a career, and perceive the opportunity to have an impact on Black students to be most meaningful (Diener, 1985; Fields, 2000; Perna, 2001). In fact, it seems that those who attended HBCUs as students return to such campuses when they seek faculty positions (Perna).

Students

Black students comprise approximately 10% of all college students, but over 17% of those Black students attend HBCUs. Given the commitment of HBCU faculty to working with these students, it might be expected that they come from exceptional backgrounds. To the contrary, HBCU students earn lower high school GPAs and SAT scores than Black students who enroll at HWCUs (Kim, 2002). They come from families of low socioeconomic status. One-third (33%) of HBCU students come from families with an annual income under $25,000, compared to 20% of students nationally (Nettles et al., 1999). In fact, students are drawn to HBCUs because of the low tuition they typically charge and high levels of financial aid they offer (Freeman & Thomas, 2002; Kim). Many also opt for a college that is close to home: 18% of first year HBCU students attend college within 10 miles of their home compared to 11% of first year students nationally (Higher Education Research Institute, 1996).

These characteristics do not seem to negatively influence achievement, however. In general, there is parity in scores on reading comprehension, math, and critical thinking between Black students at HBCUs and those at HWCUs (Bohr, Pascarella, Nora, & Terenzini, 1995; Kim, 2002). In fact, there is some evidence that Black students at HWCUs fare worse than those at HBCUs; they do not achieve academically or persist at levels equal to those of their HBCU counterparts (M. C. Brown et al., 2001).

Some of this success is likely due to the experiences that HBCU students have. They interact more frequently with faculty, are more involved, and participate in cocurricular activities at higher levels than their HWCU counterparts. The HBCU offers them a broader array of opportunities to network socially, and these networks positively influence satisfaction and occupational aspirations for students (Davis, 1991). HBCU students are more satisfied with their collegiate experience, and this has a multiplier effect; attending a HBCU retains a positive effect on satisfaction despite the fact that students believe facilities and resources at such institutions are markedly more limited (Outcalt & Skewes-Cox, 2002).

This information about faculty and students at HBCUs paint a fairly rosy picture of life at HBCUs. The future for these institutions, however, may be a bit bleaker if they do not address a couple major concerns. The desegregation that has been mandated by federal law has opened up alternatives for both Black faculty and Black students. Faculty may be attracted by higher salaries, lighter teaching loads, and better facilities at HWCUs (Fields, 2000). Students, especially the best and brightest students, have alternatives when choosing colleges (Hickson, 2002). It is in this context of uncertainty that student affairs professionals at HBCUs work.

The Nature of Student Affairs Work

A total of 71 student affairs professionals employed at HBCUs provided the data reported here. All worked at four-year institutions. Fewer than 20 of the 103 HBCUs are two-year schools. Since the majority of student affairs practitioners examined in this book were at four-year institutions, we elected to include only HBCU professionals from four-year campuses to ensure that comparisons could be draw between their responses and the responses of professionals at other campuses.

All data reported in this chapter come from the HBCU Study. Recall that data were collected at a national conference of student affairs administrators who worked at HBCUs and from professionals at 20 other HBCU campuses. In all instances, participants completed the same protocol that was used in the Association Study. They rated pairs of words that described their work, reported how much time they spent working with different constituency groups, described their relationships with those groups, and rank ordered a list of rewards from most to least valued. Many also participated in interviews that were audio recorded and transcribed. The end result was quantitative data that could be compared to the quantitative data culled in the other studies. Additionally, the comments and stories related in interviews provided invaluable insights into the nature of professional life for those at HBCUs.

The HBCU student affairs professionals are different in some ways from professionals at other institutions. For example, 89% are Black whereas only 18% of professionals at other institutions are people of color (Pickering & Calliotte, 2000). Nearly a third (30%) have been employed at their current institution for over a decade. Perhaps most interesting is the personal relationship that student affairs administrators have with HBCUs: 62% of professionals on these campuses attended or graduated from a HBCU. In fact, 44% graduated from the institutions where they currently work. Like their faculty counterparts, it would seem that those who go to HBCUs return to work there as professionals.

The nature of their work reflects their devotion to such campuses and the students who enroll at them:

> This is good to be able to feel proud about Black history and Black culture and maybe emphasizing the daily learning, and it gives you great respect for your own heritage.

> I have some of the sharpest students I have EVER seen in life come from an HBCU. And I have some of the students that were so very marginal. [They] come to a college campus like an HBCU and leave here with all the confidence in the world. That enables them to gain that job that makes them shine.

> So I think that's what's unique. That you can be a student at an HBCU and find that place. And if it's not here, there's another HBCU that will probably enable you to find that place. But it's not just about the academics. It's not just about

the social atmosphere. The social atmosphere is really the most, in my mind,
the most important because our curricula are very much alike. But it's all that
other stuff you get [at a HBCU that matters].

So professionals believe in their campuses and the students they serve. It is
in that context that the nature of their work environment should be considered.

The Work Environment

The work environment at HBCUs can best be described through three inter-
related issues: limited resources, the politics that are involved in garnering those
resources, and the bureaucracy that must be navigated once resources have been
secured. The first issue, limited resources, drives the second two characteristics
of the environment. Perhaps more important to note, none of the questions used
to gather data from professionals at HBCUs asked about resources specifically.
Rather, this was an element of their environment that the administrators
themselves raised, and, as their comments suggest, it is a significant issue for
those who work at HBCUs:

> I think we are slow to get monies from the state. I think we are paid less than
> other people in our positions. And they always base things on the number of
> students you have, the number of programs you have, the number of sports
> events you have—and that's why you have less. But we are doing the same
> thing. So that's not good. So it's based on . . . I'm thinking of HBCU schools.
> So it's always less. We do the same thing within the same environments, but on
> a lower scale.

> Oh the lack of resources. Not getting our fair share of the pie has always been
> [a problem for HBCUs]. . . . Between now and 2025 there's some HBCUs out
> of the 103—some of them are going to fail. . . . They're just. . . . Well you see
> [name of one HBCU]. Some others are in trouble. [Name of another HBCU]
> down in [name of state] is already closed. And [name of first HBCU] is on the
> way [out]. They're not going to make it.

> You compare [name of elite HWCU] to [name of HBCU]—it's like night and
> day. And I think that as HBCUs, we're limited and unfortunately . . . I don't
> know if you all have seen this in your research, but we're an endangered
> species. You're seeing HBCUs lose their accreditation. People have better
> choices.

As their comments suggest, professionals at these campuses are worried about
the institutional type as a whole, not just their individual campuses. They are
concerned about the viability of HBCUs collectively. In this sense, they stand as
guardians for the HBCU system as well as for the students they serve.

This notion of the collective is also evident when professionals talk about
the other two potent elements of their work environment only in these instances
the collective involves others on their campuses. Consider the degree of politics

on the campus, for example. Like those at liberal arts colleges, professionals at HBCUs see their campuses as political, but the politics in this case appear to be driven by relationships:

> You know, the politics that can be involved, from people—it could be in part from people being comfortable with each other and forming those types of relationships that make it kind of difficult, you know, coming from the outside coming in and trying to accomplish different things. I think that makes it really difficult to move forward sometimes. And so sometimes what I think that creates is an environment that's resistant to some change.

> Yeah, well I think that the HBCU environments are driven by contributors and those who have a great degree of charisma in terms of finances. And I think anytime finances are involved, systems are able to be manipulated, to cater to those [who] are the primary givers. So I say that, for example, if I'm a great donor, then I don't think that you'd have any problem implementing my ideology on how things should work within your system. And I think that that's what happens a lot in HBCUs, especially in private HBCUs that don't get a lot of state funds and things of that nature. So they're really dependent on outside sources.

Even when offering comments that suggest that the politics are limited, professionals couch those in terms of people:

> My director is a very fair person, a very fair person. So it's minimally political.

Relationships also form the basis of professionals' perspective on the third compelling characteristic of their environment, the degree of bureaucracy. At HBCUs, bureaucracy is not a matter of policies and procedures, as it is at community colleges or research universities. Rather, it is a matter of people:

> Mostly in the sense that it just takes going through so many different people, and if you want to try something new you've gotta propose it and then it's got to be moved . . . through the director, then your VP, then the executive staff and then the president. And it just takes a long time, sometimes, to get things done because there are so many layers and because things need to be approved by all those layers, oftentimes. Not always, but oftentimes.

> A lot of times it's not what you know, it's who you know. . . . I learned quickly you need to find out who you know . . . who to get to know to get things done, you know . . . just everywhere from public safety on up to the president. It's really a "who-you-know" type of situation most of the time.

When considered collectively, these comments paint a relatively clear picture: Much of the work environment at HBCUs is driven by the types of relationships student affairs professionals have with others on their campuses. They need to develop and maintain, or guard, their relationships with others at

their institutions. These same liaisons appear to drive the pace of work at
HBCUs.

The Pace of Work

Because student affairs practitioners at HBCUs are so connected to others
on their campuses, they characterize their institutions as slow to change. Those
relationships have to be protected and/or nurtured:

> We're like a really big family and we tend to be a little traditional. As far as
> with our students, we are . . . we're like a village and we all raising the
> children, which I guess is a part of our heritage almost. . . . We guide students
> A LOT here, which I like doing that. But the parents tend to think that we're a
> little more than just a guiding light for them. That we are their home away from
> home. And I think the university tends to adopt that. So things that other
> universities are doing, we're slow to make those changes.

> It takes forever to get anything done around here. I move pretty fast and things
> move slow. People are comfortable with the status quo, what it's always been.
> "I've worked here for 8 years and this is the way it's ALWAYS been, so I
> don't know why it needs to be any different."

> I was very sort of frustrated by the "slow-to-change," the bureaucracy, and the
> reality that at least on my campus, and I think on some other campuses too, that
> we tend to hire. . . . It's a very family oriented place. The people here . . .
> there's like 5 and 6 people from any given family that all work here. And they
> work here for like 50 years. And so you've got folks that work here because
> they got the job because they know somebody because one of their cousins or
> parents or grandparents works here—and they stayed forever because they're
> local folks.

As these comments suggest, relationships seem to take precedence when
considering change and that decelerates the rate at which new initiatives can be
adopted. This slow pace of change seems to create a fair degree of stress for
professionals at HBCUs.

Student affairs administrators at these campuses, like their counterparts at
liberal arts institutions, often play multiple roles on campuses and wear several
administrative hats. This complexity results in a very hectic workday for many:

> I work from 7:30 to 10:00 every single day of the week—and often have to
> come in on weekends. Private is different than public. I don't have a lot of
> layers of staff. I do it all. And so that's where my stress comes in.

Unlike their colleagues at liberal arts or research universities, however,
professionals at HBCUs seem to actively work at balancing their professional
and personal lives. In some cases, they do this by relying on the relationships
they guard so dearly.

If we have personal issues, it's not a problem because we all kind of cover each other. We kind of work together. I know what she's doing; she knows what I'm doing. We kind of train each other in the different areas that we all work in, so it won't be a back fall if I'm not in. Someone else can pick up and do what I have to do. But we know that there are certain times of the year that we have to be here. Like during registration, opening up the school for each semester, homecoming, and all the major functions that we have on campus. But I feel that most of the time, work and our personal life balance out to be pretty even.

And some of us work basically an 8:00 to 5:00 shift, if you would call it that. However, there is a great deal of closeness, connectivity with each other, so if we are required to work weekends—sometimes it's sporadic for some areas. But we are willing to do that. You have different classifications, if you will, of personnel so you have some folk who are contractual. You have some other categories. And so balance for one is imbalance for another, depending on what the requirements are in your different areas. And so you've got a broad cross-section probably within this group in terms of what balance or not balance is. But basically because we're an HBCU, most of the . . . or some of the programming may require you to work on a weekend, may require you to work at night, but you can balance that because it's family oriented so you're finding family, too, at some activities—that kind of thing.

In other cases, however, balancing personal and professional life is an individual responsibility, and one that HBCU professionals take quite seriously:

So the balance is the balance that you make. That's really what it is. It's the balance that you make. And as she said, we DO share responsibilities. There may be a time she has to cover for me if I had to go out, so we do share responsibilities.

So I mean you have to make your balance. You have to make your professional life fit with your personal life and those people in it. You have to make your balance.

It almost demands and requires that I make a balance in my life and not just have a life that is centered around taking care of the responsibilities that I have, and the commitment that I have to students. There is a life after my involvement with students as it pertains to my every-day work, but there must be a balance there so you can have a productive life and an enjoyable life yourself.

How Work Gets Done

Given the focus on relationships evident in both the work environment and the pace at which work is conducted, it might be surprising that some believe work at HBCUs is accomplished individually:

Well, first of all I would say that in the current role that I'm in, I work mostly—I would say just in terms of time, more by myself than anything else.

> I notice that a lot of the work that's being done, a lot of individuals have a lot
> on their backs, I should say. So it's all about kind of doing what you have to
> do—kind of covering yourself because one person is always responsible for so
> much that they can't always work as a team, because not everybody also knows
> what's going on with that person. Not everybody is trained in the same things.

Since a number of HBCUs are liberal arts colleges, it is possible that the above
comments are driven by the fact that many work in one-person offices.

For most professionals, however, work is accomplished in collaborative and
collegial ways. Although this parallels how work is accomplished at liberal arts
institutions, at HBCUs collegiality takes on a different tone. The notion of
familial relationships permeates the work atmosphere, even if, at times, that may
not be viewed as particularly efficient:

> We're certainly collegial. Everybody likes everybody else for the most part,
> and friendly and cooperative—and that's part of the benefit of that whole
> family atmosphere. Most folks have been here a really long time and are very
> friendly with each other, and have practically raised each other's kids and all
> that. But sometimes in a professional setting that can be a little bit less than
> effective I think.

Since relationships are so evident in the nature of work at HBCUs it would seem
prudent to examine those relationships more closely.

The Nature of Relationships

As the discussion to this point suggests, relationships drive much of the
work at HBCUs. The data reveal four constituencies with which student affairs
professionals on HBCU campuses interact: students, faculty, academic
administrators, and parents. First and foremost in the minds of administrators on
these campuses is their work with students. They are genuinely committed to
helping students succeed, even though they confirm what the literature says and
acknowledge that in many cases their students are not as well prepared for
college as they might wish. Consider the following comments from three
individuals at different campuses:

> Have you ever heard the term "diamonds in the rough," meaning that what's
> unique about it is you see students that come in? And when you find a
> diamond, it's filled with dirt, and cluttered, and you have to scrape it and shine
> it and clean it up, and then it's a beautiful diamond. That's the way students
> are—diamonds in the rough. So that's what's unique about them—to see them
> just glow at the end of the [day], and everybody is proud of them, parents,
> community, churches. That's what I always say, diamonds in the rough. And I
> think when the students come in as freshmen; they are really in the rough. But
> when they leave they are diamonds. That's unique.

I like seeing the outcomes. I like taking diamonds in the rough and seeing them really, really blossom into a multi-faceted diamond. And we see this happening every day. And I think that it is my greatest joy and my greatest satisfaction out of this job.

The concept on our campus is that of a family unit. Family union, family-oriented. You know, everybody kind of knows everyone because we're not a large campus. So I think that administrators have more input on that size campus, more so than on larger campuses. But again, being that it's an HBCU they want to make sure that these . . . I don't want to use the term, but "diamond in the rough" get their diamonds shining. So they do spend a lot of extra time, a lot of extra effort administratively making sure that processes are done.

At HBCUs, students are gems that need to be mined and polished. The students at these campuses are dramatically different than the students of privilege at liberal arts colleges or research universities and more closely aligned to the students at community colleges and comprehensive institutions.

The way professionals at HBCUs approach their work with students, however, is quite different than the approaches taken at other campuses. They view themselves as members of students' extended families. They see themselves as surrogate parents or siblings and assume those roles when dealing with students:

I'm like a big sister to most of them. They used to say it was a mother, but I'm too young to be anybody's mother. I'm a big sister, and that part is fun.

I don't know if you can say it would be positive—on our campus, they view me as their mom. They just look at me and if I tell them something, you know they're going to do it.

Because the approach that I use—I'm not going to pull you outside to talk to you. Or I'm not going to wait until the session is over. I'm going to embarrass you. Like your momma say, "you cut up and I'm gonna cut up." I'm going to embarrass you right then and there, and that has an effect on them because they don't want to be embarrassed.

No other group of professionals uses this sort of terminology to describe their relationships with students. Those at HBCUs truly see themselves as guardians of their students, and they take that guardianship seriously.

Finally, comments also reinforce the research on those who work at HBCUs. They recognize that they stand on the shoulders of those who came before them, and they feel obligated to "pay it forward" and prepare the next generation of Black students:

Yeah, that's the best part of the whole deal and that's why I, like many other people, that's the main reason I got involved in the first place. [I] was looking

forward to the opportunity of working with students, to kind of repay the debt
the I owe the people who worked with me when I was a student—helped me
and my peers to develop, get some appreciation for ourselves and life and all
the rest of it.

It was comments like these that led me to label this group of professionals as
guardians. Not only do they see themselves as surrogate family members for
students, their sense of professional fulfillment comes from this notion of
generativity, guarding future generations of students.

Even when discussing aspects of their work with students that they dislike,
their comments reflect aspects that parents often dislike—discipline and
disrespect:

People aren't reachable, so dealing with unruly students [is what I dislike].
Very recently I was dealing with a young man who was VERY disrespectful
and I had to have him removed and revoked his privileges to participate in
intramural sports and recreation programs. . . . He refused to leave or answer to
authority.

[What I dislike is] students who are very disrespectful. Students who are not
big on school policy and procedures.

So one of the negative things, some of the students, I think, see me as a parent
and when I try to relate as an administrator, they see their parent, and seeing
their parent or maybe even grandparent in me—sometimes it's not always
positive.

And that really bothers me. Not having the sensitivity to those who are
sacrificing for them to be here to even receive an education. [That] really
troubles me at times.

This sense of guardianship extends to student affairs professionals'
relationships with faculty members on their campuses. Although not all relations
with faculty are positive, HBCU professionals are quite even-handed in their
comments about faculty:

I like that. I really enjoy that, especially when . . . some faculty members who
really take an interest in student issues or problems—that they take the trouble
to call us and say, "Can you see this student?" and showing an interest in
making sure that he or she gets the help that they need. And I especially really
see . . . it's not something that . . . you get to work with ALL the faculty. It's
those who really take an interest, it's nice to see that.

And I can say from my standpoint, I have had good relationships with the
faculty. There are some faculty that just don't want to get involved, but that's
not to say that I'm going to get ignored because I'm going to come back to
them with another approach. The choice of course may not work, so I'm going

to sit back and think about how I'm going to involve the faculty. So it may be a different approach.

But it's good. Some of them are tough. Some feel that there's really not a need for student affairs professionals. And then you have some that embrace it, so you just have to get in there and try to work together for the common good of the student.

Their comments are very much like those from professionals at comprehensive institutions and community colleges. Those at HBCUs work well with many faculty members and understand those with whom they do not have contact.

In some ways, HBCU professionals mediate any difficulties they encounter with faculty through the relationships they have with academic administrators on their campuses. The sense of team permeates student affairs relationships with deans and academic administrators:

So, we work closely with academic deans in terms of student social and personal adjustment. And some academic problems that are happening or occurring, which have nothing to do with the student's ability or what they can achieve, what other personal problems get in the way. I'm not finding any difficulties on my campus. Sometimes they don't understand what we're trying to tell them in terms of student development and/or—how do I want to put this—their minds focus [on what] is going on in the classroom and we see 90% of what the student is doing outside the classroom. So that's always a tug of war for us. But basically we have pretty good working relationships with the academic side of the house.

I also think that once the deans have learned about you, they don't stop using you. Once they find out you exist and you can help them somehow, you get called on a lot. And it's a good thing because it continues to help make the inroads in those partnerships.

I have a close relationship with deans and department heads. And it's an open door to all their offices. If I have a problem, I can just pick up the telephone and the secretaries will put me right through to them, and they will talk to me. Or I send them an e-mail and they respond.

This sense of taking a team approach to "raising our students" extends to one final constituency group with which student affairs administrators work: parents of students. The professionals at HBCUs talked more about their interactions with parents than their counterparts at any other type of institution. Perhaps more important, however, is how they described their relations with parents. Administrators at liberal arts and research campuses talk about the difficulties they face when working with parents. Those at HBCUs talk about how they enjoy working with families to promote the best interests of students. Their comments suggest a sense of co-parenting:

And I had a phone in the conference room. And I said, "Well since I can't call your parent and tell them, you're going to call your parent." So I had them pick the phone up. I said, "You find them. . . . You're in a hospital and you need emergency surgery. Find where your mom is. Don't give me this kind of stuff." So I had the student call the mom. And I had them explain to her why I was sitting there, why you were talking to the Dean of Students. And if your mom wants to talk to me, then I can explain to her why. And then together with the parent's help, this is my goal, here's what I'm trying to accomplish. Here's how I need your help, and then we worked together with them. And it worked out really, really well.

I've even had a parent call me when I talked to a young lady, I pulled her aside one day before an interview and sent her back home. She had on these really lovely stockings but the pattern and the skirt. The pattern . . . didn't conform to any of the standards, and she was a freshman and she had never interviewed, and it was for a summer opportunity. And she looked a little bit miffed, and I said, if you don't have something, we can find something for you to wear. She went home, she found something, and in the meantime her Dad called. And the conversation, "Well don't you want them to get the job and THEN dress like they're supposed to?" And in talking with him I realized that for him, he had had an opportunity to do a lot of interviewing professionally. And he talked about that, and by the end of the conversation, he thanked me. . . . And I actually met him during the Christmas party when he came up to the area. So you're really happy when you can help them understand and come full circle, what their child's growth is.

I had one . . . it was last week. A student's mother passed. And not sure what time they're coming back so they touched bases with me a couple of times. And this was the father of the young lady as to when this child would be back to school. So, I do get quite a bit [of that]. And I think a lot of times the parents are real supportive with them, so we do a lot of follow-up to keep with them, so that when they do return to school, we are aware of their [situation].

The notion of guardianship, serving as surrogate parents for their students appears to be a driving force for professionals at HBCUs. In fact, it is a metaphor that might be applied to faculty, academic administrators, and others on campus as well. This is a markedly different approach to working with students than that taken by professionals at other types of campuses. It calls for intense, personal relationships with students and begs the question about what rewards the guardians at HBCUs value in exchange for this investment in students.

The Nature of Rewards

In some instances, the rewards that those at HBCUs cherish most are not all that different than what professionals at other types of institutions appreciate:

engaging in meaningful work and enjoying good relationships with others in a positive work environment:

> My priority is to improve the quality of life for students here on campus. And so it's very important for me that I'm doing meaningful work.

> Knowing that you can come to work every day and those values and those work ethics that you bring with you are going to have some type of impact on your students; to enhance their positive academic and everyday life skills.

> I don't know . . . that it's unique, but I guess it tends to be a small environment and it seems more like a family or an extended family of people that you work with. It's not like you become great friends, but with family members you love 'em at one point and then you're mad at 'em the next point, but you're still able to get along. So it's almost kind of like an extended family.

In the case of HBCU professionals, however, there is an added element of racial uplift. Legions of those who work at HBCUs do so because they have a desire, if not a need, to promote the interests of future generations of Black students:

> Placing African American students at the center of the experience, moving African American students from the object to the subject. It's profound; it's incredibly profound—it's exactly why I came here and it's an extraordinary thing to be able to do—particularly when you've worked at a predominantly White institution. When you make that fundamental shift, it's a powerful thing. It really, really is.

> I would say that I think when I look back at the few years that I've been here, I can look back and actually see the work that I've done. Because there's so much potential and so many things that CAN be done. I can look back and say, "Wow, I've actually made a difference." And I would say even on top of that, it's comfortable. I am an African American and it's comfortable being in an environment. . . . This is the first time I've been in an environment where I'm surrounded by other African American professionals. And that's something that I've never been used to. So, those are two aspects that are really rewarding.

> Making a positive impact on African-American students. Being influential. . . . Being a key figure in their life. I'm saying too much. . . . Being in the position to make a positive impact on numerous African-American students. Being able to be a role model for African-American students . . . a positive role model.

> I think the sense of accomplishment, and for me—and I've worked in this business for a long time—being really, really able to give back. And knowing that I'm in an area that I feel is MY purpose in life. And to be able to really give back and to be a part of molding and shaping another young person's life, especially young African Americans. And that is my greatest joy.

This is not to suggest, however, that student affairs administrators are oblivious to the potential hazards associated with working at a HBCU. They

express concerns about the inability of their campuses to expose students to the
elements they will confront once they leave the sheltered environment of the
campus:

> I guess not seeing or experiencing the total diversity thing that happens every
> day at work. It is mostly centered around less diversity, that I KNOW that's
> going to have an impact—in so many ways, a negative impact on students
> because their everyday life skills that they are going to have to learn in order to
> compete out there in this world are going to have to be balanced. They're going
> to have a certain amount of diversity in it.

They also recognize how guardianship can limit their ability to work with
students in positive ways:

> Well sometimes it can get to the point to where . . . you can't get too close, if
> you will, to the student or to the situation because sometimes you can lose
> focus. Or they lose focus because what they do is to start to look at you as a
> parent, rather than as a practitioner or as a professional. And so sometimes you
> have to have that thin line between love and hate, if you will.

> To me I think it's still very *in loco parentis*, and they don't give [students] an
> opportunity to grow. And I think that we could let go a little more and not be as
> parental.

Finally, they recognize that working at a HBCU can at times be frustrating
in terms of the very relationships that they so value and how those relationships
can influence what takes place on the campus:

> That's a really tough question, and it's tough to answer, it's not tough to know.
> I think there is still a significant amount of self-loathing and self-hatred within
> the African-American community. And as such, when you're in an all African-
> American educational environment, it manifests. It manifests itself in class
> issues. It manifests itself in terms of issues of trust, professionally and
> otherwise. It manifests itself in terms of treatment, interpersonal relationships
> and sometimes very poor quality of those. I think it manifests itself in levels of
> familiarity, whether people feel a level of comfort that I think can be less than
> professional. And sometimes [that] can allow people to feel like they can
> communicate in certain kinds of ways that aren't appropriate for the workplace.

> I think . . . least rewarding about working at an HBCU is, unfortunately, the
> lack of proactive initiatives or the lack of initiative that takes place at HBCUs. I
> attended an HBCU undergrad and I'm working at an HBCU now, and I see a
> similarity in this lack of initiative. I feel like we're a step behind. I feel like
> we're not as organized as we should be. I feel like we don't all the time strive
> for greatness. We strive for, sometimes, mediocrity. And that frustrates me.
> Whereas I look at my colleagues on majority campuses and I see the . . . and
> even small majority campuses, I see the initiatives that take place on those
> campuses [and] that has me wondering, whereas before maybe I might not

have, but it has me wondering, "Well, gosh, is this germane to HBCUs, that we're always behind, that we can't get things together, that we're disorganized."

Rewards for professionals at HBCUs differ from those for their colleagues at other types of institutions in some important ways as well. For one, they were the only group to rate salary among the five rewards they value most (it ranked fourth). Other extrinsic rewards, like benefits and the availability of support staff, are much more important to those at HBCUs than to professionals at other types of campuses. It is reasonable to speculate that this might be due to the limited resources available on most HBCU campuses. That is, extrinsic rewards may become more valued in environments where resources are scarcer.

Equally as interesting were differences between those at HBCUs and those at other types of institutions in terms of intrinsic rewards. Professionals at HBCUs rate some intrinsic rewards, like the ability to act autonomously and recognition, in the bottom third of rewards. Among those at HWCUs, autonomy was consistently ranked among the top five rewards they valued and recognition was not far behind. Perhaps the close working relationships found on HBCU campuses diminishes the ability to act autonomously and the need for recognition, but any such speculation should be further investigated.

Overall, it would seem that the rewards of working at a HBCU relate to the ability to promote development among students, most particularly among Black students. The limited resources at these institutions have rendered some extrinsic rewards (e.g., salary, benefits) more important to professionals. These findings suggest that life at HBCUs is different in some fundamental ways from professional life at the other types of colleges and universities examined in this volume thus far.

Conclusions

Throughout this chapter I have referred to student affairs professionals at HBCUs as guardians. The metaphor is appropriate on two levels. First, there are powerful professional reasons associated with the notion of guardianship. Administrators on these campuses recognize that their students often come to college from challenging backgrounds, backgrounds to which they can often relate:

You know my mom was single, a single-family household, single-parent household. It's important to me that I'm dealing with children or students that are from backgrounds such as mine—you know, similar to mine. So I feel like I'm giving directly back.

For our students, that's why I enjoy being at an HBCU. Their needs are very simple. They don't come with a lot of attitude. I mean they've got an attitude about some other things. But they're not snooty. They're not arrogant. Because a lot of them come from single-parent homes. And they're the first generation

coming to college, and so they feel blessed being here. And I'm so blessed, I'm
happy to be here. Because I went to a majority school only. So I know the other
side.

This prompts professionals to adopt roles of surrogate family members
when dealing with students, be that parent, grandparent, or sibling. They take
their roles as guardians quite seriously and attend not only to the academic and
social development of their students but to their emotional and spiritual growth
as well. This sense of family also seems to permeate their relationships with
others on campus, bringing with that all the rewards and challenges that families
deal with over time.

The metaphor of guardian, however, has a much deeper meaning for
professionals on these campuses, one that is embedded in the history of HBCUs
in America. In this sense, student affairs administrators see themselves as
guardians of the HBCU system, of the need for race-based institutions of higher
education, especially for Blacks in this country. Their defense of the system is
grounded in the relationship HBCUs have had with this country for the past 145
years.

HBCUs were initially the product of a racist society. After only 15 years,
their primary sources of support nearly abandoned them, yet they survived. In
the post-*Plessy* era they were almost exclusive providers of higher education for
Blacks in this country. They struggled in terms of garnering resources, and still
they persisted. By the middle of the 20th century, their status within the system
of higher education in the country was minimal (M. C. Brown et al., 2001).
Indeed, Jencks and Reisman (1968) reported that "by almost any standard these
110 colleges are academic disaster areas" (p. 433). Yet they endured. When the
Brown decision sought to dismantle the two-tiered system of higher education in
the country, HBCUs were confronted with a new set of challenges; now they
had to compete for resources with HWCUs as well as further diversify their own
campuses. Throughout their history, HBCUs have suffered under just about
every shift in policy. Even today they lack the resources of any other sector of
the postsecondary system. Yet they endure.

Professionals on these campuses are cognizant of that history. They are
fully aware that their campuses do not have the physical, fiscal, or human
resources that other types of institutions wield. They choose to work at HBCUs
because they are fiercely committed to the opportunities that their institutions
offer to Blacks who might otherwise not have access to higher education. In this
sense, they serve as guardians of the system of higher education for Blacks in
this country.

Those who elect to work at HBCUs (often the products of these campuses
themselves) work with students whose credentials may be marginal. They work
on campuses with limited resources and for lower salaries and fewer benefits.
Colleagues are like family and may work together for long periods of time, as
staff members seem to commit to lifelong careers at their campuses. At the heart

of their work, however, is their need to fervently protect the interests of the students with whom they work and the institutions they serve. They are guardians at two levels and they seem to embrace both roles.

Chapter Seven

The Producers:
Professional Life at Community Colleges

The final institutional type that emerged in the post-Civil War era is the most recent species in the higher education realm, the community college. Unlike the institutional types addressed in other chapters of this book, community colleges do not have entrenched roots in the postsecondary education system. Rather, they reflect America's response to changes in the K-12 educational system at the end of the 19th century and to the industrialization that swept the country after the war.

Community colleges are characterized by their relatively broad missions and their clearly defined service areas. Over time they have evolved to serve multiple purposes. They offer the coursework associated with the first two years of the baccalaureate degree and prepare students to transfer to four-year institutions to complete their undergraduate work. Vocational training and workforce preparation also are central to the community college. Additionally, they proffer developmental education to students whose previous schooling has not provided them with sufficient skills in reading, writing, and mathematics to succeed in college. Providing lifelong learning opportunities for members of the local community constitutes a fourth purpose for community colleges. This is coupled with a final objective of serving their community, primarily by providing venues for community events.

The most distinctive element of community colleges, however, is their local focus. All their programs are designed to serve the people and organizations of their local service area. The local service area is a designated geographic region that an institution is mandated to serve. Given the breadth of the programs they provide, every person and organization in the service area is a potential client of the community college. This responsibility results in an incredible workload for those employed at such institutions and leads me to refer to student services professionals on these campuses as "producers." As the evidence reveals, community college practitioners are expected to sustain high-quality services that meet the demands of a broad array of learners. Moreover, they accomplish these ends through fewer offices and with fewer professionals than other institutional types. Understanding the gaps in the higher education hierarchy that community colleges were designated to fill helps to explain this focus on production.

Historical Evolution

The seeds of the community college were planted in the decades immediately following the Civil War. Some of the forces that led to their creation were internal; that is, they stemmed from the existing educational system of the era. During the 18th century, the nation established educational institutions at the lowest and highest levels: primary schools and colleges. The 19th century saw the emergence of middle and secondary schools as well as the introduction of graduate education. At the end of that century, then, there was an educational ladder from the lower to the higher forms of learning and no need for additional levels of education. Rather, educators faced two challenges. The first centered on the articulation between secondary schools and colleges (Brubacher & Rudy, 1997; Urban & Wagoner, 2000).

As the college curriculum expanded in the 18th century to include subjects in math, sciences, and humanities, entrance requirements were stepped up (A. M. Cohen, 1998; Rudolph, 1977). Students needed to be proficient not only in Greek and Latin but in math, geography, history, and English, as well. Requirements in foreign languages and science were added in the years succeeding the Civil War (Rudolph, 1962). Most secondary schools, however, were designed to offer terminal education, not to prepare students for college (Lucas, 1994). Only a few of the academies founded in the colonial era to educate the elite offered a college preparatory curriculum.

This deficit prompted a debate about where academic preparation for college should take place. Some leaders thought that postsecondary schools ought to redesign their curricula to offer preparatory courses. Others argued that the first two years of the college curriculum paralleled the German secondary school and should be relegated to the secondary level in America (Brubacher & Rudy, 1997; Urban & Wagoner, 2000).

The gap between what secondary schools were providing students and what colleges and universities required of students led to the second challenge for education leaders. There was a clear educational ladder in the country: primary institutions, middle schools, secondary schools, colleges and universities, and graduate programs. At issue, however, was where breaks in the institutional hierarchy should be placed (Brubacher & Rudy, 1997). For a period of time after the Civil War various models were tried. In some cases, eight years of primary school were followed by four years of secondary school. In other states, students spent six years in primary school, three in middle school, and three in secondary school. Other models included: eight years of primary school and six of secondary school; six of primary, three of middle school and five of secondary school; even six years of elementary school, four years of middle school, and four years of secondary school (Brubacher & Rudy, 1997; A. M. Cohen, 1998).

There was no clear educational ladder when community colleges emerged and as a result, they adopted two early forms. In some cases, they became extensions of the secondary school. As such, they were managed much like lower level educational institutions. They had superintendents, teachers often came from secondary schools, and the curriculum was designed to provide vocational training for students so that they might succeed in the industrial economy that was rapidly developing in the country (Lucas, 1994).

In other instances, they were founded to offer the first two years of the undergraduate degree. Referred to as junior colleges, they operated more like colleges and universities (Brubacher & Rudy, 1997). The curriculum involved courses in math, science, and humanities. Campuses were managed by deans and students expected to move on to upper division coursework at a 4-year institution to earn the bachelor's degree.

So, initially community colleges were designed to provide vocational training and transfer education. In both cases, though, these institutions evolved outside the step-wise progression from elementary to middle to secondary school to college. As such, they were always on the margins of the educational enterprise (Brubacher & Rudy, 1997; A. M. Cohen, 1998).

In the eyes of educational leaders, community or junior colleges offered several potential outcomes. For students who had never considered postsecondary education, they represented a chance to pursue more advanced academic opportunities. For others who might not be sufficiently talented to achieve the bachelor's degree, they offered a dignified manner of ending their collegiate career after two years or after receiving vocational training to prepare them for life in an industrialized society. For gifted students, they served as feeder institutions and allowed colleges and universities to focus on upper division undergraduate training and graduate and professional education. In terms of forces internal to the education enterprise, then, community colleges filled certain niches that complemented the hierarchy (A. M. Cohen, 1998; Urban & Wagoner, 2000).

There were external economic and social forces that influenced the evolution of the community colleges as well. Unlike any of the previous institutional types described in this volume, the community colleges are products of the industrial age. The economic issues prevalent at the time shaped them in profound ways. The most pressing of these involved the need for trained workers in the expanding industrial sector (A. M. Cohen & Brawer, 2003; Pedersen, 1988). The rapid growth in both the number and type of industries being founded in the country depended on workers who could operate the machinery these plants employed.

Two other social catalysts influenced the emergence of the community college. Technology modernized productivity and resulted in an extended period of adolescence for America's youth. Children in the nation were no longer required to work to support families, so they spent more time being schooled. This shift was coupled with the drive for social equity that characterized America in the early decades of the 20th century. There was a pervasive belief that a combination of hard work, diligence, and education would lead to upward mobility (Brubacher & Rudy, 1997; Jencks & Riesman, 1968). To that end, more students were attending schools and staying in school for longer periods of time.

The confluence of these external social and economic dynamics, coupled with the internal shifts in the educational ladder in the country, laid the foundation for the emergence of community colleges. As the number of high school graduates increased in the early decades of the 20th century, the community college sector expanded. In 1922, there were 207 such institutions operating in 37 states. Eight years later, in 1930, there were 450 junior colleges enrolling 70,000 students and operating in most states in the nation (A. M. Cohen, 1998). There were fairly dramatic shifts in locus of control, however. In the early part of the century, 66% of junior colleges were private institutions. Over successive decades, states stepped in and established systems of community colleges, most notably in California, Illinois, and Missouri. As a result, by the mid-1970s, 84% of such institutions were public and only 16% were privately controlled (A. M. Cohen, 1998; A. M. Cohen & Brawer, 2003).

By the end of the 20th century, community colleges were so prolific that nearly every U.S. resident lived within commuting distance of such an institution. Over the same time period, their services expanded to include developmental (sometimes called remedial) education and continuing education. Their accessibility made them the logical providers of such programs and broadened their visibility in the community. This created somewhat of a conundrum: As community colleges became more visible they attracted more students. As they attracted more students, their visibility was enhanced. Resources to support these additional students, however, were not forthcoming. This escalation resulted in uncommonly heavy workloads for staff at community colleges. The producers in the student affairs profession at these institutions lead markedly different lives than their counterparts at other types of colleges and universities. To a large extent, this difference is driven by the nature of the community college campus.

The Nature of the Community College Campus

The Carnegie Foundation (2001) reported that there were 1,669 two-year institutions in the United States in 2000. Of these, 485 were private, for-profit colleges. Also known as proprietary schools, the for-profit sector of two-year institutions represents a unique group of colleges. Since none of the data in any of the studies that form the basis for this book were elicited from professionals at proprietary institutions, they are not addressed in this chapter, though their growing presence in the higher education hierarchy renders them a wonderful subject for future research.

Eliminating the for-profit institutions still leaves 1,184 community colleges. The vast majority (87%) of these are publicly controlled and only 159 (13%) are private not-for-profit institutions (Carnegie Foundation, 2000). Overall, community colleges represent 36% of the public not-for-profit colleges and universities in the country. In terms of enrollment, however, a disproportionately high number of students attend community colleges. Over 6 million of the 15.3 million college students in American institutions, roughly 40%, are enrolled in community colleges (NCES, 2001a). The ubiquity of these campuses is evidenced in the number of students they serve. On average, community colleges enroll 3,785 students. The median enrollment, however, is 1,681. That is, there are a few very large community colleges but the vast majority are relatively small. Their size, however, may not reflect the breadth of their mission.

Mission

There are experts who argue that community colleges are too diverse in terms of size, setting, governance structure, physical plant, and related factors to be considered a single institutional type and should, in fact, be assigned to multiple types (Clowes & Levin, 1989; Katsinas, 1996). Despite their differences, however, the community colleges share common elements.

One aspect of community colleges that has remained stable over the century of their existence is that they are designed to serve adult learners (Ayers, 2002). Beyond that, their mission has expanded over time to reflect the needs of their local service areas (Gleazar, 1980; Vaughan, 1997). As noted above, community colleges originally served two basic missions. For those who viewed them as feeder institutions for colleges and universities, community colleges were transfer institutions (Goldman & Beach, 2001). For those who perceived them to be extensions of secondary schools, they offered vocational training (A. M. Cohen & Brawer, 2003).

Over time, however, their mission has expanded. During the 1970s and 1980s, as the baby boom generation completed high school and demand for higher education grew, increasing numbers of students were ill equipped to handle the rigors of college-level academics. They needed remedial assistance. The community colleges, with their focus on service to the local community, stepped in to address this need and offered developmental education. At first, such endeavors targeted domestic students who needed to improve basic academic skills. In recent decades, developmental programs have started teaching basic English reading and writing skills to the immigrant population that has grown exponentially in this country (A. M. Cohen & Brawer, 2003).

Additionally, as the notion of lifelong learning gained prominence during this same period, community colleges developed community education programs. The term "community education" encompasses all types of programs including adult and continuing education, contract training, and a plethora of other offerings, some for credit, others not, some taught on campus, others at remote locations or through distance learning. It is through community education that community colleges are highly distinctive, as the needs of a rural service area (sometimes several counties) may be dramatically different than those of an urban or suburban service region (a city or single county) A. M. Cohen, 1998, A. M. Cohen & Brawer, 2003).

An offshoot of community education programs is the community service mission of community colleges. This mission involves using campus facilities for community events. For example, community colleges often have the venues for community concerts and lectures. Community service also involves identifying the needs of the local service area and developing programs and services to address those needs (A. M. Cohen & Brawer, 2003).

Perhaps the clearest way to illustrate the common elements of various types of community colleges is to examine examples of their mission statements. Consider the following statement of a rural community college:

[Name of college] is dedicated to serving the varied educational needs of our diverse populations in affordable, accessible and supportive settings.

Mission Goals

1. To provide pre-professional and liberal arts courses which lead to Associate of Arts or Associate of Science degrees. The courses are designed to transfer to a four-year college or university and will apply toward a baccalaureate degree.
2. To provide certificate, diploma, and Associate of Applied Science degree courses for students working to develop and enhance occupational or technical competence leading toward employment or further education.
3. To provide learning opportunities for people of varying ages, backgrounds, and abilities with a particular focus and commitment to retraining and lifelong learning.
4. To provide continuing education, management education, and customized training for professions, businesses, and industries.
5. To provide facilities for programs, activities, conferences, teleconferences, and courses to meet community needs.
6. To provide extended educational opportunities by means of flexible scheduling and delivery.
7. To provide effective and efficient use of resources through partnerships with agencies, other educational institutions, businesses and industries.
8. To provide continuous improvement processes via assessment, evaluation and upgrading of programs and services, and to support the professional development of college personnel.

9. To provide the resources to meet the contemporary standards of facilities, informational resources, technology, and teaching strategies to ensure quality educational outcomes.
10. To provide comprehensive student services enabling academic and personal growth toward lifelong learning.

Two things stand out about this example. First, notice how straightforward this statement is when compared to those of other institutional types, like research universities. Second, the objectives that this particular institution shares with other community colleges are enumerated in the statement: transfer education, vocational training, developmental education, community education, and community service.

These same objectives are evident in the following mission statement from a suburban community college:

> The mission of [name of college] is to provide quality post-secondary education at low cost for the citizens of [name of county] and others. Its offerings include liberal arts and occupational/technical degree programs, certificate programs, lifelong learning, and service to the community. Open access and low tuition support the College's effort to see that all qualified persons are given an opportunity for higher education.
>
> The College offers the first two years of baccalaureate education, transferable to four-year colleges and universities, and career education in occupational, vocational, technical, and semi-technical fields to meet changing employment needs. In addition, credit-free courses, seminars, conferences, workshops, and contractual training programs are created to meet the needs identified by the community.

Again, transfer, vocational, developmental, and community education, as well as community service are central to the institution.

These objectives parallel those of an urban community college, as the following example illustrates:

> As a comprehensive community college, [name of college] is committed to offering courses and programs designed to provide students with the information, knowledge, attitudes, and skills necessary to function effectively and creatively in public, vocational, and personal life situations.
>   To that end, we offer:
> 1. Programs designed to provide career opportunities for:
>   a. entry prior to or on receipt of a [name of college] degree.
>   b. entry on receipt of a four-year degree.
> 2. Programs designed to ensure that a student obtains the analytic, imaginative and humanistic skills necessary to participate fully in the community as an informed citizen with knowledge of the world, past and present, and that enhance the creative aspects of one's life.
> 3. Programs designed to provide basic academic and learning skills to enable students to participate in programs as defined in "1" and "2" above.

4. Programs designed to assist students to function effectively in personal life situations.
   COLLEGE PHILOSOPHY
   We believe that we have an obligation to respond to the academic and cultural needs of our community; to maintain a leadership role in defining and clarifying the needs and aspirations of the community; to provide for their realization through services within the functions of this college as an educational institution; and to warrant community support through dedication to excellence in learning.

Again, the common mission objectives are clear. It would seem, therefore, that despite the variation in structure, governance, and setting, community colleges do share certain goals. Given these shared goals, is the work of faculty similar across community colleges?

Faculty

Community colleges represent 36% of institutions and enroll 40% of students, but they employ only 29% of faculty members at all types of institutions. Perhaps more important, community colleges employ a disproportionately high number of part-time faculty. Overall, they employ 29% of all faculty but 44% of all part-time faculty and only 18% of all full-time faculty. On average, at any given community college only 35% of faculty work on a full-time basis and the remaining 65% are part-timers (NCES, 1999). The imbalance between full-time and part-time faculty has raised concerns that community college faculty are becoming de-professionalized (Clark, 1988).

Community college faculty members differ from faculty at other types of institutions in other characteristics, as well. Nearly half (48%) are women and over 15% are minorities (A. M. Cohen & Brawer, 2003). Women represent only 20–30% of faculty at other types of institutions. There are also far fewer minority faculty members at other campuses, an average of 4%–8%. Academic preparation among community college faculty also differs from their counterparts elsewhere. In 2000, 15% of community college faculty held the bachelor's degree, 63% held the master's, and 16% held the doctorate (Outcalt, 2002). At the liberal arts, comprehensive, and research institutions the majority of faculty members hold a doctorate or other terminal degree.

Some of the differences may be attributed to the work that community college faculty do. These faculty members teach, and teaching is their primary activity. Nearly 72% of their time is devoted to instruction, as compared to the national average among faculty of 56%. They spend far more time teaching than their counterparts at research universities who spend only 40% to 45% of their time in instruction. Over half (57%) of community college faculty members teach 15 units, or five classes, per week. This translates to over 350 student contact hours per week for most community college faculty (NCES, 1999).

Given their attention to teaching, it is not surprising that community college faculty members spend relatively no time (less than 4%) on research activities. The time their counterparts at other institutions devote to research exceeds 15% on average, and at some campuses, like research universities, research activities consume more than 25% of faculty time (NCES, 1999).

Other data suggest that the differences in the ways that community college faculty spend their time are not surprising. Although they report working slightly fewer hours per week than the national average for faculty (49 vs. 53), the 72% of time they devote to teaching is just a tad more than the amount of time they report they would like to spend teaching (69%) (NCES, 1999). Their dedication to their work may stem from their own experiences; 40% of community college faculty attended community colleges as students (Keim, 1989). Moreover, they view themselves as teachers rather than scholars (A. M. Cohen & Brawer, 1989).

If teaching is what they prefer to do, and teaching is how they spend the bulk of their time, it might be assumed that satisfaction levels among community college faculty would be high. The data suggest otherwise, however. Community college faculty are generally motivated by intrinsic factors, such as student achievement and their own professional development (Diener, 1985). Colleagues and the quality of the institution all influence job satisfaction (Milosheff, 1990). Paradoxically, faculty members are drawn to the instructional mission of the community college (McGrath & Spear, 1991), yet this same mission, that undervalues research, makes them feel as if they work at second-class institutions (Seidman, 1985). On a parallel note, they have become increasingly concerned over the quality of students enrolling at community colleges in recent years, further adding to their frustration (A. M. Cohen & Brawer, 2003). Some additional details about community college students might help explain this conundrum.

Students

Any attempt to describe community college students must address two issues: their numbers and their diversity (A. M. Cohen & Brawer, 2003). Enrollments in community colleges have increased dramatically over the past 40 years. In 1960, there were 500,000 students attending community colleges. By 1980, that number had expanded eight-fold to 4 million (NCES, 2002). At the end of the 20th century, there were over 6 million community college students (NCES, 2000).

In 1997, 44% of all students matriculating to institutions of higher education enrolled in a community college (NCES, 2000). The diversity among these students is compelling by almost any measure. Consider, for example, demographic characteristics. Women are represented in higher numbers in community colleges, where they comprise 58% of all students, than they are in higher education in general (56%). That same year, 1997, community colleges enrolled 38% of all college students but 46% of all minorities enrolled in institutions of higher education. In fact, enrollment among some groups of minorities exceeded their representation in the general population. Even the age distribution among community college students is difficult to capture. Student ages range from 17 to 70, and the average age is close to 30 (A. M. Cohen & Brawer, 2003). The variety among students is perhaps best understood in light of the programs that they pursue at community colleges.

In 2000, 66% of community college students were seeking transfer credits or certificate credits. An additional 21% were enrolled in classes to improve their job skills and 12% were enrolled out of personal interest (Voorhees & Zhou, 2000). These numbers suggest that a fair number of community college students aspire to earn the bachelor's degree. In fact, about 42% of students who start their higher education career at a community college plan to earn a bachelor's degree, and 30% to 60% of those who earn bachelor's degrees have some community college experience. But success rates are very erratic; transfer rates range from 11% at some institutions to 40% at others (A. M. Cohen & Brawer, 2003).

To some degree, the disparity can be explained by differences in student abilities and circumstances. Most community college students come from the lower half of their high school graduating class in terms of both academic ability and socioeconomic status (Cross, 1971). In 2000, the composite SAT score for community college students was 839. For those who aspired to a bachelor's degree, the composite score was 961. Socioeconomic differences are evidenced through financial aid statistics; 56% of all full-time and 31% of all part-time community college students receive financial aid, as compared to 39% of undergraduates in general (Presley & Clery, 2001). For most, the choice is not between attending a two-year and a four-year college, it is between attending a two-year college or not attending college at all (A. M. Cohen & Brawer, 2003).

Attempting to classify community college students presents another set of challenges. Some start in degree or certificate programs but are forced to drop out due to demands of work or family (Sydow & Sandel, 1998). Many students take one class at a time or enroll full-time for a semester, leave for a semester, and return on a part-time basis. They move from degree programs to certificate programs to continuing education classes, seemingly at will (A. M. Cohen & Brawer, 2003).

Collectively, data like these have led experts to suggest that it is "hard to disaggregate the effects of community colleges from characteristics of students who enter them" (A. M. Cohen & Brawer, 2003, p. 50). This may help explain why faculty members at community colleges feel conflicted: They love to teach but are concerned about the quality of students in the classroom and the persistence of those students. These same characteristics influence the work of the student affairs professionals at these institutions.

The Nature of Student Affairs Work

Professionals at community colleges participated in three of the six studies. In the National Survey Study, their responses about the nature of their work, relationships, and rewards were statistically compared to responses from professionals at other types of campuses. There were also community college practitioners in the Association Study. They provided quantitative data on their work, relationships, and rewards, and engaged in a dialogue about each of those topics that yielded rich qualitative data. Finally, both the Community College Case Study and the Community College Follow-up Study included only professionals from community colleges. The first of these investigations included observations of and interviews with professionals at work. The second employed the same protocol used in the Association Study and rendered both quantitative and qualitative data.

The findings from these studies reveal that life for professionals at community colleges is very different than it is for their counterparts at other types of institutions. For example, like their faculty colleagues, student affairs professionals at community colleges feel that their institutions are marginalized in the higher education hierarchy:

> There's sort of a second-class citizenship there that always haunts two-year schools. There's a definite second-class [status].

> Oh, I think it's the general perception that you're a second-class citizen. You know, universities are in the limelight. It's more prestigious to be at a university as opposed to a community college.

> Well, I think that we're the poor stepchild of education. Kind of the—almost a continuation of high school in many peoples' minds. We're not the real deal. I think that the role that the community college plays is TERRIBLY underestimated and the kind of the impact that it has is terribly underestimated.

This last comment reveals a second pervasive theme in the data: Those who work at community colleges understand the mission of those institutions, and they embrace that mission. In fact, they are significantly more likely to know and endorse their institutional mission than student affairs professionals at research, comprehensive, and liberal arts campuses. Their own words best illustrate this point:

> So, that whole notion of access to higher education and that being the sort of thing that citizens ought to be able to expect from the government is a pretty neat thing. It's really politically empowering also because . . . especially folks from disadvantaged economic situations, this [the community college] is what's been referred to as their "ladder for success." This is the way that you improve yourself. Not everybody can go to the big universities and folks have to often start out at a place like our community college to sort of prove themselves. And

then when they transfer to the four-year school and complete their undergraduate degree, that's really an exciting thing to help to create opportunities where prior to arriving here, a lot of folks had a pretty short end of the deal. So that's exciting to be involved in community colleges, you really feel like it's a way of giving opportunity to folks that haven't had a whole lot before.

Well, the thing that I'm passionate about at a community college is the fact that we are an open-door institution. Of course, that poses some opportunities and challenges for us also. We get to deal with every type of student that you can conceive of, from the highest functioning to the lowest functioning. And it's our challenge to find different interventions, mechanisms, learning environments, or what-not, to make sure that they can reach some goal—and it doesn't have to be their initial ultimate goal . . . but redefining that through the educational process is the best thing about being at a community college.

Recall that those at comprehensive institutions talked about serving students from under-represented groups but in a more generic sense. Likewise, those at HBCUs commented on students but focused almost exclusively on Black students. When community college practitioners address their service to students from under-represented groups, they do so in a very individualized, personal way.

As these comments also suggest, student affairs professionals at community colleges recognize the transfer function and vocational training role of their institutions. They acknowledge that some students need developmental assistance and believe in the access that their institutions provide. Their comments hint at the amount of work that professionals at community colleges produce and the environment in which that work unfolds.

The Work Environment

Working as a student affairs professional at a community college, according to some experts, involves a balance between regulating student behavior and promoting student development (Doucette & Dayton, 1989; O'Banion, 1971). Moreover, this balancing act should link all college functions in order to maximize the effectiveness of student services (Dassance, 1994). To this end, community colleges typically have a common set of student services. These include recruitment and retention activities, counseling and guidance services, orientation programs, cocurricular activities, and financial aid (A. M. Cohen & Brawer, 2003). Although these are discrete functional areas, staffing is often not as clear. On many campuses, for example, counselors are responsible for orientation, or staff that handle cocurricular activities manage orientation.

Keeping in mind that the majority of community colleges (62%) enroll fewer than 2,500 students (NCES, 2000), these figures translate into a limited number of student affairs staff at most campuses. It is not at all unusual for the entire student affairs division to employ fewer than a dozen professionals. These administrators, however, provide programs and services to all types of students (e.g., older, traditional-aged, immigrant) in all types of programs (e.g., transfer, vocational, developmental, and continuing) and in all types of statuses (e.g., degree, certificate, job training). This is the crux of their work environment. One can only imagine the amount of information practitioners need to grasp and the dexterity they employ to disseminate that information. Their productivity levels are, of necessity, exceptionally high.

That environment can be further characterized in three ways. First and foremost, student services professionals at community colleges serve students. For most, this is the reason they work in the community college environment:

> I have two types of clients. One is the 18–22 year old, out of high school, needing a little help in making a choice as far as majors and colleges and professional areas. The other type is the 25–85 year old adult. They really need to know how to work or at least begin to develop some knowledge of working. . . . People who have been displaced at their job, become unemployed. [I] really have to help them deal with loss first and then with career issues second.

> The values here have always centered foremost on the student, giving the very best services that we can offer with whatever staff we've got—even though it's put together with bailing wire and chewing gum or whatever. The students themselves, some of the students coming through here would never know some of the things. And I've just told you what has happened in the past 20–30 years. But the services have been the same.

> You really can see the contributions you're making. I think it's just a hands-on working with students, and just knowing you're making a difference in that person's life. I mean you can see it, and they're in and out of here a lot, transferring and getting jobs and coming back 20 years later. It's frustrating too, though, because sometimes I feel like we just don't have enough. We just can't meet all their needs, but you know, we're doing the best we can.

The notion of serving students is the highest priority for professionals at all types of campuses, but it manifests differently at each sort of institution. At liberal arts colleges, administrators look to understand students holistically. At sectarian campuses, issues of spiritual and ethical development are added to that mix, whereas at HBCUs, racial uplift is a guiding tenet. For those at community colleges, the focus on students is associated with success in career and life. At other types of institutions, professionals talk about helping students find purpose in life. At community colleges, they help students achieve those purposes.

Perhaps it is this orientation to outcomes that resonates with faculty at community colleges. Student affairs administrators on these campuses are significantly more aware of the importance of teaching than their counterparts at other types of institutions. They also report a significantly higher level of collegiality with faculty than professionals at any other type of campus. Student services staff work with faculty in a variety of contexts:

There are some faculty that are absolutely fantastic. They really know what we are trying to do, what we are trying to achieve. They see us as educators in concert with them. And yet we have that other half out there. Our discipline is not valued.

Well, most of the faculty are very willing to help, and they will do whatever they can. Now occasionally you will get people who just are, you know, but the vast majority of the teachers here are really concerned about their students' well being and they want them to succeed. We have a lot of test things that we do. Like if a student misses a class or whatever they come here to do their make-up test and occasionally we proctor if a teacher is going to be out and they ask us if we can proctor for them and we do it when we can. I guess the majority of them do whatever we ask, if it's reasonable.

If we have a student, if they are just really struggling . . . I may call the instructor and say "what do you see, what goes on in the classroom". You know, so I can kind of see what's going on here.

At liberal arts colleges and research universities, most faculty members do not understand the work of student affairs professionals. At comprehensives, staff do not expect faculty to understand their work. At community colleges, however, many more faculty do seem to work with practitioners and to appreciate the services they provide. Working with faculty is the second hallmark of the environment for student affairs professionals at community colleges.

The third characteristic of the community college work environment is the bureaucracy that is endemic to these campuses. In fact, professionals at community colleges report much higher levels of bureaucracy than administrators at every other type of institution. This is not to say that they like bureaucracy. In fact, some of their comments suggest they attempt to subvert the bureaucracy when they can:

Well, policy says that if a student doesn't . . . if you don't withdraw voluntarily from a course by a certain date, then you don't have the option to withdraw from that course as it gets closer to exam time. I think that's bad policy, but it's policy. Or a student leaves and doesn't know that they formally have to notify someone that they're withdrawing from the course. So did they fail the course? I mean, did they get that "F"? No, they flunked administrative procedures, is what they flunked. And I've just fought against that all my career. Now I know a dozen ways around it, but I can't get it changed. It's stuff like that . . . that somewhere somebody sitting behind a desk thinks they need to be efficient and comes up with stuff like that that.

[For] every activity that I have on campus, I have to go look at the entire mission that I have for student activities and I have to show how this activity that I am bringing on campus, what goal and what objective it's reaching from my mission statement. And if that, if it's not reaching any of the goals or the objectives, then I don't bring it. And then I have to have it approved and I have to justify, and then there's an assessment and surveys done to show that it met the requirements that we're looking for and that the people that attended say what it meant [in terms of] goals and objectives.

When I say paperwork, . . . there's more accountability today than there has EVER been. It's a lot of work, but it really plans your life and your job. It defines it.

None of the practitioners at other types of institutions talked about bureaucracy as much or in the same tone as those who worked at community colleges. In some ways, the levels of bureaucracy that govern their work are understandable. Remember that many community colleges were founded as extensions of K-12 education systems and reflect the same degree of administrative coordination evidenced in systems that manage children. Nevertheless, they work in a highly proceduralized environment that means they must produce a high volume of precision work.

It is also important to note that the bureaucracy seems to engender a sense of limited authority for some professionals:

The basic groundwork, yeah, I'm involved quite a bit. The final say so, I have none whatsoever.

I have a lot of responsibility and not a lot of authority. There are things I can change in [my office] but when it affects other offices . . . it's a problem to actually get things changed.

Community college administrators do not seem to resent their lack of authority, however. Rather, they take pride in their ability to adapt quickly to changing circumstances; it is a mark of their professionalism.

In summary, these three elements—student-centeredness, recognition from faculty of the work they do, and a high degree of bureaucracy—are the most prevalent characteristics of work environments for student affairs professionals at community colleges. It is this environment that influences the frenetic pace of work for the student affairs producers on such campuses.

The Pace of Work

The pace of work at community colleges is frenzied; a fact that contributed to the moniker "producer." Three themes permeate the data in terms of the work pace. First, community colleges make major decisions significantly more quickly than all other types of campuses. They also introduce change more quickly than all other institutional types except comprehensive universities, particularly when it comes to academic programs. Whereas change at liberal arts and research institutions is slow, at community colleges change is rapid. To some degree this pace is driven by their mission to serve their local area:

> Two weeks ago I had faculty propose a new curriculum for a new certificate
> they want to start awarding in eight weeks because the program will be done in
> six. They just got it approved by the state. They didn't tell me and now I gotta
> have a whole administrative system ready to admit and award degrees—in six
> weeks—on TOP of all the other processes that are in place for ongoing
> students.

> It's more than getting a new class because people are interested in it and they
> need to know. It's changing entire administrative systems on a dime to
> accommodate a new group of students.

> We had to operate in the same mode to start a nursing program. They spent the
> break turning a room into a lab. It's already full but we don't have the faculty
> yet. Jobs are out there, but it got approved by the state.

Most of the comments in previous chapters have bemoaned how long it took to
enact change on campus. Even at comprehensives, where change was enacted
more quickly, none of the respondents talked about making major changes in a
matter of weeks. Most practitioners at other types of campuses think in terms of
semesters or academic years. At community colleges, change is enacted in a
matter of days and weeks.

In addition to happening quickly, the majority of change for student affairs
professionals at community colleges is externally induced. Numerous
respondents related stories about reacting to changes mandated by other campus
agencies, or by state or federal entities. This external pressure leads to higher
levels of stress among community college professionals than among
administrators at all other types of institutions:

> It's the multi-tasking that creates the stress because there are so many things
> that we're asked to do—part of it is a function of how big you are as an
> institution, part of it is how you're organized. But we seem to be involved in
> everything because everybody admits that it's all about students, so therefore if
> faculty come up with a new idea, well they have to have our input, we gotta
> feel part of the process. If the administration comes up with something, we've
> got to be a part of it. . . . So you're just dragged into everything whether you
> want to be or not.

The pace of work for the producers at community colleges is frenzied and
multi-dimensional. This pace is tempered somewhat, however, by the ability of
community college professionals to control their work week more effectively.
They are significantly less likely to work evenings and weekends than their
colleagues at other institutional types. In fact, they are significantly more likely
to work a reasonable number of hours than those at other types of colleges and
universities. Overall, however, there is a connection between the pace of work
and the ways that work gets done by staff members at community colleges.

How Work Gets Done

Creativity at liberal arts colleges is encouraged. At research universities it is expected. In stark contrast, the producers at community colleges value conformity and security over creativity and risk taking. Perhaps because they are called upon to fulfill so many functions, work at such a turbulent pace, and comply with so many procedural requirements, they seek security when they can:

> We're kind of lucky because most of our services are mandated by federal law so federal law trumps state problems. But with that has become a real cocooning, insulating. . . . All I can say is entrenchment, I think, this real [sense of] almost [building a] barricade and let's not shake anything up or do anything too differently.

> People talk about wanting to get new ideas and do things differently and get fresh new energy. But then you want to implement something, and it's, "Well, we've always done it that way and we don't really want to change." And so I'm confused as to whether people want creativity or they want conformity.

To some degree, this preference for conformity and security may stem from the way in which work gets done at many community colleges. First, the producers at community colleges are multi-taskers. Nearly universally their daily lives involve juggling any number of responsibilities:

> We're a small community college so I'll have to qualify it a bit. You end up with a very diverse and very vague job description. They want you to do . . . you kind of fill in the blanks. You kind of fill in for. . . . Well you have all these services that need to be provided, and there's only two counselors here. . . . And between the two of us, we have to take care of ALL these services. So our job description reads like . . . you wouldn't believe it. It's insane. The potential for it to blow up in our faces is just incredible. But thankfully, I'll be completely honest with you, the students don't take advantage of what's here because if they did we would never have a moment's rest.

> [The] worst aspect of working at a community college would have to be that you are responsible for just SO much stuff. Here at [name of college] I wear a lot of different hats. And sometimes it's irritating trying to get it all done in a day, trying to meet the needs of so many different people, and still feel like you're doing something worthwhile. Some days I feel like I don't get a lot done because I am . . . so much is being asked me that I'm not sure even where to start.

Recall that those at liberal arts institutions often have ancillary job responsibilities, and that practitioners at HBCUs also discussed handling multiple tasks. The difference at community colleges is often the overall size of the student affairs staff. On many campuses, there are fewer than a dozen practitioners. The person who offered the above comment about serving as one of two counselors worked on a campus that enrolled over 1,200 students. These two individuals handled all academic and personal counseling for those students as well as managing the testing process required of all matriculating students. It is the multiple roles that professionals at community colleges play, coupled with the pace at which they work, that render the metaphor of administrators as producers most convincing.

The way in which they produce their work contributes to this image. Their work is team-oriented and highly collaborative. Indeed, those at community colleges work significantly more on committees than their counterparts at any other type of institution:

> In the community college we're all on committees together—faculty, staff, counselors, administrators, students—are all blended into committees. And we're not segmented in that respect. So we work together a great deal there. As an administrator, we're also involved in all the faculty meetings, so we're not separated there. Also at least one counselor goes to every [academic] Division meeting, so we always have representation with the faculty. It is a good relationship. We also know what's our turf and what turf we share, and everybody works together for the betterment of the students.

> We cross-train, cross-team for just about everything that we do on the campus. There's a mixture of people from all over the college that sit together and share ideas and kind of move us forward in the direction that we need to move in.

> You know you've heard it takes a community to raise a kid? It takes everyone in the community college to raise the student.

The multiple roles professionals at community colleges fulfill and the collaborative ways in which they conduct their work may help explain why they value conformity and security. That is, they are expected to do so much and to work with others so extensively that valuing conformity balances the extensive demands otherwise placed on them. The collaborative nature of their jobs also helps explain their relationships with others.

The Nature of Relationships

There are two sets of relationships that merit attention on community college campuses. The first is the relationship that student affairs professionals have with students. As noted above, students at community colleges are very unlike students at four-year institutions. Student affairs professionals not only recognize these differences, they embrace them:

> I think the most rewarding aspect is the fact that a lot of our students come here without much educational experience, as in not well-prepared for college, and might not have had a wonderful high school experience, and that we're able to provide them a form of higher education that they can readily grasp and help to

evolve themselves in a more fruitful experience. So I think it's just reaching and touching those students that haven't had a great educational experience in the past and might not be well prepared at having them succeed in some aspect on our campus.

So a lot of those people all they've done is work in factories all of their lives. Like I told them, I said, "Look at this as an opportunity that a door has been opened." Because a lot of them wanted to come to school, but because they had financial obligations, family obligations, they couldn't come to school. They had to eat and take care of the kids. But now they're able to come back to school. And like I told them, "Don't look at it as a bad thing. Look at it as something that you're now able to do. You're able to come back to school. Look at it that way and run with it." But the biggest problem is self-esteem, and if I can just let them know that they CAN do it, and most of the time at the end of a semester they'll come back to me and. . . . Or if they see me in the hall, they come in talking about "Well, I don't know if I can do this math; I don't know if I can do this English because when I was in high school I only went blah-blah years and. . . . ." But they see me in the hall, "I made an A in my English class, or I made an A in my algebra class." Not only are they making me smile, but I'm smiling because they're smiling.

Oh, I think it's the variety of students. I mean, the average age is around 30, so I could be working with a high school student taking college courses for the first time while they're still in high school, to an engineer who just got laid off from their [sic] job, to a woman or man who's worked in a given industry for 25 years and it's the only thing they know. They don't have a high school diploma and business has moved off-shore and we've got to figure out what we're going to do with this person to keep him a viable member of the community. You know, how we're going to retrain them, to working. . . . So it's really the student—just the VARIETY of students and just the neat part of. . . . Just what they can bring you and do.

These sentiments most closely resemble what professionals at HBCUs had to say about their students. At HBCUs, however, race was a unifying force. Helping Black students succeed was preeminent. At community colleges, though many students are racial minorities, race is not a factor, nor is age, or sex for that matter. Staff members at these campuses embrace all types of students. There is no talk of entitlement or elitism when community college professionals describe their students as there was among those at liberal arts and research institutions. Quite to the contrary, they deal with students who may not feel any sense of empowerment and the professional needs to address that.

The second characteristic of relationships on community college campuses is the sense of unity among faculty and staff. Perhaps it is the relatively small size of most community colleges, but professionals describe their work relationships as a team with a shared goal:

There is a very strong culture based on a collective set of values that are written and used in the hiring process. We consider the student at the center of all decisions; we have a commitment to community involvement; quality instruction; leadership and innovation. Our personal commitment is to be cooperative and supportive; proud; caring; positive; and dedicated. People tend to come to our institution and stay for entire careers. The leadership on both the academic side of the college and on the student services side of the college promote cooperative activities and ventures. Both areas of the college are aware of and have read articles and books about cooperative efforts between academic services and student services and recognize the power of such partnerships. The two groups who have the most information about students need to share information in order to best serve the student.

I think you get a good relationship that sometimes it's harder to gain maybe at other types of institutions. We work closely with each other—not all the time, but I feel like a lot of the time. Since the community college faculty don't have to worry about research and publishing and so forth, their sole focus is on teaching and helping students succeed. And so in that end we all try to work together. I don't know how many times faculty have called me or I've called faculty about a student that needs some extra help, or they've struggled with something. And I try to be the advocate for the student. And the faculty are very open to that. And so I think that's one advantage, which helps our students, because a lot of them couldn't survive in kind of a dog-eat-dog four-year university. They just don't have the skills yet to. . . . They need that extra help from faculty and from student affairs folks to get to that next step. And so I believe we can provide that for them here. I think that somewhat makes us unique and that's what we try to do.

I think we have a lot more access to each other because we're a smaller institution and we're focused on I guess more of a student-centered dynamic that it's easy for us to access each other. Professors are easy to approach; they're close by; they're willing to work with students—they're not passing student problems on to a TA or to an assistant or something. But they're more interactive, and the same with staff people I think. That staff people get more involved because they are part of the community too. I just think we have easier access to each other.

These descriptions speak to the relationships among faculty and staff overall. Other data support the notion of collaboration among all elements of the campus. Student affairs professionals at community colleges are significantly more likely to work with faculty, to be known by faculty, and to work with and be known by other administrators than their colleagues at other types of institutions. They are significantly more likely to work with academic deans and the president of their campus, and to be known by these academic leaders. In general, student affairs professionals are significantly more likely to work with all constituency groups on campus.

Among student affairs professionals, relationships are even closer. Administrators routinely refer to those with whom they work as family:

Well, because we are a small community college, it is very much like that cliché of working with family. People stay here a long time and there's very little turnover.

Is like being a part of a family. You know everyone.

Supportive; very inclusive. People take care of each other in all aspects of their lives.

In all honesty it is like a family because it's not just a profession. We know probably more than we need to know about [each others'] life outside the office.

Those at liberal arts colleges also talked about staff as family. In the case of community colleges, however, there is often so little turnover that this notion of family takes on added meaning. In one study, most student affairs professionals had been employed by the college for 20 or more years. The person with the least amount of experience on the campus had been there nearly a decade. When numbers of staff are small and people work together for years, familial relationships are deep and powerful.

Overall, those who work at community colleges are expected to produce extraordinary amounts of work, but they do so in a setting that is highly collaborative and team-oriented. This seems to offset the stress of working in a highly demanding environment. There are also other rewards associated with a career at a community college.

The Nature of Rewards

When it comes to rewards, those at community colleges are not unlike their colleagues at every other type of institution. They value intrinsic far more than extrinsic rewards. Conducting meaningful work in a positive environment and having good relationships with those around them are what matter for community college professionals:

I'll go back to one of my earlier statements—just seeing people empowered. When I can see at graduation—see individuals that I've seen along the way walk out the door with a degree in hand or certificate or diploma, or get their GED or their high school diploma or certificate—then it brings a certain satisfaction knowing these individuals are leaving with something that they can use for a lifetime. That their perspective on life has been changed somehow—whether it's new skills, whether it's just learning for knowledge's sake. Those are all satisfiers for me. I just feel really good about it. It's not the pay, it's not the work hours—it's knowing that students are getting what they need.

You should come to a community college graduation. It's just wonderful. So many of the students . . . it took them so long to get to that point. You know, [at the four-year institutions of the world] your students come in as a freshman and you expect them to graduate in 4 years—that's kind of the expectation of the student, that's the expectation of the university. And for the most part, that's what happens. At least in 4 or 5 years. But our students—so many of them have outside responsibilities, like. . . . Our median age is 29 or 30. So many of them work. Even our 18-year-olds work because they live at home and so they work outside of the home. But then many of them have children. You know, they're president of their PTAs—they've got other responsibilities other than school. So they take school at a slower rate, which we recommend to them. I'm like, "If you're working any amount of hours, you can't take 17, 18 college credits. It just can't be done successfully." So they take it at a slower pace, and so when they hit that graduation, it's just joyful for them and for us as well, because it just took them a lot of the time a long time to get there, and they had to surpass a lot of hurdles many of them to get there as well. And like I said, some of them weren't prepared academically in high school. And then to think that they could come to a community college and succeed. It's just a neat experience. That kind of gives me the motivation to keep going everyday—just to know the impact that you can have on somebody's life.

There are other intrinsic rewards, as well. Community college professionals are significantly more likely to earn recognition from their colleagues and from academic administrators than administrators at other types of institutions. They value the ability to influence decisions and the autonomy they are afforded:

I think there is a certain way in which people generally speaking give honor and recognition to the kind of work that we do. I find that it is a very rewarding thing.

I think the biggest thing for me and everybody in the counseling office is that we know that we're respected for decisions that we make. And administratively we have no one that dictates what we do because they've hired us for what we're capable of doing and they trust us in that respect. And we know that we have the respect of the President and the Vice President and the decisions that we make—particularly in their absence.

Autonomy makes me feel like a real professional. Like I don't have anybody looking over my shoulder. I don't have individuals who don't trust my judgments. It's a way of saying to me, "We know you can do what you say you can do."

In the sense of rewards, then, those at community colleges are very much like other student affairs professionals, with one exception: Salaries for many are relatively high. Since most community colleges are public, they operate on statewide salary scales. The service-area structure of community college systems, however, means that many campuses are located in rural areas where the cost of living is much lower. As a result, professionals feel they are well-compensated for their work, even if being engaged in meaningful work is their most valued reward.

Conclusions

In a sense, the label "producer" reflects the mission of the community college. Student affairs practitioners serve the broadest spectrum of students. They offer the greatest scope of academic programs: transfer education, vocational training, developmental programs, and lifelong learning opportunities. They are expected to serve their local communities, which means that every individual and organization in the service area is a potential client. All of this translates to a very heavy workload.

This workload is carried out through a limited number of student affairs functional areas and with a limited number of professionals. The environment is rife with bureaucracy and work is highly regulated. On the other hand, the work environment for those professionals focuses almost exclusively on students. This leads to an environment in which staff members interact with scores of students and expect to maintain the highest standards of quality in all those interactions.

It is not surprising, then, that the pace of work for professionals at community colleges is quite different than it is for those at other types of institutions. Community colleges are expected to know the social and economic climate in their service area and to respond to changes in that climate on a regular and ongoing basis. As a result, most change in the work of professionals is externally imposed. This can lead to high levels of stress among student affairs administrators, though these levels are somewhat ameliorated by a work schedule that demands fewer evening and weekend commitments and a better balance between their personal and professional lives.

The pace at which professionals work is also influenced by the ways in which they conduct their work. Most professionals are required to multi-task. The limited number of staff members on most campuses means that they cross-train and cover bases for one another. Moreover, much of their work is done in collaboration with other elements of the campus. Collaboration and teamwork are the norm on community college campuses.

This norm is achievable because of the close working relationships student services professionals at community colleges have with faculty, academic administrators, and other constituencies. There seems to be a greater sense of shared mission at community colleges than at other types of institutions, and the focus of that mission is on serving students.

Not everything about life at the community college is different than at other campuses, however, When it comes to rewards, those at two-year campuses are not all that different than their counterparts at four-year institutions. What matters is that their work is meaningful. The words of those who work at community colleges are best captured by this sentiment:

> I think the most rewarding thing to me is to go to graduation every year and see those students that I have worked with walk across that stage. Because they're just thrilled. They're absolutely just thrilled. And it really, really does something to you when you realize that you have had a hand in something that

these students have done. And I'm really proud of our faculty and our classified staff, and our deans, because everybody seems committed to doing the best that we can possibly do for our students at this community college.

Chapter Eight

The Change Agents:
Student Affairs Administration at
Hispanic-Serving Institutions

The final group of institutions at which student affairs professionals work that is addressed in this volume includes colleges and universities that have been identified as serving Hispanic students. Hispanic-serving institutions (HSIs) are not an institutional type per se. In fact, liberal arts colleges, religiously affiliated institutions, community colleges, research and comprehensive universities have all been designated HSIs. Like their HBCU counterparts, HSIs are identified by the students they serve rather than their missions or their curricula.

HSIs, like the other types of institutions, developed as a result of larger social movements in the U.S. In this case, demographic shifts and immigration and migration patterns over the last third of the 20th century were key to the emergence of HSIs. As a result, these colleges and universities tend to be clustered in select states and regions across the country. They are situated in some of the fastest growing regions of the country, hence are rapidly expanding to meet the shifting demands of their geographic settings.

It is the ways in which professionals at these institutions have adapted to those changes, as well as the transformations they seek to promote in their students, that led me to characterize student affairs administrators at HSIs as "change agents." They talk about the programmatic, cultural, academic, and administrative changes occurring on their campuses. They talk about the changes their students experience as a result of their engagement in higher education. Finally, they relate that their work life at HSIs has changed the way they see themselves. Change is what led to the emergence of HSIs and change encapsulates what professional life is like at these institutions.

It is important to note that there are a number of terms that have been used to describe individuals of Spanish-speaking heritage. Hispanic and Chicano have both been widely employed, though they may be associated with imperialistic roots and regional bias. The term Latino has been utilized most frequently in recent years, though that phrasing is subject to criticism for being overly generic. For purposes of this volume, I have chosen to use the term Hispanic. Given that the federal designation for the institutions included in this group is Hispanic serving, employing parallel terminology to refer to the students who attend these colleges and universities seems reasonable.

Historical Evolution

The development of HSIs in the hierarchy of American higher education is relatively recent. It is only over the past 30 years that these colleges and universities have emerged (Benitez, 1998). Their growth was prompted by a series of social factors and legislative actions. The first of the social issues was the Civil Rights movement of the 1960s (Laden, 2001). Until that era, colleges and universities in the U.S. were *de facto* segregated. The vast majority (87%) of students were White and the curriculum was almost exclusively White and Western (Association of American Colleges and Universities, 1995). In fact, some states limited Hispanic access to higher education through legal actions similar to those that curtailed access for Blacks (Southern Education Foundation, 1995). The Civil Rights movement led to greater diversity among college students and additional financial aid programs to encourage participation in higher education among students from historically under-represented groups (Justiz, Wilson, & Bjork, 1994; Laden, 2001).

Immigration patterns and demographic shifts in the country are other social factors that influenced the emergence of HSIs. In 1960, Hispanics accounted for only 3% of the U.S. population. Their numbers quadrupled over the next four decades and today they account for nearly 13% of the country's population (*Hispanic Yearbook*, 2002; U.S. Census Bureau, 2002). This number is expected to increase to 22% by the year 2015 (U.S. Census Bureau, 2002). Moreover, only 75% of these individuals are American citizens; the rest are immigrant resident aliens. Initially Hispanics were clustered in urban areas of the country. Over the past decade, however, they have moved to less populous regions of the country where employment and housing options are more plentiful (Laden, 2001).

The founding of the Hispanic Association of Colleges and Universities (HACU) in 1986 was another milestone in the development of HSIs. With support from Hispanic corporate and education leaders, HACU created a consortium of two- and four-year colleges and universities that aimed to promote access to higher education for Hispanics and support for institutions that instructed such students (Laden, 1999). It was HACU's lobbying efforts that led to several legislative and executive actions associated with HSIs. To start, HACU gained recognition for HSIs in Title III of the 1992 Higher Education Reauthorization Act, rendering these institutions eligible for federal funding (Laden, 2001; Schmidt, 2003). Access to federal funds increased when HSIs were included (along with HBCUs and Tribal Colleges) in Title V of the 1998 reauthorization of the Higher Education Act (Basinger, 2000; S. E. Brown, Santiago, & Lopez, 2003).

These legislative efforts were complemented by two executive initiatives in the 1990s. In 1994, President Clinton established the President's Advisory Commission on Education Excellence for Hispanic Americans. The 25 Commissioners are appointed by the president and charged with assessing the degree to which quality higher education is accessible to Hispanics and recommending ways to improve such access. They report the findings of their endeavors to the Secretary of Education. The White House Initiative for Educational Excellence for Hispanic Americans is a multi-agency group that provides assistance to the President's Commission and strives to educate other agencies about the roles that HSIs play in the higher education system of the U.S. (White House Initiative, 2000).

The culmination of these efforts is a group of colleges and universities, representing the full spectrum of institutional types, designated as HSIs. What is not as clear is the definition of such institutions. There are several, but two dominate. The first is the less restrictive and is used by HACU to define such campuses as those non-profit, accredited colleges and universities at which Hispanics account for at least 25% of enrollment. Title V parameters are more restrictive and define HSIs as those institutions that are non-profit at which at least 25% of undergraduates are Hispanic and that meet certain standards for percentages of low income and first generation students among undergraduates, along with other criteria.

Depending on which definition is employed, the number of HSIs in this country varies. Benitez (1998) reported there were as many as 738 or as few as 131. In either case, Puerto Rico is host to the largest number of HSIs. Beyond that territory, the colleges and universities are clustered in the nine states that are home to the greatest numbers of Hispanics: Arizona, California, Colorado, Florida, Illinois, New Jersey, New Mexico, New York, and Texas. These facts provide the context in which HSIs currently operate.

The Nature of the Hispanic-Serving Institution Campus

Unlike HBCUs that were founded to educate descendents of former slaves, only a few institutions (e.g., National Hispanic University, Hostos Community College) were founded to serve Hispanic students. All other HSIs evolved into such as the numbers of Hispanic students they enrolled increased. Overall, HSIs represent approximately 6% of all higher education institutions in the U.S. but enroll 50% of all Hispanic college students (Laden, 2001; Stearns & Watanabe, 2002).

During the 1990s, enrollment at HSIs increased by 14%, the number of Hispanic students enrolled at HSIs increased by 14%, and the number of degrees conferred by HSIs increased as well. In fact, the number of degrees conferred by HSIs increased by 36% during this decade compared to an increase of 13% among all institutions. By 1999, the degrees conferred by these colleges and universities included AA degrees (46%), bachelor's degrees (39%), master's degrees (13%), professional degrees (1%), and doctorates (1%). The number of degrees awarded to Hispanics at HSIs grew by 95% during the 1990s. As these data suggest, HSIs are major providers of higher education to the Hispanic population in this country and will continue to play a critical role in terms of access for Hispanics in the foreseeable future (Stearns & Watanabe, 2002).

Mission

Like their HBCU counterparts, HSIs include a variety of types of colleges and universities. Unlike HBCUs, however, very few HSIs were established to educate Hispanic students. Their missions, therefore, reflect their particular institutional type. For example, the mission of one religiously affiliated liberal arts HSI reads more like that of a religiously affiliated college than a HSI:

> PURPOSE: The primary purpose of [name of] University, as stated in the Charter, is to offer its students a quality education. Furthermore, [name of] University commits itself to assuring a religious dimension and to providing community service and presence within a more caring environment.
>
> VISION: [Name of] University seeks to instill in its students St. Dominic's vision of a world that celebrates God's dwelling within us and among us, where life is reverenced and nurtured, where hatred and injustice are eradicated and where the intellectual life is promoted and supported.

Likewise, the mission statement for one comprehensive HSI parallels those of other comprehensive institutions. That is, it tries to capture an undergraduate instructional focus, graduate professional programs, and service to its region:

> [Name of] University serves the people of the State of [name] and its surrounding areas as a comprehensive, regional, rural, public, coeducational university. Its student body is diverse in age, culture, language, and ethnic background. Teacher education continues to provide the basic foundation of [name of university's] programs. That focus has broadened to include a range of certificate, associate, baccalaureate, and several graduate programs which also meet the needs of students in allied health, arts and sciences, business, and vocational education. All undergraduate degree programs include a strong comprehensive general education requirement.
>
> Excellence in teaching is a preeminent goal at [name of] University. The University encourages the exchange of ideas; fosters the cultural, emotional, intellectual, physical, and social growth of students; nurtures a lasting

appreciation of learning; encourages increased relationships with people of diverse backgrounds; and furthers an appreciation for the benefits and opportunities derived from community involvement. [Name of university], through advanced technology and telecommunications, creates opportunities for its students, the faculty and staff, and the communities it serves to participate more fully in educational efforts which provide access to information and outreach to the global community.

[Name of university] recognizes as a strength the multilingual, multicultural population of the region and state and accepts the responsibility to be particularly mindful and supportive of the unique opportunities afforded by this diversity. The University aspires to promote increased access to all levels of education and to help people better understand and appreciate diversity, tolerance and cooperation. The University is committed to help preserve and enhance the rich cultural heritage of the region it serves and to broaden its student diversity by reaching out to students from other states and nations.

[Name of university] values the contributions of its faculty, staff, and students and is committed to their professional growth and personal enrichment. Faculty and staff encourage student success by providing quality educational opportunities that are affordable and accessible. The University supports innovative and scholarly work, promotes integrity and equity in its dealings with people, actively pursues accreditation by recognized national and regional accreditation agencies, and seeks continual improvement of institutional management practices and processes.

[Name of university] works diligently to maintain fiscal and ethical integrity in its activities, to provide for the future educational needs of the people of Southwestern [name of state], and to build a collaborative relationship with its constituencies. The University addresses the educational, cultural, community, and economic development needs of the region through its library, museum, gallery, fine arts center, theater, and through supportive partnerships with community and educational organizations, business, industry, and local governments

In this same vein, the mission statement of a research university that is a HSI reflects the tripartite mission of teaching, research, and service. It emphasizes the world-class nature of the institution and lists its prestigious affiliations. This statement is very similar to the mission statements of research universities described in Chapter Five:

The University of [name of state] at [name of city] is the premier public institution of higher education in [region of state], with a growing national and international reputation. Renowned as an institution of access and excellence at both the undergraduate and graduate levels, [name of university] is committed to research and discovery, teaching and learning, and public service. [Name of university] embraces the multicultural traditions of [region of state], serves as a center for intellectual and creative resources, and is a catalyst for the economic development of [name of state].

[Name of university] is accredited by the Commission on Colleges of the Southern Association of Colleges and Schools to award bachelor's, master's, and doctoral degrees. The University offers students the knowledge and skills required to succeed in their chosen fields. In addition, [name of university] provides the opportunity for all undergraduates to develop into highly educated individuals by mastering its Core Curriculum in an environment that promotes personal growth, academic success, and life-long learning.

[Name of university] provides access to its various degree programs to a broad constituency at multiple sites and maintains rigorous academic standards in requirements for successful completion of its programs. [Name of university] encourages attendance of both traditional and nontraditional students by offering flexible scheduling, varied course offerings, and extensive student support services.

[Name of university] emphasizes a balance of excellent teaching, research and creative activities, and scholarship. In addition, [name of university] recruits and retains faculty who exemplify this balance and encourages faculty to engage in public service activities appropriate to their academic fields. The University also encourages and facilitates multidisciplinary instruction, research, and public service efforts through its administrative structure, degree programs, and personnel policies.

Through its broad research efforts, [name of university] adds to the knowledge base and applies that knowledge to today's problems. [Name of university] seeks to facilitate the transfer of research findings to the work environment through continuing education and graduate-level programs that enhance the specialized skills of professionals employed in [name of city] and the [name of] region.

Mission statements of HSIs, then, reflect the historically entrenched functional roots of the institution rather than the relatively recent shift to educating Hispanic students. Evidently, the focus offered by HSIs to Hispanic students is reflected in what they do, not in how they describe themselves.

Faculty and Staff

The relatively new status of HSIs in the system of higher education in America is what prompted me to include them in this volume. Interestingly, data about HSIs are relatively scarce, despite their rapid rise to prominence. Because they have only recently been designated as a distinct cluster of colleges and universities, and due to the fact that they represent the full array of institutional types, data on HSIs have not been disaggregated from large national databases in many instances. This is particularly true of data about faculty at these colleges and universities. Although information about faculty at HSIs is limited, facts about Hispanic faculty in general are more readily available. In this discussion I will attempt to distinguish between the two forms of information.

As of 1999, about 46% of the 162,506 employees of HSIs were faculty members, and instructional and research assistants accounted for an additional 4%, rendering half of all employees in some sort of faculty role (Stearns & Watanabe, 2002). These numbers take on a different interpretation when examined from the perspective of Hispanic employees in higher education in general.

During the 2001/2002 academic year, less than 3% of full-time faculty at colleges and universities in the U.S. were Hispanic (Wilson, 2003). In fact, only 5% of all employees at degree-granting institutions in 1999 were Hispanic. However, HSIs employed 30% of all Hispanics working at these degree-granting institutions. The numbers further shift if institutional types are factored into the equation. In that case, over half of all Hispanics working in higher education in 1999 were employed at two-year institutions (Stearns & Watanabe, 2002).

This is not to say that Hispanics represented the majority of staff members at HSIs. In fact, they represent only 25% of all employees at all HSIs and somewhat less than that at two-year institutions. This does make Hispanics the second largest ethnic group employed by HSIs, where only Whites are employed in higher numbers. Another 16% of employees at HSIs are members of other ethnic and racial groups (Stearns & Watanabe, 2002).

The racial divide is more prominent when examined by type of employment status, however. Although 41.4% of nonprofessional staff members at HSIs are Hispanic, only 22.3% of administrative/managerial employees are of Hispanic descent. Among faculty, the numbers drop further: 13.4% of instructional and research faculty are Hispanic. Slightly more Hispanics (19.8%) are teaching and research assistants at HSIs. Perhaps more relevant to this volume, over a quarter (26.4%) of non-faculty HSI professionals (which includes student affairs administrators) are Hispanic (Stearns & Watanabe, 2002).

There are several factors that may influence the limited number of Hispanic faculty at HSIs. The first relates to salary. In 1995/1996, the average salary for all faculty members at HSIs was the same as that of the national average: $53,929. By 1999/2000, the average faculty salary at HSIs had fallen and was $1,236 below the national average. Full professors make 93% of the national average and associate professors at HSIs earn about 97% of the national average for their rank. Only assistant professors earn salaries that exceed the national average. Differences in salary also emerge based on institutional control. Faculty salaries at private colleges and universities in the U.S. historically are higher than those at public institutions. In the case of HSIs, however, the opposite is the case: Salaries at private HSIs are lower than those at public HSIs (Stearns & Watanabe, 2002). If they have a choice, Hispanics who aspire to faculty careers might wish to pursue those aspirations at higher-paying public colleges and universities.

This is particularly true given the number of Hispanics who earn doctorates, and hence qualify for faculty positions at most institutions. One of the barriers to increasing the representation of Hispanics on the faculty at HSIs, or at other types of institutions for that matter, relates to the graduate pipeline. In 1993, Hispanics earned only 2% of all the doctorates earned in the U.S. In 1994, only 946 of the 43,261 doctorates conferred in this country went to Hispanics

(Benitez, 1998). Seven years later, in 2001, Hispanics earned only 1,116 doctorates (Wilson, 2003). Additionally, the vast majority of these doctoral degrees were in education and the social sciences. The doctorate is generally the passport to a faculty career. The fact that so few Hispanics are earning doctorates leads to a very small pool of potential faculty members ("Educating the Largest Minority Group," 2003). Those Hispanics who do earn doctorates often take positions at non-HSI institutions where salaries, benefits, and professional development opportunities are greater.

Workload may well be another factor that influences where Hispanic faculty members elect to work. Although the data have not been disaggregated to distinguish HSIs from other types of institutions, many HSIs are liberal arts and community colleges as well as comprehensive universities. As noted in previous chapters, faculty members at these types of institutions devote far more time to instruction than their colleagues at research universities. It is likely, therefore, that faculty at HSIs teach heavier loads and that may impact where Hispanics with doctorates choose to pursue a faculty career.

A final set of obstacles to increasing the number of Hispanic faculty, at HSIs or elsewhere, has to do with institutional and cultural barriers. For example, Hispanic faculty members are often called upon to serve on numerous committees in an effort to diversify committee membership. As such, they frequently become spokespeople for Hispanics in general, a role in which few are comfortable ("Educating the Largest Minority," 2003). At times, interethnic identities (e.g., Cubans vs. Puerto Ricans vs. Dominicans) interfere. That is, the interests of a particular ethnic group take precedence over the interests of Hispanics overall (Wilson, 2003). Finally, many Hispanic faculty members prefer to identify with their discipline rather than their race and do not take on campus roles that associate them with the Hispanic community. All of these factors influence the visibility of Hispanic faculty, both at HSIs and at other colleges and universities.

This is not to say that there are not sufficient Hispanic representatives among faculty and staff for students. As Laden (2001) noted, there is a prevailing myth that there are too few role models for Hispanic students. At HSIs, Hispanics represent from 5% to 67% of all faculty members, and anywhere from 25% to 40% of administrators. For students, then, the nature of the HSI campus is different than it is for faculty members.

Students

The literature on Hispanics in higher education parallels that on faculty: Some focuses on Hispanics at all types of colleges and universities and others focus on students at HSIs. I will try to distinguish between the two throughout this discussion. Perhaps the clearest way to look at students is through the three stages of the higher education process: preparation, matriculation, and graduation.

Differences in educational preparation for Hispanic and White students begins early and persists throughout the educational process. For instance, the importance of early childhood learning on later success in school is well documented. Whereas 55% of White children ages 3 to 4 are enrolled in some sort of preschool program, only 35% of Hispanic children are provided such an opportunity. Indeed, by age 9 test scores suggest that Hispanic students are, on average, about two grade levels below their White peers (*Educational Attainment*, 2002).

These disparities endure through secondary education. In 1994, 37% of all Hispanics aged 18–24 had not completed high school, and only 47% of those 25 and older were high school graduates (Lane, 2001). By the end of the decade, these numbers had not improved substantially: 57% of all Hispanics were high school graduates, compared to 82% of Whites and 75% of Blacks (Anaya & Cole, 2001; Wilds & Wilson, 1998).

In addition, Hispanic students face other barriers when preparing for college. For many English is a second language, and lack of fluency hinders their success in high school (S. T. Gregory, 2003). They are not well prepared for college academically (Garcia, 2001) and are often unfamiliar with the admission process. Most are from lower socioeconomic income levels (Rodriguez, Guido-DiBrito, Torres, & Talbot, 2000) and lack financial resources to enroll even if they are admitted (Olivas, 1997). A disproportionately high number are first generation students (Weissman, Bulakowski, & Jumisko, 1998).

For all these reasons, college-going rates for Hispanics are low. Nearly 41% of Whites and 30% of Blacks go to college, but only 22% of Hispanics do so (Devarics, 2000). Only 27.5% of Hispanic high school graduates were enrolled in college in 1997, versus 46% of Whites (Hernandez, 2002). Although Hispanics report higher education aspirations that are equal to, if not higher, than other racial groups, they do not achieve those aspirations (Gloria & Rodriguez, 2000).

These issues influence where Hispanics go to college. Tuition, the availability of financial aid, and proximity to home are the most important factors for Hispanic students in the college choice process (Benitez, 1998). More than 50% of Hispanic students go to schools that are less than 10 miles from their home versus 38% of White students (O'Brien & Zudak, 1998). To a large extent, this explains why HSIs have emerged in those locations where large numbers of Hispanics live.

Once they matriculate, Hispanic students face another series of challenges and barriers. They experience high levels of discrimination and harassment (Malaney & Shively, 1995). They do not adjust socially or academically to the same degree as Whites and have more negative perceptions of their campus than their counterparts of other races. Hispanics perceive higher levels of racial tensions on campus. That in turn influences their level of institutional attachment. Handling the academic rigors of college, and effectively managing

time and money are challenges for first-year Hispanics (Hurtado, Carter, &
Spuler, 1996).

In the face of these challenges, HSIs provide an alternative for Hispanic
students. They represent institutions that are relatively inexpensive and offer
reasonable levels of financial aid. In most cases, they are close to home for
Hispanic students. Support from family influences Hispanic student success, so
proximity to family is important (Weissman et al., 1998). Additionally, many
students need to work to support families or have other family obligations that
require them to travel home frequently (Hernandez, 2002). As a result, minority
enrollment at HSIs grew by 49% between 1990 and 1999 whereas White
enrollment decreased by 20%; minorities comprised 64% of students at these
institutions by the end of the decade. The rate of growth among Hispanic
students was the fastest, and they now represent 42% of students at HSIs. In
fact, HSIs enroll 50% of all Hispanic college students in the country.

HSIs succeed in educating large numbers of Hispanic students even though
they are overburdened and underfunded. For example, they spend 43% less on
instruction per FTE than other institutions and 51% less on academic support
(e.g., libraries, course development), and reserves at these institutions are 42%
less than at other campuses. Most germane to this volume, HSIs spend 27% less
on student services per FTE than other institutions (Stearns & Watanabe, 2002).
It is in this environment that student affairs professionals at HSIs conduct their
work.

The Nature of Student Affairs Work

A total of 194 student affairs professionals at 20 institutions provided the
data reported here. The data collection was limited to administrators at four-year
HSIs for two reasons. First, this reduced variations in responses that might
inadvertently reflect differences between two- and four-year HSI institutions.
Second, practitioners at five of the other institutional types in this book are
employed at four-year institutions. Those at community colleges were addressed
in a separate chapter. It seemed more reasonable to look at professionals at four-
year HSIs. It is important to note, however, that there are a number of two-year
HSIs, and data from administrators on such campuses are not reflected in this
chapter.

The data reported in this chapter came exclusively from the HSI study.
Participants completed the same protocol that was employed in the Association
and HBCU Studies. They rated certain characteristics of their campus (e.g.,
extent of centralization, bureaucracy, politics) to render quantitative information
about their work. They reported the amount of time they spent with different
constituencies (quantitative data) and what they liked and disliked about
working with those groups (qualitative data). They rated a list of rewards
enabling us to calculate mean scores and rank order those rewards from most to
least valued. Finally, many participated in interviews with members of the

research team. They offered more extensive descriptions of their lives and provided stories that illustrated the nature of their work. Because the same protocol was used, we could compare their responses to those from practitioners at other types of institutions.

Professionals employed at HSI institutions located in seven states provided information about their work life. The respondents worked at liberal arts and religiously affiliated campuses as well as comprehensive and research universities. The majority (83%) worked at public institutions, and most (60%) were employed at large campuses (15,000 or more students), though nearly a quarter of respondents (22%) were at schools that enrolled fewer than 5,000 students. They were relatively evenly distributed by level of responsibility: 31% identified themselves as entry-level, 36% as mid-level, and 33% as cabinet-level administrators. Most (58%) had earned a master's, though those with a doctorate or professional degree (15%) and those with a bachelor's (23%) were also well represented.

In some ways, HSI professionals were like their colleagues at HBCUs. Nearly half (49%) had been employed at their current institution for at least six years and a third (33%) had been working on their campuses for over 10 years (versus 30% of those at HBCUs). In terms of ethnicity, White non-Hispanics comprised the largest group of participants (51%), but Hispanics were well represented. Nearly a third (30%) were administrators of Mexican, Puerto Rican, or other Latino descent. Like their counterparts at HBCUs, more than half (51%) of the HSI professionals attended or graduated from HSIs and 40% attended or graduated from the HSI at which they worked.

Unlike those at HBCUs who took pride in the long history of educating Black students, however, professionals at HSIs talk about how rapidly their institutions have evolved:

Well, there are probably several things that are unique. One of them is that because we're so new and growing so fast, there are opportunities that wouldn't exist in a school that had been established longer.

And it seems that what I'm working in now is an institution [at] which the goals are noble; they strive to provide excellent education to a population that may not have had this opportunity 10–20 years ago. It is exciting, and it's . . . I don't know how to explain it. It's just very different and very rewarding work.

I mean we have a real rich heritage of cultural diversity that wasn't always the case before the '60s. I mean this was probably a lily-white conservative campus in its beginnings, in its origins. And the whole civil rights movement and Vietnam protest movement definitely changed that.

It is this sense of quickly evolving transformation that guides professional practice at HSIs and why they merit the moniker "change agents."

The Work Environment

The two most prominent characteristics of the work environment noted by
HSI professionals involve the degree of centralization on their campuses and
their service orientation. When they talk about the issue of centralized versus
decentralized administration, their sentiments are similar to their colleagues at
comprehensive institutions. They acknowledge both types of administration:

> Our campus is very large. We have about 33,000 students. So in that regards,
> physically we're decentralized. And in terms of a mode of operating, because
> of the largeness of the institution and the Division, we do count on directors to
> behave or to manage their departments fairly independently from us. But
> nevertheless, we do exert a great deal of oversight just to ensure that the
> departments are working effectively and they're also working in conjunction
> with each other toward our mission.

> It's hard because some things are really centralized and some things are totally
> decentralized.

There is a certain ambivalence expressed by HSI professionals. As another
noted, "Let's see—gosh it feels like a little bit of both." This is not to say that
administrators are bothered by this ambivalence. Rather, they seem to appreciate
both approaches to organizational management:

> Centralized. Well, again, coming together. We always meet to talk. . . . But
> again the individual departments are decentralized because they're doing their
> own specific missions. Or they have their own specific goals within their
> departments. So that's decentralized. But I think we have a unified mission. So
> we're centralized because we have a unified mission, a Student Affairs mission,
> and we come together to meet on that, and that's centralized.

In a similar vein, HSI professionals seem to be of two minds about the
degree of professionalism on their campuses. They recognize that a high degree
of professionalism is desirable but only under certain circumstances. In other
instances, professionalism can marginalize others, or at least give the appearance
of marginalizing them:

> We're going through a lot of administrative . . . higher administration, and
> restructuring. And I think within the last seven months, there's been operational
> changes, possible academic changes, and the way they've [been] handled hasn't
> necessarily been—in my opinion—the most professional.

> Right, and I think it's just a different style. I'm not saying that it's necessarily
> wrong because I think there's benefits, there's plusses and minuses for
> whatever style of management that you have. And you involve people too early
> and your ideas are not down and it prevents change. And if you involve them
> too late you lose good people that felt they were not part of the new process.

Like their counterparts at comprehensive universities, HSI student affairs administrators seem to appreciate both ends of the continuum; at least when it comes to the issue of professionalism. In matters of service orientation, responses seem to be driven more by institutional type than HSI status.

When asked whether they considered their institution service oriented, the response from HSI administrators at liberal arts institutions was resoundingly in the affirmative:

> My work environment is service-oriented for many different reasons. One, because we provide a service for college students and so we are service [oriented] people. And second "service" because that's our mission at the university: to [provide] service. And we have what are called "Service Thursdays" where we actually, as an organization and community, are going out into less fortunate communities to provide a service—community service and outreach. So we embrace service literally, but also what we do for the college students IS service. We're providing them opportunity and valuable information that help [them] grow as individuals, and that's more service.

For professionals at HSI comprehensive and research universities, however, the issue is not as crystallized. They acknowledge that there is a service orientation among some on campus but that others adopt a business perspective:

> I would actually have to say that I think in my particular institution, there is actually some conflict between those two different perspectives. I would say that most of the people for example in student affairs where I work take a much more student-oriented approach to it, where I think senior administrators who have to deal with the business community and have to deal with the legislature take much more of a business approach. And I think that there are times where that's a conflict, you know. Because, for example, like the administration is very big on recruitment. And I think student affairs tends to sit back and say, "Yes, well recruitment is important. Obviously if we don't have students we don't exist, but at the same time we need to focus on retention and servicing the students that we've already got here because we take more of a student services approach. And so I would say that I think both philosophies operate at my institution, and I think that at times they can come into conflict with each other.

In some senses, HSIs are like HBCUs. It is difficult to discern whether attitudes about service are due to institutional type or due to the Hispanic-serving status of these colleges and universities. Regardless, note the subtle reference to the rapid growth at this campus ("we need to focus in on retention and servicing the students that we've already got"). The burgeoning enrollment at HSI institutions was relatively pervasive in the comments of administrators, despite institutional type. This expanding demand for services influences the pace of work for professionals at these campuses.

The Pace of Work

The fact that the designation "Hispanic-serving" was coined only in the past couple decades is indicative of the pace at which the colleges and universities in this institutional category have changed. Student affairs professionals at HSIs recognize this pace of change, albeit in a relative context. They know that higher education organizations are typically monumentally slow to change. Change on their campuses occurs comparatively quickly:

> We've got new people in leadership positions. Our enrollment has grown by about 7,000 students in the last three years. So we've almost [grown] . . . by a third. Five years ago we had 18,000 students. Now it's at 25,000. So significant increases in enrollment. We've added eight new doctoral programs in the last two years. So we're just making significant leaps in terms of the kinds of things that we're doing and then all of those major changes are requiring everyone to change.

> Well, I would say that a lot of times changes at school first of all get resisted just because they're changes. Sometimes people feel that way about it. But here really big changes might take a year or two. But for a school, that's not that slow. Some changes can go through in 6 months.

> Quick to change. I'll give you an example we're working on. We had an institution call—that's a consortium of distance ed high schools that are in our service area—asked us if we could put together a program for their high school seniors to be concurrently enrolled with the college. And if we would be interested in offering those classes so that they could take classes while they're a senior in high school and then transfer those classes to [our university] and come to [our university]. And I said, yes, we'd be very interested in doing that. And they called us on Wednesday and we had them an answer this morning, as well as a program.

The only other campuses where rapid change was mentioned were comprehensives where change was discussed in terms of years, and community colleges where change could occur in a matter of weeks. Change at HSIs seems to occur more quickly than at comprehensives but not quite as quickly as at community colleges.

The rate at which change takes place leads to high levels of stress among student affairs administrators on these campuses. Professionals report multiple demands on their time and energy; demands that they routinely strive to meet. Over the long run, this leads them to believe there is a fairly profound imbalance between their professional and personal lives. Indeed, they reported the highest levels of imbalance among administrators at all types of campuses.

To a large extent, the fast-paced changes that are occurring on these campuses place administrators in a quandary. As student affairs professionals, they are committed to being proactive. Indeed, they are powerfully socialized to anticipate issues and address challenges before they become major issues. In the rapidly changing environments on HSI campuses, however, reactive is often the only option administrators seem to have, even if they wish it to be otherwise:

> That's a tough question. In theory we're trying to be more proactive and less reactive, but the only reason we're doing that I guess is because we've been primarily reactive. So I guess I'll have to say reactive.

> Often—because what I just mentioned, because [of] our limited staff—we are reacting to a situation, but our SPIRIT is proactive. Every year at retreats—and again I'm talking within the Division of Student Affairs—we're constantly talking about those two words and how do we become more proactive in what we are offering students, how we're supporting students. But because of the hats each of us wears and we are all spread so thin that often we don't have that time to plan and be proactive. And often we are reacting to situations or reacting to what we hear, that then really drives a change in our services. But again, the spirit is there from our Dean and I think as an employee we all embrace it that we really want to move to a more proactive environment. But I would say because of, again, staffing issues, we really are more reactive.

> OK, well there is this, for example, a hate-crime issue that happened on a college campus. And then based on it hitting the news, hitting kind of the community, we then moved in a reactive way, saying, "Gosh we need to start looking at how we're really working with our students and how are students are feeling regarding hate crimes, and really, where do we stand as a university." Now it shouldn't take a hate crime for us as a university to step up to the plate and really engage our students in conservation. That should . . . again, the proactive—it should be already happening. Those dialogues should already be happening. And unfortunately it took an incident like that for us, as a Division, to look inward and say, "Oh my gosh, now what are we going to do?" Not address the issue—but address the topic, address the climate of what's going on regarding diversity. So that's the most recent example where absolutely we should be proactive, and we are to an extent. But it shouldn't take an incident, a student incident, to make us really create greater dialogue and . . . programming based on an incident.

Some of these comments echo those of professionals at liberal arts colleges. The intent is to be proactive, but limited staff time and resources often mean professionals operate in a reactive mode. It would seem that the designation "change agent" does not necessarily infer proactive change.

It might be presumed that the degree of change, high stress, reactive mode of operating on these campuses would lead to a feeling of helplessness among HSI administrators. To the contrary, however, they seem to thrive in this environment and find it challenging in a positive manner:

> Positively challenging—no question. . . . We have some enrollment issues that we're concerned about right now, especially as they relate to our budget reductions that we're experiencing here in [name of state]. They're affecting our ability to provide quality instruction to our students. So we have decided to

cut back on our enrollment. So I feel like I'm playing a significant role in the
conversations that are taking place with regard to the strategies that we're using
to do just that.

Sentiments like this were routinely reported by HSI professionals. They rise to
the demands placed on them as a result of the pace at which they work. Still, this
fast pace influences how student affairs administrators accomplish their job
responsibilities.

How Work Gets Done

Patterns that relate to accomplishing work on Hispanic-serving campuses
are interesting. What is valued is relatively clear, but perceptions about how that
work is accomplished are more equivocal. It will come as no surprise that HSI
administrators have a difficult time refusing to take on additional work: Change
is too constant and demanding to do so:

I've never refused to do anything. You know, anything that's asked of me I do.
It really isn't easy for me, but if I have a real problem with a new procedure or
taking on something new, I think that if I can justify it and it's reasonable—the
justification is reasonable, I don't think that they'll force it on me. So I think
that it's workable.

Well, I would say it's the culture of the university for people to nominate you
and encourage you by letters to be part of a committee, and they thank you for
being part of a committee before you actually say yes or no. And usually the
letters come from higher level administrators. So it's to the point where you
can't say no.

Assuming greater responsibilities, however, seems to be most readily
accomplished in an environment that values risk taking and creativity.
Respondents were almost unanimous in their sentiments about these values:

Risk-taking is highly valued. Since I've come in I've tried to question
everything that I do about my job, appropriately, with research, with data, with
surveys, etc. to say, "Are we doing it well? Are we delivering the service
well?" And I would say half the programs—probably 2/3 of the programs that I
oversee either radically changed, have been suspended and re-implemented, or
we really moved into an entirely new direction with them.

And again because we're a relatively young school—only 30 years old—so we
don't have any ruts into which we are permanently planted. And also, because
you need to be creative to get along in this economic pinch. And I think that the
administration is very open to ideas from below. You don't always find that in
schools, you know. And that helps with encouraging creativity.

Creativity and risk taking have been reported by practitioners at several types of
institutions but in different ways. At liberal arts colleges, creativity is

encouraged. At comprehensive campuses, it is valued. At research universities, creativity and risk taking are expected. At HSIs, however, risk taking and creativity are necessary for survival.

When it comes to who accomplishes the work, professionals at HSIs are ambivalent. As their comments about other issues suggest, they seem to see both sides of the coin. At times, work is accomplished through individual efforts. At other times, teamwork and collaboration are called for:

> So, definitely my decision-making individually impacts our team. And so does my coworkers. So the bigger team is the university. And we also look at our decisions from that perspective. We try to truly be devil's advocates for each other, which is a team effort.

> I'd say 50% individual and 50% team.

> Good question. I think philosophically we promote collaboration. I think . . . to the extent that you can't see how your department interrelates with other departments. For instance, if you can't see how the Student Recruitment Office could connect with the Orientation Office, I think we have some of that here and I think that's not uncommon. I'm not saying we think in silos here, I think there is a good *esprit de corps* here amongst our staff in Student Affairs. And I think there is philosophically an interest, a desire to collaborate. But I think like in many places, even though that desire is there, we still have a ways to go to really truly engage departments to coordinate with each other more on combined projects and activities, and processes.

So the pace of work for HSI administrators reflects to a large extent the nature of the campus: The campuses are quickly evolving and the work that professionals undertake is changing equally as rapidly. The change agents at HSIs thrive in such an environment. This means that their relationships with others on campus are extensive and complex.

The Nature of Relationships

The words that student affairs administrators at HSIs employ to describe their relationships with others on their campuses in many ways mirror what their colleagues at other types of institutions say. For example, they find their student affairs colleagues to be "collegial," "collaborative," and "supportive," although they can also be "territorial." Likewise, some faculty members are "cooperative" and "concerned for students," whereas others are "uninterested" and "don't understand" or "don't care about student affairs."

There are some unique elements to the relationships that those at HSIs have with others on their campus, however. Perhaps most interesting was the frequency with which they mentioned "respect."

> The other thing I found that with Hispanic students, they are a lot less influenced by the popular culture. They are more respectful and I'm assuming

that's because of the home situation. So they come with a level of respect that
some of the other students may not have. So even if they're challenging me on
issues, they challenge me in a respectful manner as opposed to being rude and
antagonizing.

The term "respectful" was used by numerous practitioners to describe any
number of constituencies, including faculty, academic and other administrators,
alumni, and community members. The issue of respect seems to be more
important on HSI campuses than on all other campuses, except, perhaps HBCUs
where disrespect was seen as problematic.

The term "role models" was used in conjunction with faculty,
administrators, and alumni. Even when asked what they disliked about working
with different groups on campus, HSI professionals expressed empathy as often
as not. For example, support staff members were "terribly overworked" and
"grossly underpaid." Alumni would like to be more involved, but "everything
changes so fast it is difficult for them to keep current." This sense of empathy
also characterizes the two groups about which HSI professionals talked the
most: students and their families.

It is clear that those who work at HSIs know their students. Their comments
operationalize what the literature reports. Their students are often first
generation, low income, Hispanics who come from the local area and who
would not otherwise have access to higher education:

OK, I would [say] number one [is] the fact that we are so diverse. We are one
of the most diverse institutions in [name of state], and one of the most diverse
nationally. I think that the fact that we are in essence an open-access institution
and really pride ourselves on being geared for serving students who probably
wouldn't have access to many other institutions. It's a very unique and positive
[aspect] of [name of university].

But I can tell you from my perspective that it is really very rewarding to know
that I'm helping a group of people that need a break—because many of them
are sons and daughters of migratory workers. They do not have the complete
education that some of our more fortunate students have. So it's wonderful to
see them come in and be able to counsel them and help them to develop the
skills they need to be successful here and then to see them go on and graduate
and do big things—become attorneys and city council people and take their
places in business and industry as well. And that's very, very wonderful.

I think it's the opportunity to serve an underserved population. I think that's the
most unique thing is that we have an opportunity to reach out to a group of
students that have been underserved and ARE being underserved.

I would say a lot more of the students would be low-income has been my
experience. For the most part . . . and that just working with low income
students is actually—there's so many different things that come into play when
students are lower income. Or more students are lower income.

This is not to suggest that practitioners at HSIs do not recognize that they serve non-Hispanic students as well. They readily acknowledge that their responsibilities extend to all types of students. In fact, the broad diversity of students on their campuses is what appeals most to many of them. The large presence of Hispanics at their institutions, however, flavors much of what they do.

In large part, this may be due to the fact that professionals deal not only with their Hispanic students but also with the families of those students. The focus on family was more evident in the comments from this group of professionals than from administrators at any other type of institution:

> Family is very important to Hispanics I believe and their views of education may be different. And so I think just trying to look at the things that are a value to them and trying to work with that in the different things that we offer. The programs that we offer, the services that we offer, our mindset about things. It's just important, I think, to pay attention to that particular group of students.

> I'm a Euro-American Caucasian male [and since being here I have learned] how much more impact family has on the Hispanic community than it does in the Caucasian community. I'm not saying I'm not close with my family, but since I've been here for two years, I've learned how much more important that is. And when we have events on campus and the large families come, I think that's awesome to have that much involvement, especially the pride that folks see in their students . . . the families see in their student when they're coming to commencement to graduate or being inducted into an honors society, or being here for such-and-such.

> Lower income students have different concerns, different anxieties. There's a stronger concern for financial aid and there's a stronger need to educate the students about their options financially. There's an added concern about family when there's financial issues. And so students may even still be holding a role in the family when they come to college in terms of paying rent or helping out in any way that they can with their family, which sometimes is very far away. So just helping the student balance that or prioritize becomes a factor with lower income students.

> I think the family ties . . . it's very different than like when I worked in the Midwest. Parents dropped their kids off and then that's it. But here family—the parents and the family are very much a part of the students' lives.

These sentiments are unique to professionals at HSIs. Those at HBCUs talked about working with parents in a positive way and viewed parents as partners in the educational process. At HSIs professionals talk not about parents but about families. Siblings, grandparents, aunts, and uncles all play a role in students' lives. Those as HSIs are change agents for not only students but also their families.

If families are part and parcel of working at HSIs they are as often sources of challenge as they are sources of support for student affairs administrators:

> A lot of them still live at home obviously and I think issues of letting go, for parents, here are heightened because we have to address things differently than we would I think at other institutions. Because they'll ask questions about curfew and things that are just foreign to me but parents here want their daughters—even if they're 19 or 20—to have chaperones if they go do certain events. And so I think that just ties to family and recognizing that our students are sometimes . . . they don't have as much freedom to do things. And it's a cultural thing. And it doesn't seem to faze them. More often than not they're not even that bothered by it; they just accept it as a fact of their family and their culture.

Practitioners at other campuses talked about parents. At both liberal arts and research universities professionals talked about the sense of entitlement on the part of parents. At HSIs the opposite seems to occur: Parents have no sense of entitlement to higher education and simply want their children to hold on to traditional family values. Because so many HSI students are the first in their families to attend college, there are times when professionals find family members to be "parochial" and "provincial." They report that "college is foreign to them" and they "want us to take their place while their students are in our care."

In general, relationships at HSIs are dominated by work with students and their families, and most professionals seem to find their work with these groups rewarding, albeit challenging at times. There are other rewards associated with working at HSIs, however.

The Nature of Rewards

Like their colleagues at all other types of institutions, the reward HSI professionals value most highly is the meaningfulness of the work that they do:

> I would say the fact that the majority of our student population are [sic] first-generation college students. And it's rewarding to be able to play a role in their success in college, and then to see the pride in their families as they move forward in their careers.

> Seeing a first-generation college succeed and have their family learning right along with them. Even if they go through tough times, and stress times. And you have to understand—yes we are a predominantly Hispanic serving institution, but our target is first-generation. So that's the perspective I'm coming from. It is seeing that student grow inside and outside the classroom, and seeing them succeeding. And seeing them go from freshmen. . . . I've been at this institution for almost nine years, so I've had that opportunity to see them move from freshmen through to senior and some who have remained to pursue their graduate degrees. And seeing that empowerment in a positive way, when

all the odds were against them. Or so they thought when they first came. Seeing
the multicultural aspect enhance everybody's learning at the institution. Seeing
the Hispanic student who had one perspective on life and the world open up
and accept, and be accepting, that traditional roles within cultures is not a
prescribed mandate for their life. But instead seeing that they have options that
they can marry successfully with their culture.

The opportunity to help make a difference in somebody's life. An opportunity
to be a part of a person's growth process. And as sort of a general thing, I think
that also in this institution, I do get an opportunity a lot to work with people
who have either been in some cases the first-generation of college students in
their family, and also people who, like me, that they've transitioned through
community college to university and has kind of taken that path, rather than
sort of the more "traditional" path. To be a part of that process and being here
for people and encouraging them to, well, to struggle and to watch them
struggle and succeed is the most rewarding part. And knowing that I just played
a small part in that is good. I don't see myself as being the major impetus, but if
I can make a difference—even if it's just knowing that in a small interaction
with me, then I feel good about that.

When I look at . . . where my university is we're surrounded by other, I would
say more competitive universities—maybe more, how do I say this . . . I think
the best word is competitive. More competitive universities. And I always
come back, you know . . . I might have a meeting down the street at one of
these universities that has a lot more money than we'll ever have and just has
so many more resources. And I always come back to my university and I just
feel so satisfied, and it's because the students that we serve are so grateful. We
have a lot of first-generation students and when you work with a first-
generation student, they . . . ANY support that you give them, they embrace it,
they appreciate it, they want to be involved, they want to grow, they want to
learn. And that is such a rewarding environment to be in.

When those at HBCUs talked about serving first generation students, it was
about serving first generation Black students. Those at community colleges also
commented on the satisfaction they took in serving students who might not
otherwise pursue higher education, but those were community college students.
All the comments in this chapter were made by professionals at four-year HSIs.
Their interest is in first generation students of all races at four-year campuses.
This is what sets them apart from their colleagues at HBCUs and community
colleges.

On the downside, at times there is a focus on Hispanic students.
Professionals need to be very cautious not to overlook the other students on their
campuses:

Personally, I think when you are at HSI and whereas of course you have to
accommodate to that particular culture, I do notice sometimes that the culture
seems to dominate OTHER cultural aspects of the university. So I think that's
one disadvantage. Since half of the group comes maybe from a Hispanic or

Latino culture, sometimes that tends to dominate the vibes of the campus, the
activities that take place on campus. And then of course even in [name of city
where campus is located], which is predominantly Hispanic and Latino . . . so I
would say a disadvantage because sometimes that culture really dominates and
it doesn't really allow for other cultures to be—not NOT recognized, but AS
recognized.

Um, I would have to actually say that in some ways [the disadvantage of
working here is] that it is a Hispanic-serving institution. I mean I think there are
really good things about the focus on Hispanic students. But at the same time, I
think that sometimes that can become—how do I want to put it? Let me be very
careful here. Sometimes it can leave the impression—and I don't necessarily
mean that it's intentional—but sometimes it can leave the impression that other
students who are not Hispanic are not valued.

Administrators at HSIs are like their counterparts at other institutions in that
the rewards they value most highly are all intrinsic in nature. Other than
engaging in meaningful work, they also rate a positive work environment, good
relationships with others, the ability to influence decisions, and autonomy as the
most rewarding aspects of their work.

There are some different values for those at HSIs, however. For example,
they place a higher value on advancement opportunities than their colleagues at
all other types of institutions except HBCUs. They are also like their colleagues
at HBCUs in that they value salary and benefits more highly than professionals
at other types of campuses. Conversely, rewards that are important to
administrators at other colleges and universities are not particularly valued by
those at HSIs. Recognition from others is less important to HSI professionals
than to all others except those at HBCUs. Support for professional development
is valued less by administrators at HSIs than by those at any other institutional
type.

The most significant challenges to working at a Hispanic-serving college or
university relate to two issues: lack of resources and burgeoning enrollments.
Numerous HSI professionals talked about the challenges they face in their work
due to the limited resources they have:

Having no money. And I don't think that has anything to do with our diversity,
but we just struggle financially at the university. We want . . . you know as a
university we want to embrace our diversity, but at the same time we just don't
have the funds to give these students what they deserve as far as service and
opportunities. We do our very, very best, but we struggle.

I don't know. That's a good question. I think a general frustration that really
has nothing to do with us being an HSI, it's just our limited resources. I wish
we could do more for the students and we are stretched about as thin as we
could go.

These sentiments mirror what those at HBCUs said about the impact that the lack of resources has on what they can accomplish in their jobs. These comments take on added importance in light of the fact that the study did not ask about the availability of resources. This was sufficiently important to practitioners that they raised the topic on their own. The extent of change the change agents can introduce is constrained by the resources they have available.

To a large extent, the challenges associated with limited resources are exacerbated by the continued increases in enrollment reported by professionals at HSIs. The literature reveals the exponential growth of these campuses. The comments from administrators who work at them substantiate those reports:

> I guess probably the fact that for this institution, since we're growing so fast, we can't provide a lot of services that we could if we had a slower growth rate. I mean we're outstripping what we can provide in services. You know, it's functionality like classrooms, instructors and parking. It's not dissatisfying in a way to me, but it's not fair to the kids that are coming here, the students. They could go to someplace where the growth was a little slower or flat and get a lot better service and attention than we could give them.

> I think the fact that we have grown so fast and that the state is really pushing access and opportunity, which we have been called the poster-child for [higher education in this state]. But then we don't have the resources. So the lack of resources; the fact that there's just not enough to do what we want to get done.

It would seem, then, that working at a HSI offers professionals a somewhat unique set of rewards and challenges. Collectively, though, how does the nature of their work, their relationships with others, and the rewards they garner render employment at a Hispanic serving campus different from working at other types of colleges and universities?

Conclusions

I have described student affairs professionals as change agents. A variety of data strands need to be woven together to illustrate this point. When that tapestry is complete, though, the evidence is compelling. To start, HSIs are newcomers to the higher education hierarchy; they have emerged only in the last three decades. In that short time, however, they have grown both in terms of the number of institutions so designated and in the number of students they serve. This means that change is entrenched in the culture of HSIs, and those who work at these colleges and universities serve as agents of many of those changes. This may be why student affairs administrators at HSIs talk about how quickly their institutions change, and how risk taking and creativity lead to change.

These changes are targeted at Hispanic students and the Hispanic communities in which HSIs are situated. This is not to say that other students on these campuses are ignored. It simply means that the change is most evident among Hispanics because they are so dominant on HSI campuses:

I think [working at a HSI is] unique because it offers the opportunity to learn,
interact, and create community support for our Hispanic population that will be
very soon our predominant culture, or "minority group." They WILL become
the majority-minority. And seeing good solid education with which our
students that will be our leaders and our majority in the future, that will in
many ways rule decisions we make—both community and statewide, as well as
within our country. But seeing that instead of reacting from a point of view that
is with no education and it's only based on feeling and seeing that our students
learn to exercise and be confident about the voices that are so important that
they bring to the table. And they're able to, because of what they experienced
in college, not just the book learning, but what they experienced allows them to
give support to the voices that they do bring to the table. So that they are not
seen by "the rest of the public" as only reacting on feelings or only waiting
until the last minute to respond to a political issue, or something of that nature.
But instead, given the validity that they so deserve.

Those who work at Hispanic-serving colleges and universities work with
legions of first generation students for whom higher education can be a life-
changing event. Their students often come from low-income families, and
higher education serves as a path to greater earning power and upward
socioeconomic mobility. Student affairs professionals on these campuses are
often the agents of such change, particularly in terms of enlightening students
and their families about the doors that higher education can open for them:

I think the thing that I find most rewarding about working at a Hispanic-serving
institution, is the thing that I find most rewarding about the field that I'm in—
and that's the students themselves. I'm a big believer in promoting student
success. I actually am working at an institution where I grew up. This is my
hometown. And being able to help students' success and to understand that
there is a larger world out there, that getting an education is something that's
positive for them, is something that's very important for me personally. And I
have to honestly say that for my own personal perspective as an employee, I
did not come to work for this institution because it was a Hispanic-serving
institution. I came to work for this institution because it was in my hometown
and there was an opportunity for me to give back to my local community. And
that was more important to me than the fact that it happened to actually be a
Hispanic-serving institution.

This is not to say that the findings reported in this chapter should be
unquestioned. Indeed, in some cases it was difficult to determine if the
sentiments being offered were more influenced by the fact that the campus was
Hispanic serving or by the particular institutional type of the college or
university. It may be difficult to distinguish what to attribute to the fact that it is
a liberal arts or religiously affiliated campus, or a comprehensive or research
university at which the professional works rather than the fact that it is a HSI.
Nevertheless, work at HSIs seems to be unique and student affairs
administrators who work at these campuses embrace that uniqueness. It almost

seems as if they become part of the larger Hispanic community in which their campus resides:

> Probably what's unique and what is not seen at other institutions obviously is the language, so whether it's phrases or Spanish that we have a much more regular understanding than other people would do. Like if I go visit colleagues or go to conferences, I'm saying "Ola, Buenos Dias" or "Gracias," and you can catch yourself because people will look at you. And then also at [name of institution] in particular is the culture is very warm, very welcoming. Students, staff, faculty embrace—whether it's a hug, a kiss—is more common than a handshake. And for people coming to our campus for the first time, it takes them a little while to get used to that. That that's how people are welcomed.

Indeed, even the element of their work they find most challenging—the lack of resources—is challenging because it limits the amount of change they can introduce on their campus for their students. Cumulatively, the evidence paints a fairly convincing picture of student affairs professionals at HSIs serving as change agents on their campuses. Moreover, the projected demographic shifts in the U.S. suggest that HSIs will play an increasingly important role in the country's higher education system in the future; that will increase the prominence of the change agents on these campuses.

Chapter Nine

Where You Work Matters

In the opening chapter of this volume I argued that there was a pervasive assumption among student affairs administrators that the nature of professional practice transcends institutional type. Many student affairs administrators are convinced that what they do on a daily basis is driven by the functional area in which they work (e.g., orientation, student activities, career services) but not by where they practice their craft (e.g., community college, comprehensive university). The evidence presented in the preceding chapters is fairly persuasive that this is not the case. Although there are elements of student affairs administration that are similar across some institutional types, the work that professionals conduct does, in fact, differ based on where they work.

These differences suggest any number of implications. How should aspiring professionals be educated so that they are prepared for the differences in professional life at various types of colleges and universities? What should current professionals know when they consider career opportunities at other types of institutions? What mechanisms can be incorporated into recruiting and hiring practices to assist employers in acknowledging the skills and experiences that might be transferable from one institutional type to another? How can professional development programs be conceptualized to inform staff members about the relationship between administrative practice and institutional type? Any attempt to address these questions should be prefaced with a summary of how professional practice varies at different types of colleges and universities.

How Student Affairs Administration Differs by Institutional Type

This book describes a theoretical framework through which student affairs administration at different institutional types can be understood. It is critical to note, however, that framework is parsimonious. It takes a very complex concept and attempts to simplify that concept so that it can be universally understood. I paint a portrait of seven forms of professional practice, each relevant in a different college or university setting. That is what a good conceptual framework does; it attempts to render the complicated comprehensible. In doing so, however, the nuances can be lost. The model generalizes what professional life is like at liberal arts institutions, but there are 606 liberal arts schools in this country. Some are in rural areas, others in suburban or urban settings. Some enroll fewer than 500 students; others enroll more than 5,000. Some community colleges are multi-campus mega-institutions, whereas others are independent and small. HBCUs and HSIs represent institutional types from across the Carnegie spectrum. Each college and university campus has a unique history, set of traditions, and setting. The framework described in this volume cannot do justice to all the unique qualities that distinguish institutions within a certain type from one another; it makes no claim to do so.

That said, the model does address what appear to be common professional phenomena that occur across campuses within a single institutional grouping. Many student affairs administrators should recognize elements of their own professional work lives in the metaphor that describes their type of campus. Not all conclusions will resonate with all practitioners in each institutional setting. The conclusions, however, are based on evidence drawn from over 1,100 student affairs professionals at hundreds of colleges and universities across the country. To the degree that the metaphors paint general portraits of professional life for student affairs administrators on different campuses, they are useful. Table 9.1 summarizes the key differences.

The Standard Bearers at Liberal Arts Institutions

The philosophical underpinnings of the student affairs profession are grounded in two primary standards. First, each student is a unique individual and should be treated as such in the educational process. Second, higher education should concern itself with the holistic development of students and not concentrate only on their intellectual growth. Professional life for student affairs administrators at liberal arts institutions focuses on dealing with individual students and promoting development of each student in multiple arenas. As such, the term "standard bearer" seems to best describe their work.

Those at liberal arts colleges work one-on-one with students daily. They know what their students are studying, how many siblings they have, in what activities and organizations they participate, and who their friends and

Table 9.1.
Summary of Institutional Differences

Standard Bearers: Liberal Arts Colleges	Interpreters: Religiously Affiliated Institutions	Generalists: Comprehensive Institutions	Specialists: Research Universities	Producers: Community Colleges	Guardians: Historically Black Colleges/Universities	Change Agents: Hispanic-Serving Institutions
Nature of Campus: Mission						
-Historic focus on liberal arts, recent focus on professional studies -Represent 15% of all colleges and 7% of all students -Most have large endowments	-Promote spiritual development -Represent 25% of all colleges -At least 23 denominations sponsor colleges	-Hybrid: liberal arts & some graduate education -Many are members of state systems -Regional focus -Represent 15% of all colleges, 21% of all students	-Tripartite: teaching, research, service -Close ties to corporate/ military/ government complex -Represent 7% of all colleges, 24% of all students	-Vocational, transfer, developmental, continuing education -Structure varies considerably -Represent 36% of all colleges and 40% of all students	-Specified mission to educate Blacks -Distrust of dominant culture -Represent 3% of all colleges and 2% of all students, confer 17% of all bachelor's earned by Blacks -Includes 4- and 2-year, public and private colleges	-Missions vary; tied to institutional type, not HSI status -Represent 6% of all colleges, enroll 50% of all Hispanic students -Campuses are located in the 9 states that are home to the greatest number of Hispanics
Nature of Campus: Faculty						
-9% of all faculty are at liberal arts campuses -68% are full-time -Heavy teaching load, research limited	-Not all are members of the institutional denomination; this causes conflict with sectarian leadership -Appreciate campus mission - Many concerned about student development and strive to incorporate faith into the classroom	-21% of all faculty at comprehensives -Between 33% and 50% are employed part-time -Typically teach 4 or more classes per term -Increasing focus on research	-24% of all faculty at research universities -79% work full-time -43% of time spent teaching -Typically teach 2 classes/term -Research productivity is preeminent	-29% of all faculty at community colleges -On average 65% of faculty work part-time -Employ more women and minority faculty -72% of time devoted to teaching -40% attended community colleges as students	-Most Black faculty earned BAs at HBCUs -37% of all Black faculty work at HBCUs -Typically teach 4 classes/term -Growing focus on research -Salaries significantly lower - Committed to racial uplift and students	-Over 81,000 are on faculties at HSIs -3% of all full-time faculty are Hispanic, 30% of these work at HSIs, over 50% work at 2-year colleges -Represent 25% of all employees at HSIs

Table 9.1 (continued)

Standard Bearers: Liberal Arts Colleges	Interpreters: Religiously Affiliated Institutions	Generalists: Comprehensive Institutions	Specialists: Research Universities	Guardians: Historically Black Colleges/Universities	Producers: Community Colleges	Change Agents: Hispanic-Serving Institutions
			Nature of Campus: Students			
-Most from privileged backgrounds -Most are 18-22 years old -They value the collegiate experience	-Well steeped in campus traditions -Many hold conservative personal values -Many went to sectarian K-12 schools	-Many from underserved populations -Most from region or state -Graduate programs serve working adults	-Most from middle/upper middle class backgrounds -RU degree has only slight effect on degree completion, occupational status, earning potential -Psychological size can influence students' involvement on campus	-Many underprepared -Many are low-income -Academic achievement equal to that of Blacks at HWCUs	-Most from underserved populations -Disproportionately high numbers of women and minorities enroll at community colleges -Average age of student is 30 -Most from lower half of high school class rankings	-Many Hispanic students underprepared for college -Many Hispanics are low-income -Many Hispanics are first generation students -Hispanic students may face language barriers
			Nature of Work: Environment			
-Focus on holistic development -Close, personal contact with students -Ancillary job common -Fairly political environment	-SAs teach undergrads -More committee work -Denominational politics play a role	-SAs teach graduate students -Exposed to many other functions -Highly political within system	-Highly competitive -Highly political internally and externally -Complex, decentralized organizations -Hard to navigate campus physically and psychologically	-Many professionals are HBCU alumni -Very limited resources -Establishing and sustaining relationships critical	-Staff feel campuses are marginalized -Most campuses small -Local service area	-Resources very limited -Enrollments burgeoning -Some elements of environment more tied to institutional type than to HSI status

Table 9.1 (continued)

Nature of Work: Pace

Standard Bearers: Liberal Arts Colleges	Interpreters: Religiously Affiliated Institutions	Generalists: Comprehensive Institutions	Specialists: Research Universities	Guardians: Historically Black Colleges/Universities	Producers: Community Colleges	Change Agents: Hispanic-Serving Institutions
-Campus slow to adopt change -Frequent evening/ weekend commitments	-Campus very slow to adopt change -Sectarian leadership influences campus operations	-Highly bureaucratized -Relatively quick to change -Reactive more than proactive	-Highly stressful -Fast paced daily -Bureaucracy slows pace of change	-Slow to adopt change because relationships must be maintained -Staff work at balancing person and professional life	-Quick to adopt change -Responsive to community needs -Most change externally generated -High stress balanced by limited evening and weekend hours	-Very quick to adopt change -High stress seen as a challenge -Reactive rather than proactive

Nature of Work: How Work Gets Done

Standard Bearers: Liberal Arts Colleges	Interpreters: Religiously Affiliated Institutions	Generalists: Comprehensive Institutions	Specialists: Research Universities	Guardians: Historically Black Colleges/Universities	Producers: Community Colleges	Change Agents: Hispanic-Serving Institutions
- High degree of autonomy - One-person offices common - Creativity encouraged	- Less administration and bureaucracy - High degree of autonomy paired with team work	- Work extensively with student affairs colleagues across campus - Creativity highly valued	- Risk-taking expected - Creativity the norm	- Work accomplished through relationships with others	- Highly bureaucratized - Policy/ procedures guide most work - Security and consistency valued - Extensive committee work with faculty, academic administrators	- Risk-taking necessary - Creativity required - Sometimes work collaboratively, sometimes independently

Table 9.1 (continued)

Standard Bearers: Liberal Arts Colleges	Interpreters: Religiously Affiliated Institutions	Generalists: Comprehensive Institutions	Specialists: Research Universities	Guardians: Historically Black Colleges/Universities	Producers: Community Colleges	Change Agents: Hispanic-Serving Institutions
Nature of Relationships						
-Faculty care about students but not necessarily about student affairs -Student affairs colleagues work very closely together (rewarding but time-consuming) -Students bright, active, but may have sense of entitlement -Extensive contact with parents who also feel entitled	-Faculty often partner with student affairs -Parents viewed as partners in educational endeavors -Student affairs professionals view each other as "brethren" -Relations with students are life-affirming	-Faculty not expected to understand work of student affairs -Accepting of multiple roles students fulfill	-Little expectation to work with faculty -Know students professionally rather than personally -Work very closely within department -Do not know student affairs colleagues in other departments	-Often work with faculty, president, and academic leaders -Many staff are related to one another -Student affairs operates like a family -Staff treat students as family members -Extensive contact with parents guided by notion of co-parenting	-Often work with faculty, president, academic leaders -Student affairs staff small -Student affairs colleagues like family	-Work closely with some faculty, not bothered by faculty who do not understand student affairs -Believe support staff are overworked and underpaid -Work closely with families of students -Relations with other guided by respect
Nature of Rewards						
-Able to see growth in students -Relatively low salaries; limited benefits -Rural location of many campuses has advantages and disadvantages	-View work as a calling -Salaries low and benefits limited -Able to integrate faith into work	-Value work with underserved students -Value autonomy -Limited advancement opportunities leads to higher turnover	-Salary and benefits good -Access to student and support staff good -Advancement opportunities good -Believe they serve students rather than seeing student growth	-Meaningful work associated with racial uplift -Salary and benefits important to professionals, though limited -Autonomy not valued or sought	-Highly value service to underserved groups -See students transformed -Evening and weekend hours limited -Work recognized by others on campus -Salary and benefits good	-Salary and benefits more highly valued -Advancement opportunities more highly valued -Recognition not valued

significant others are. In a phrase, they come to know their students. Many professionals at liberal arts institutions have ancillary job responsibilities in addition to their major functions. As such, they work with students in multiple settings and promote development in multiple arenas. Knowing students as individuals and educating students holistically are the standards of the profession, and administrators at liberal arts colleges embrace those standards in their daily practice.

They accomplish their work on campuses that are typically small and steeped in history and tradition. Change at these institutions is slow, to a large extent due to the politics that come into play. Professionals tend to operate with a high degree of autonomy, primarily because most are the only administrators on their campus charged with a certain set of tasks. This also means that they spend extensive hours at work, including many evening and weekend commitments. Those with spouses, partners, and children find that they can involve those people in campus life and that helps them balance their professional and personal lives.

Relationships at liberal arts colleges vary by constituency groups. Faculty members have a fair amount of power, yet not all faculty members understand and/or appreciate the role that student affairs administrators play on their campuses. Students are bright, energetic, and enthusiastic, but many come from relatively wealthy backgrounds and that can lead to a sense of entitlement, a sentiment echoed by their parents. Relationships with student affairs colleagues, however, are quite close. The upside to this is that there is a great deal of support and collaboration among professionals. The downside is that maintaining relationships with colleagues consumes both time and energy.

The rewards associated with working at a liberal arts institution are primarily intrinsic. Engaging in meaningful work is of prime importance. Student affairs administrators work on such an individual basis with students and get to know them so well that they can see the changes that their students undergo while enrolled in college. This is what makes their work so worthwhile, and it is powerful because it offsets other rewards that are more problematic. Salaries tend to be lower at liberal arts colleges, and benefit packages and advancement opportunities are more limited. Many of these campuses are in rural locations. This location is beneficial in that the lower cost of living can offset the diminished salary. For those with spouses/partners and families, the location may enable them to integrate family life with campus life. For those who are single, the location may impose some social limitations.

Those who aspire to work at liberal arts institutions would be well served to prepare themselves in certain ways. First, an understanding of multiple functional areas in student affairs might make them more competitive for positions on campuses where ancillary duties are the norm rather than the exception. Second, developing strong interpersonal skills would be beneficial. Such skills should enable professionals to more readily establish the close relationships with students that are the hallmark of working at a liberal arts college. The ability to relate well to others would also serve administrators in maintaining the close relationships with student affairs colleagues that are characteristic of liberal arts campuses. Honing political sensitivities would also be helpful. Faculty, alumni, and parents all represent fairly powerful constituency groups on these campuses, and groups with which student affairs professionals interact fairly regularly. Finally, those considering careers at liberal arts institutions might want to assess the intersection between their professional and their personal aspirations. Most of these campuses are small, and they are frequently located in rural areas. These characteristics influence cost of living, social life, advanced educational opportunities, and other aspects of life that may impact professionals in profound ways.

The Interpreters at Religiously Affiliated Institutions

Administrative life at religiously affiliated institutions poses a different set of circumstances. Many of these institutions are small, and their primary focus is on undergraduate education that integrates spiritual development into campus life. The separation of church and state that prevails in secular institutions is an anathema at religiously affiliated campuses. In fact, their missions delineate their role in promoting the religious and ethical development of their students.

On occasion, this emphasis can pose challenges for student affairs administrators. The professional cant calls upon practitioners to promote self-exploration and discovery among students. At times, such discovery leads students to conclusions that are at odds with denominational canons. Topics like abortion, sexual orientation, capital punishment, stem cell research, and others are typically addressed in denominational teachings, but students do not always adopt those teachings. In fact, one of the fundamental hallmarks of higher education is to encourage students to question issues and to develop a personal set of values based on the principles they have adopted as their own after thoughtful and thorough consideration. Student affairs professionals on religiously affiliated campuses often serve as interpreters when those principles contradict religious teaching. They translate student learning theory to religious leaders on campus to explain how students have come to some conclusions. They translate denominational canons in instances when those tenets cause dissonance for students. Perhaps most important, they interpret their own personal faith into the work they perform on campus.

That work takes on different forms than the tasks that professionals at other types of institutions perform. Those at religiously affiliated colleges spend much less time on administrative tasks and somewhat less time working with individual students but devote a significantly greater portion of time to teaching activities. There are typically fewer student affairs professionals on small religiously affiliated campuses, but their input is valued, and they serve on numerous committees and influence decisions in important ways.

Work is conducted on campuses that are perhaps more steeped in tradition than even their liberal arts counterparts. Faculty, academic administrators, alumni, staff, and students are all far more likely to know the history and traditions of the institution. As a result, change occurs very slowly, and professionals often find themselves addressing issues reactively rather than proactively. Interestingly, there is less bureaucracy at religiously affiliated institutions than at other types of colleges and universities. This difference may be due to the centralized leadership on such campuses. They tend to be led by clerics. As a result, there is an additional layer of politics that professionals need to be attuned to—the politics of the church.

This climate influences the relationships that student affairs administrators have with others on their campuses. Many (though not all) faculty on these campuses are as concerned about student development as professionals. As a result, partnerships with faculty are more frequent at religiously affiliated campuses. Relationships with parents of students also tend to be less contentious; they are often viewed as partners in the educational endeavor. There is a strong sense of team and collaboration among members of the student affairs staff. Even the terminology used to describe colleagues—devoted, dedicated, faithful—reflects the denominational nature of the institution. Without a doubt, however, it is relationships with students that are at the heart of professionals' work at religiously affiliated institutions. They view those relationships as life giving and precious, again a reflection of the religious climate of the campus.

The rewards for student affairs practitioners at religiously affiliated institutions are highly intrinsic, which may be a good thing because extrinsic rewards like salaries, benefits, equipment, and support staff often are limited at these colleges. Administrators view their work as a calling, a personal mission, and they thrive in an environment that enables them to work with students in spiritual matters. They talk about how their work allows them to integrate their own spirituality into the work they do with students. Their professional lives truly feed their souls.

All these factors suggest a unique set of skills that might be required to succeed professionally at religiously affiliated institutions. First, a thorough understanding of student development theory and practice is needed. Second, a thorough understanding of the tenets of the particular denomination is needed. When professionals are well versed in both they are in a better position to translate one context into the other and interpret both contexts to appropriate constituencies on their campuses. Additionally, an understanding of the denomination may enable administrators to better understand the additional political implications of working on the campus. Finally, and perhaps most important, student affairs professionals who work at religiously affiliated campuses need to have a clear sense of their own spirituality and an abiding faith. This belief system seems to be essential to their work, and their professional fulfillment stems from their ability to integrate that faith into their daily work.

The Generalists at Comprehensive Institutions

The comprehensive university is a hybrid that blends the focus on a liberal arts education for undergraduates with professional training at the graduate level. Most are public, regional institutions that enroll fewer than 5,000 students. Perhaps more germane to the professionals who work on these campuses, comprehensive universities tend to educate students from historically underserved populations at the undergraduate level and working adults at the graduate level. Collectively, the nature of the comprehensive institution requires student affairs professionals who are generalists. They need to be equally as skilled working with undergraduates as graduates. They need to have as great an appreciation for the liberal arts tradition as they do for graduate professional training. The multifaceted nature of these institutions requires administrators who can operate from varied perspectives.

The work of the generalists on these campuses is markedly different than for student affairs professionals on other campuses. For one, they are as likely to teach like their counterparts at religiously affiliated campuses, but at comprehensives professionals teach graduate students rather than undergraduates. Presumably, they are teaching in human resources, counseling, or student affairs graduate programs that would be reasonable components of the professional programs typically housed on such campuses. Beyond teaching, those at comprehensive institutions have opportunities to work with professionals across campus and to gain exposure to many functional areas of student affairs administration. This diversity contributes to their ability to view issues from multiple perspectives.

Such abilities are helpful given the nature of the work environment on comprehensive campuses. These institutions tend to be highly bureaucratic and centralized. Many (though not all) are members of statewide systems, which may help explain the bureaucracy and centralization to a degree. It also may explain the highly political nature of these campuses; the politics are often associated with system-wide or state-wide issues. Regardless, the generalists readily cope with these elements of campus life. They have an uncanny ability to appreciate both the positive and negative aspects of their campus's characteristics. This skill serves them well in an environment that is relatively quick to change. These changes tend to be more reactive than proactive, however. They are frequently in response to demands for programs from their service region.

Relationships at comprehensive institutions are also different from those at other types of campuses, and this seems to be tied to professionals' ability to view issues from a variety of perspectives. For example, faculty members at comprehensives are not as likely to recognize or appreciate the work of student affairs professionals, but the generalists accept this attitude as the norm. After all, faculty members are meeting the demands of both undergraduate and graduate students and cannot be expected to meet those of student affairs professionals. Administrators work extensively with their student affairs colleagues on comprehensive campuses, as might be expected given the opportunities they have to work across functional areas. Their relationships with students are also influenced by their institutional settings. They are highly sensitive to the multiple roles that their students often fulfill. They structure many of their programs and services to address those needs (at both the undergraduate and the graduate level).

In exchange for their efforts, the generalists at comprehensive campuses value the intrinsic rewards they earn. They are committed to serving the special groups of students who are drawn to their campuses and see themselves as educating those who would not otherwise have access to higher education. The student population enables them to approach their work tasks in creative and unique ways. They delight in the autonomy they have to work across areas and to influence decisions in multiple arenas. The only downside they report is that advancement opportunities are somewhat limited. That may explain the relatively high rate of turnover reported by professionals at these institutions.

To succeed as a generalist at a comprehensive institution, professionals need certain skills. For one, organizational skills and an understanding of institutional systems will enable student affairs administrators to appreciate the bureaucratic and centralized nature of comprehensive campuses. Since many comprehensives are part of larger state systems, practitioners would be wise to garner an understanding of their particular system early on in their tenure. This knowledge may enable them to better anticipate the system-wide demands that may be placed on them. Knowledge of multiple functional areas would also enable administrators to transition more readily into the comprehensive institutional climate. A thorough understanding of populations underserved in higher education, as well as adult learners, would provide professionals with an intellectual understanding of the student clientele with which they are likely to work. They can couple this knowledge base with their actual experiences with students to fine tune their grasp on their clientele. Finally, they ought to have a passion for working with underserved populations. It is the fueling of that passion that will fulfill them in the work at a comprehensive institution.

The Specialists at Research Universities

Research universities are large, complex, decentralized organizations that value power, prestige, and the generation of knowledge over the transmission of knowledge. Specialization is perhaps the dominant trait of research universities. They are difficult to comprehend and navigate both physically and psychologically. These collective attributes influence student affairs professionals at research institutions who describe themselves as specialists.

Since the majority of graduate preparation programs in higher education and student affairs are housed at research universities, many professionals are socialized to the norms of these campuses; or at least socialized to the extent possible in graduate student roles. There are aspects of professional life at these campuses, however, that still take new professionals by surprise. For example, they tend to understand (and appreciate) the need for the extensive bureaucratization needed in large organizations like research universities. They have less of an appreciation for the politically charged environments of these campuses. The politics are often driven by the competition that is characteristic of research environments. Indeed, the two most enduring attributes on research campuses are the degree of competition among units and the risk taking and creativity that this competition promotes. This is not to say that this sense of competition is particularly vicious. In fact, it is fairly covert; but powerful nonetheless, as illustrated by the relationships professionals have with others on their campuses.

Those at research institutions not only do not work very extensively with faculty, they do not expect to do so. They recognize the competing demands that faculty members address. Their relationships with students are also different than those at liberal arts, religiously affiliated, or comprehensive institutions. They get to know a limited number of students fairly well but not large numbers. Nor are they typically known by large numbers of students. Their relationships with students tend to be more professional than personal. It is their relationships with other student affairs colleagues, however, that are most different than what is found at other institutions. Since research campuses are relatively large, most student affairs departments are relatively large. Professionals on these campuses tend to work very closely with their departmental colleagues and, at times, with colleagues in one or two other departments. But there is not a campus-wide student affairs identity that is evident at other institutional types.

These conditions also lead to different rewards for this group of student affairs professionals. For instance, in terms of extrinsic rewards, salary and benefit packages tend to be satisfactory for those at research universities. Access to student staff, graduate student staff, and support staff is greater. Professional development opportunities are fairly rife; in fact, those at research campuses devote more time to professional association activities than their counterparts at all other types of institutions. Their intrinsic rewards are manifest in very different ways, however. Whereas those at other institutions develop deep, personal relationships with students and can *see* the changes in their students at graduation, those at research universities *believe* that what they do on a daily basis makes a difference in the lives of students. Positive working relationships for those at research institutions are those within their departments, not those across campus as at other types of colleges and universities. Advancement opportunities are plentiful in research organizations so not particularly valued by those who work there. In general, they thrive on the risk taking and creativity that are not only accepted but in fact expected at research institutions.

The skills student affairs administrators need to succeed in the research environment are different as well. First, developing expertise in a single functional area might prepare professionals for the specialization that is endemic on research campuses. It would also enable them to establish strong intradepartmental relationships that characterize work on the campuses. Since the generation of knowledge is valued on research campuses, the ability to conduct research, assessment, and evaluation would enable them to communicate in the preferred language of the campus. A high tolerance for risk and a well-honed creative talent would also serve them well. Finally, they need an appreciation for competition and an ability to engage in healthy forms of rivalry.

The Guardians at Historically Black Colleges and Universities

The 103 HBCUs in this country were founded to educate the descendents of slaves. Over the century and a half that they have existed, they have struggled to survive. Much of that struggle can be attributed to policies adopted at the state and federal levels that were often costly and contradictory. This history has generated a deep and abiding distrust of the dominant culture among those devoted to HBCUs. Although they enroll a diverse group of students, their missions specifically focus on promoting the interests of Blacks. The student affairs professionals employed at HBCUs take that mandate seriously. As a result, they find themselves assuming the role of guardian in two senses of the word. First, they act as guardians for the students they serve. Second, they are guardians of the HBCU system and serve as sentinels protecting race-based education in the U.S.

Perhaps the prevailing attribute of the HBCU work environment is the lack of resources. This concern has politicized the work environment as individual units compete for those resources. This competition is highly relational, however. The campus politics are based on the relationships that professionals have with others at the institution. In fact, many of the environmental characteristics at HBCUs are dependent upon interpersonal associations. For example, once resources are secured, the bureaucracy that must be navigated to expend those resources relies upon maintaining positive relations with those on campus who administer them. HBCUs are slow to adopt change because the relationships on campus need to be protected and nurtured; change often takes a back seat if it jeopardizes those associations.

The nature of relationships between student affairs professionals and other groups on campus, then, merit attention. Almost without exception, administrators report family-like relations with others on their campuses. They frequently team with academic administrators. Campuses are typically small enough that professionals know their president and work with that person on student-related issues. Their work with student affairs colleagues is highly collaborative; they rely on one another extensively for both professional and personal support. Since many staff members on HBCU campuses are literally related to one another (by birth or marriage), and since many serve their entire careers at a single institution, it is not unusual to deal with the same individuals for decades. It is their relationships with students and their families that dominate life for HBCU professionals, however. They see themselves as surrogate family members—parents, grandparents, siblings—when working with students. And they believe students see them in such roles. This may make it easier when dealing with parents. Professionals adopt a perspective of co-parenting; they partner with parents to guide students to success.

It is their role as guardians that they treasure most. Meaningful work for those at HBCUs is directly linked to the notion of racial uplift. They understand that their students are frequently underprepared for college and often come from lower income families. They thrive on the idea of polishing these "diamonds in the rough" and seeing Black students grow, develop, and succeed. This attitude may be influenced by the fact that many HBCU student affairs professionals are products of HBCUs themselves. Often they are alumni of the institutions where they work. Their perceptions of other rewards differ in some important ways from their counterparts at other types of institutions. For one, they place a high priority on salary and benefits, perhaps because both tend to be limited at HBCUs. Autonomy, an intrinsic reward that is highly rated by administrators at other types of campuses, is not at all valued at HBCUs. Again, their sense of connection to others on campus likely diminishes any desire (or need) for autonomy.

The skills and experiences needed to succeed at a HBCU, therefore, differ from those needed to achieve at other institutional types. First, an appreciation of the historical evolution of this unique group of institutions might help professionals understand how external forces have buffeted them over time and how that has created a sense of distrust of external entities. Second, a sound understanding of the characteristics of first generation, low income, and academically underprepared students would enable student affairs administrators to deal with the majority of students at HBCUs more readily. Additionally, those who work at these campuses have to have strong interpersonal relations skills. They need to be able to establish and sustain working relationships with a wide variety of constituency groups. Indeed, their professional success may be linked to their ability to maintain relationships. Finally, and perhaps most important, those who aspire to work at HBCUs would be well served to have a powerful commitment to promoting success among Black students. It is this personal investment that seems to draw professionals to HBCU settings and to keep them there.

The Producers of the Community Colleges

The community colleges are truly the workhorses of the American higher education system. They represent 36% of all non-profit institutions and enroll

40% of all college students. In some ways, it is difficult to characterize community colleges since they vary dramatically in terms of size and organizational structure. Some are multi-campus institutions whereas others are stand-alone campuses. Their focus on service to their local area means that their programmatic offerings can differ radically. Despite their variations, there are some common elements that can be identified among these institutions. The most prominent is that student affairs staffs at most community colleges are small (fewer than 12). These personnel handle all functions for all students, however. Since students can range in age from 18 to 80 and may be pursuing any of a number of outcomes (i.e., transfer, vocational, developmental, or continuing education), professionals at community colleges manage an incredible workload. For this reason, they are the producers.

The work environment at community colleges can be characterized in several ways. To start, staff members at these institutions often feel their campuses are marginalized and refer to them as "the stepchild" of higher education. This feeling may be partially attributed to the historical roots of many community colleges that emerged from K-12 education systems. It may also be attributable to the two- versus four-year focus. Whatever the causes, professionals perceive their institutional environments to be out of the mainstream. Beyond that, there are other environmental factors shared by many community colleges. They are highly bureaucratized, more so than any other institutional type. This characteristic is somewhat surprising since they are also the quickest to make major decisions and to adopt change of all types. Much of this change has to do with the introduction of new academic programs, but student affairs administrators must adapt their practices to accommodate those programs. This need leads to another characteristic of the community college work environment: Most change is externally generated. That is, professionals respond to changes that are imposed on them rather than initiating changes from within. This reactivity may be why conformity and security are more valued by those at community colleges than by administrators at all other types of campuses. When change is frequent and externally generated, conformity and security are harder to come by, hence more important. Collectively, these environmental factors create a high stress atmosphere for student affairs professionals at community colleges, though that stress is ameliorated to some degree by the relationships they have with other constituencies on campus.

One reason why relationships at community colleges are so positive has to do with the issue of mission. These institutions have clearly defined missions, and those who work at community colleges understand and embrace those missions. This tendency puts everybody on the same page. It is not surprising, then, that student affairs professionals know and frequently work with the president and academic administrators on their campuses. Their relationships with faculty are far more cordial than at any other institutional type. Like their counterparts at HBCUs, administrators at community colleges view their student affairs colleagues as family. The small size of most staffs, coupled with the fact that there is very little turnover, means that professionals work with one another for years, even decades. Over that sort of time period, close bonds are formed. Their longevity might well be attributed to their relationships with students. Students at community colleges are by far the most diverse of any institutional type. There are disproportionately high numbers of first generation, low income, women, minority, adult, and academically underprepared students at community colleges, and student affairs professionals thrive on serving these individuals. The rewards they value most are tied to students.

Like administrators at all other types of institutions, engaging in meaningful work is the most highly valued reward among professionals at community colleges. They are able to see growth and development in their students, similar to their colleagues at liberal arts institutions and HBCUs. They also value the positive relationships they have with others on campus. They receive recognition from colleagues and academic leaders, probably because they frequently work closely with them so leaders have a clearer understanding of the worth of their contributions. Finally, there are two extrinsic rewards about which those at community colleges talk. The first has to do with work schedules. They are much less likely to work evening and weekend hours than professionals at other types of campuses. Much of their work is accomplished during normal business hours. Second, many such institutions are public but are located in rural regions. As state agencies, staff members are paid according to statewide salary ranges. Because they are located in rural regions where the cost of living is lower, this often translates to a very reasonable salary, hence quality of life.

The nature of work life at community colleges suggests that successful administrators at these institutions have a skill set that differs from those required at other types of campuses. To start, individuals with an understanding of systems are more likely to appreciate the high level of bureaucracy at community colleges. Likewise, professionals need to be able to work in settings where externally imposed mandates are the norm and should enjoy rising to the administrative challenges such changes present. They need a solid understanding of the students they serve (e.g., first generation, low income, adult, minority). Knowledge of the historical evolution of community colleges might enable them to better understand the mission of these institutions and the niche that they fill in the higher education hierarchy. Finally, community college professionals must be able to function at high levels of productivity and high levels of quality nearly all of the time.

The Change Agents at Hispanic-Serving Institutions

The HSIs are perhaps the most elusive group of colleges and universities to characterize. Unlike liberal arts colleges, comprehensive campuses, research universities, or community colleges, HSIs are not mission-driven. Unlike religiously affiliated institutions, most (though not all) HSIs are public and do not include a sectarian focus. Unlike HBCUs, HSIs were not founded specifically to educate Hispanics and, although at least 25% of their student populations are Hispanic, this percentage is nowhere close to the 80% to 90% Black enrollment found at most HBCUs. The clearest way to characterize HSIs is to say that they are a group of institutions, representing the full spectrum of institutional types, that over the past 30 years have increased their enrollment of Hispanic students to such a degree that they merit this label. Professionals at HSIs can be referred to as change agents, but caution should be used when doing so. At times it is difficult to discern whether it is institutional type or HSI status that influences the work life of student affairs administrators.

Given that caveat, there are elements of the work environment that are shared across HSIs. Like comprehensive institutions, there are both centralized and decentralized systems, service and business orientations, and high degrees of professionalism that are both advantageous and disadvantageous at HSIs. Professionals seem to understand and appreciate the divergence they find on their campuses with respect to these issues. Other elements of professional life are more similar to community colleges. HSIs are very quick to adopt change, for example. In many cases this is driven by the explosive growth in enrollment that is occurring at these institutions. This growth means that HSI student affairs administrators often operate in a reactive rather than proactive mode. It also means that risk taking and creativity are fairly rampant on these campuses. As a result, professionals work in a relatively high-stress environment, but they see this environment as a positive challenge, not one that overwhelms them.

Although it may be difficult to differentiate what elements of the work environment reflect institutional type versus HSI designation, relationships at these campuses are distinctive in their own right. Professionals at HSIs look upon all types of constituency groups fairly magnanimously. They enjoy working with faculty who comprehend the nature of student affairs work but understand that not all faculty members are at that point. They believe support staff members provide invaluable help but are overworked and underpaid. They are empathic in their comments when asked what they dislike about other groups on campus. This quality may be attributed in part to the value they attach to "respect" at HSIs, particularly in their dealings with students and families. Student affairs administrators at these institutions realize that their students are often first generation, low income, and academically challenged. In fact, this is what they like about working with students. They find such students more respectful, more self-effacing, and more appreciative of the opportunities available to them. They also are impressed with the degree of involvement that family members of students at HSIs have in their educational endeavors. For many professionals, it is heartwarming to see parents, siblings, grandparents, aunts, uncles, cousins, and distant relatives attend campus ceremonies that celebrate student success. They view this opportunity as one of their most valued rewards of the job.

In terms of other rewards, those at HSIs are like their counterparts at other institutions in some respects; intrinsic rewards are much more highly rated.

Engaging in meaningful work, enjoying good working relationships in a positive environment are also important. There are some differences between those at HSIs and others, however. Salary and benefits are more highly rated at HSIs, as are advancement opportunities. They do not value recognition very highly at HSIs; perhaps this mirrors the modest and unassuming nature of the Hispanic students they serve. The real challenges for those at HSIs are diminishing resources and burgeoning enrollments. They are finding it increasingly difficult to do more with less, and that leads to a degree of professional frustration among administrators at HSIs that was not evident at other institutions.

Those who aspire to succeed at HSIs, then, would be well served to develop certain skills and to acquire certain knowledge bases. For example, fluency in Spanish (even if only moderate) would be an enormous boon to a professional at a HSI, particularly when working with family members for whom English may be a second language. Tolerance for rapid change and risk taking would facilitate the transition to the working environment. A thorough understanding of the challenges that first generation, low income, and academically at-risk students face would assist professionals in their interactions with students. An appreciation for the role that family plays in the Hispanic culture might enable administrators to incorporate family into the campus culture more readily. Finally, professionals at HSIs would benefit from familiarizing themselves with the distinct differences between various elements of the Hispanic culture (e.g., Mexican, Puerto Rican, Guatemalan). Such a knowledge base might enable professionals to interface with students and their families in ways that are most appropriate.

The skills and knowledge bases that might lead to success at different types of colleges and universities are relatively easy to identify. Developing those skills and gaining that knowledge, however, might take place in any number of settings. Since most student affairs administrators begin their careers in graduate preparation programs that is the first place where preparation for differences in practice by institutional types might be addressed.

Implications for Practice at the Graduate Preparation Level

It is important to remember that almost three-quarters (70%) of graduate preparation programs in higher education and student affairs administration are housed at research universities. Nearly all the rest are at comprehensive institutions. The socialization of new professionals that occurs during the graduate education process is powerful, and the role of the campus environment in that process is commanding. That is, most graduate students are socialized to the research or comprehensive university environment. There are some exceptions to this. For example, there is a smattering of graduate programs that offer special tracks for those interested in working at community colleges. These are exceptions, however, not the norm. For the most part, graduate programs best prepare professionals to work in select environments. This deficit suggests that a conscious and concerted effort will need to be made if differences in professional practice by institutional type are to be addressed in graduate programs.

There are several constituencies that might engage in such efforts. The first is faculty in graduate preparation programs. To start, faculty members might assess their curricular offerings to identify those classes and experiences into which they might infuse notions of institutional differences. For example, courses that talk about college environments and those that address the historical evolution of higher education in this country would seem to be logical classes in which to start introducing institutional differences. There are other classes, however, that may not be as obvious but that also offer opportunities to address issues of environmental differences. Many graduate programs require students to complete courses in program intervention design, the history of the student affairs profession, and higher education law. All these classes could include elements that examine how the issues at hand vary from the perspective of different types of colleges and universities. Certainly any internship or practicum requirements provide opportunities for students to experience professional life at different types of campuses.

Assignments are another arena in which faculty members could introduce concepts associated with institutional type. Research papers that explore matters at varied kinds of institutions or that explore a single problem from the perspective of multiple types of colleges and universities could help students better understand and appreciate how campus environments influence professional practice. Reading assignments that address organizational type can promote broader thinking on the part of graduate students. Research conducted at different types of colleges and universities, or in which the respondents are students at different types of institutions, would also require graduate students to recognize the full spectrum of establishments in the higher education enterprise. Classroom activities and discussions can also be designed to ensure consideration of multiple institutional types.

Finally, faculty members typically serve important roles in the lives of graduate students in higher education and student affairs programs. As advisors, they are in a position to encourage students to think about their own skills, interests, and talents and to help students process the kind of work environment that would best showcase those abilities. Additionally, many programs require students to complete some type of capstone project, be that a research project or other undertaking. Advisors might encourage students to explore issues at different types of institutions for such projects. Activities like these on the part of faculty legitimize other types of campus environments for students. They enable students to realize that the campus at which their graduate program is housed is not the only type of college or university environment in which they might work and help compensate for some of the power of the socialization process.

Those who supervise graduate students in assistantship and internship or practicum settings might also promote understanding of institutional differences. These professionals can offer perspectives based on their years of experience at their current campus as well as previous campuses. When working with students, it is important that supervisors inquire about the materials that students are learning in their graduate classes and try to make connections between that material and the on-the-job training that graduate assistantships and internships offer. This strategy should entail applying the classroom materials not only to the actual setting in which the student is working but also talking with the student about how that material might be interpreted differently at another type of college or university.

On a related note, graduate students should be encouraged to seek out assistantship and internship opportunities at other institutions when circumstances permit. Most graduate preparation programs are at universities, but many times there are liberal arts colleges or other types of institutions within reasonable proximity. Almost certainly there would be a community college within commuting distance. Although there may be administrative obstacles that would need to be addressed to ensure that assistantships on such campuses were equitable to those offered at the student's home campus, working at another type of institution would require students to see student affairs administration through another lens. In turn, those students would be able to share their perspectives with others in the classroom setting. Any opportunity for students to learn from one another about differences in campus settings is likely to increase their appreciation of those differences.

Finally, students themselves should take the initiative to ensure that they learn about as many institutional settings as possible while they are in their graduate programs. Very often students enroll in a graduate program because their experience as undergraduates was so positive (or, at times, so negative) that they seek to offer future generations of students the same meaningful collegiate experience that they had (or to be sure future generations are not subjected to the negative occurrences). Frequently such students assume they will return to the type of institution from which they graduated to accomplish that goal. So those who attended religiously affiliated campuses aspire to return to religiously affiliated campuses, for example. They may see their graduate school experience through the lens of their undergraduate alma mater. Notwithstanding the pressure to adopt the graduate institutions' values exerted through the socialization process, students may elect to adhere to what they know. The graduate experience, however, provides an ideal opportunity to step outside one's comfort zone and try new things.

For example, students might actively pursue topics for class assignments that address issues at other types of campuses. If they were undergraduates at research universities, studying issues associated with life at community colleges might be enlightening. If they are products of comprehensive institutions, learning more about HBCUs might engender new respect for other forms of higher education. Likewise, seeking assistantship and internship opportunities at other types of campuses would promote broader perspectives for students. In particular, summers offer students a wide range of options to learn more about other types of campus environments. A number of professional associations offer summer internship programs. Students may also have families that live near institutions where summer employment opportunities are offered. Any chance to work in a different setting would likely benefit students in multiple ways. For one, they would have a chance to test whether different campus environments are a good match for their interests and abilities. Second, they would gain new perspectives on professional life in different institutional settings. Understanding the complex and multifaceted system of higher education in America is a knowledge base that will serve new professionals well in both their initial administrative capacity and as their careers advance. The recruiting and hiring process may be the first test of such a knowledge base.

Implications for the Hiring and Recruiting Process

Differences in settings where student affairs professionals practice are perhaps most noticeable in the recruiting and hiring process. A perusal of any job announcement publication (e.g., *The Chronicle of Higher Education, Black Issues in Higher Education*) reveals that many colleges and universities seek professionals who have experience in a particular institutional type. That is, announcements for vacancies at research universities often seek candidates with an appreciation for the land grant mission that many of these institutions fulfill. Or, they seek applicants with an appreciation for the complexity of the tripartite mission of the research university. Positions at liberal arts colleges often seek incumbents who have an appreciation for the traditions of liberal education. Community colleges are notorious for requiring prior experience at a community college when hiring professionals. Yet the evidence presented in this volume suggests that the nature of work, relationships, and rewards can cut across institutional types.

For example, professionals at both comprehensive universities and community colleges work in environments that adopt changes rapidly. Professionals at both types of institutions are exposed to a wide variety of functional areas. Administrators at liberal arts colleges and HBCUs develop intensely personal relationships with students and witness development in those students over the course of their college careers. Student affairs practitioners at both HSIs and religiously affiliated institutions work fairly extensively with families of students. Those at both research universities and liberal arts colleges frequently work with students who exhibit a relatively high sense of entitlement, whereas those at HSIs, HBCUs, and community colleges all often work with first generation, low income, academically at risk students. One would think that these types of shared experiences would be considered assets when professionals attempt to move from one type of college or university to another. This is not the case, however. So what must be done to facilitate career shifts across institutional types?

To start, professionals need to recognize what experiences and skills they bring to bear in the marketplace. It is highly likely that those seeking to advance their careers by moving to a new college or university may be misled by verbiage in job announcements that make it sound like prior experience in a particular type of institutional setting is required. An assessment of the work environment, relationships, and rewards at the campus(es) at which the professional has worked might parallel any such requirements. Conversely, some administrators may self-select out of certain job searches because of their beliefs about what the work life at a particular type of college or university might be like. Developing an understanding of what professional life is like at different institutions might enlighten administrators and encourage them to pursue opportunities that they might otherwise dismiss out of hand.

At the other end of the recruiting and hiring process are search committees and employers. These entities would also be well served by an understanding of student affairs professional practice at different types of campuses. When advertising position vacancies, they might want to consider whether experience at a certain type of institution is paramount. It is likely that search committees overlook highly qualified candidates because they are deemed to lack experience at the requisite type of campus. Positions that call for high levels of collaboration among professionals, however, might be successfully filled by student affairs administrators who have worked at liberal arts colleges, religiously affiliated institutions, or HBCUs. The evidence reveals that life at all three types of campuses entails working closely with colleagues. Likewise, those who have worked at HSIs and research universities come from environments where creativity and risk taking are requisites, whereas those at comprehensives are typically capable of appreciating issues from multiple perspectives. Search committees might be well served to focus on the types of skills and experiences that candidates might bring to positions rather than limiting their pools to those who have worked at a certain type of institution.

The recruitment and selection process might also employ techniques to identify applicants who are more likely to succeed. For example, professionals at liberal arts institutions report low levels of satisfaction with extrinsic rewards like benefits but high levels of satisfaction with lifestyle issues (e.g., cost of living in the rural areas where many such schools are located, involving family in campus life). When recruiting candidates to these campuses, employers might want to explore what types of rewards are most meaningful to candidates. Those at community colleges and comprehensive universities are frequently called upon to work in multiple functional areas, and those at liberal arts colleges often hold multiple job titles. These kinds of experiences might serve candidates well in the research university setting where the daily pace of work can be frenetic. Search committees may benefit from exploring how candidates have multi-tasked in previous capacities if the job calls for such abilities.

Finally, it is important that employers realize that the recruiting and selection process is only one step in the integration of new staff members to the campus. Professional development programs on campuses can also be designed to address any experiential gaps in newly hired professionals.

Implications for Professional Development Programs

Although certain skills may transfer from one institutional setting to another, other skill sets and knowledge bases may need to be developed once a newly appointed staff member arrives on campus. For instance, a professional who has worked at a research university may be hired at a liberal arts or religiously affiliated institution because he or she had expertise in a particular functional area; specialization is one of the defining characteristics of professional life at research campuses. However, those at research universities may not have experience developing the close personal relationships with students that are so inherent in the liberal arts and religiously affiliated environments. Remember that those at research universities *believe* that their work makes a difference in the lives of students whereas those at liberal arts and religiously affiliated campuses *see* the differences in their students. The newly hired staff member might benefit from some work in counseling and/or communication to build the skill set necessary to establish and maintain close relationships with students.

In a similar vein, liberal arts and religiously affiliated institutions share an academic focus on liberal education. Professionals at both types of campuses often assume multiple roles and their work with student affairs colleagues can be characterized as familial. If a professional from a liberal arts institution were to be hired at a religiously affiliated campus, however, professional development opportunities that would allow the new staff member to explore how her or his spirituality could play out in the new environment might be warranted. Conversely, if a professional moves from a religiously affiliated college to a liberal arts institution, developing an understanding of the role of faith in a secular setting may prove beneficial.

In other cases, entire staffs might benefit from programs that focus on life at different types of colleges and universities. For example, those at comprehensive institutions are generalists who often work with both traditional and non-traditional students who are both graduates and undergraduates. Development programs designed to provide information about these varied student populations might educate professionals across the student affairs division. The same could be true at HBCUs, HSIs, and community colleges where disproportionately high percentages of low income, first generation, and academically underprepared students enroll.

Finally, the responsibility for honing skills through professional development programs should be noted. On many campuses, there are divisional committees charged with designing and implementing staff development programs each year. Although these efforts are important, there are other approaches to increasing staff effectiveness that should not be overlooked. For one, those who supervise professionals have an obligation to assess the skills and interests of the staff members they supervise and the needs and demands of their functional area, campus, and the profession in general. They can then identify where staff members might benefit from developmental opportunities. Understanding how experiences at other types of institutions might have shaped staff members is a key element to designing professional development opportunities to provide those staffers with the skills and abilities they need to succeed in their current institutional setting.

Likewise, professionals need to assume responsibility for their own development, and understanding differences in the nature of work life at different types of institutions can assist them in their planning. For example, young professionals working at community colleges, liberal arts institutions, religiously affiliated campuses, HBCUs, and many HSIs and comprehensive universities typically earn a master's to launch their careers. Many, however, aspire to higher-level positions and will consider seeking a doctorate at some point in their career. Most doctoral programs are at research universities (though some are at comprehensives). These professionals might work on such campuses while seeking their advanced degrees. If so, understanding professional life at research universities might enable them to undertake professional development opportunities to prepare for that eventuality. In other cases, students might remain employed at one institution while seeking an advanced degree at a research university. Again, recognizing the differences between the environments where one works and where one studies might make life in both settings more meaningful. In all these cases, administrators can assume responsibility for engaging in their own professional developmental opportunities.

Conclusion

The framework presented in this volume offers implications for those who work at different institutional types, for those who train aspiring student affairs professionals, for the recruitment and hiring process, and for the professional development of administrators. I believe the evidence supports the argument that professional practice does not transcend institutional type and that where you work does, in fact, matter. That said I hasten to point out that far more research is needed to explore the other factors that influence professional life for student affairs administrators. For example, if there are commonalities within functional arenas across institutional types, those need to be identified. If student activities administrators at religiously affiliated and comprehensive institutions share common work lives, then discovering those communal elements would advance what is known about the student affairs profession in general. It is certainly conceivable that men and women perceive professional life differently, and the same is likely true for Caucasians and people of color. Further exploration of these differences needs to be undertaken.

To a large extent, the belief that function supercedes setting has guided the development of the student affairs profession. Professional life has been organized to a large extent around functional areas. There are professional associations for those who work in housing and residence life, orientation, advising, career services, student unions, and many other functional areas. Even the cross-functional national associations are organized around function in many regards. There are commissions in the American College Personnel Association (ACPA) devoted to functionally specific groups. In the National Association of Student Personnel Administrators (NASPA), internal organization revolves around geographic region to some extent and populations in other respects. Only in recent years have these associations acknowledged different institutional factors; there are committees that target those at small colleges and two-year colleges. The findings reported in this volume suggest that greater attention to issues of institutional setting is warranted and associations may strive to address these issues in the future.

Overall, then, the framework presented in this book should be viewed not as an ending, but as a point of departure. Questioning the professional cant that function is the driving force behind practice has led to some compelling findings about the role of institutional type in student affairs practitioners. Further inquiries about the work life of administrators can only lead to a richer understanding of our shared profession.

References

Academic Excellence (2002). The tyranny of small numbers. Retrieved April 2, 2003, from www.rescorp.org/AE-rpt3.pdf

Aleman, A. M., & Salkever, K. (2002). *Multiculturalism and the liberal arts college: Faculty perceptions of pedagogy.* Chestnut Hill, MA: Boston College. (ERIC Document Reproduction Service No. ED465357)

Allen, W. R., Epps, E. G., & Haniff, N. Z. (1991). *College in Black and White: African America students in predominately White and historically Black public universities.* Albany: State University of New York Press.

Allen, W. R., & Jewell, J. O. (2002). A backward glance forward: Past, present, and future perspectives on historically black colleges and universities. *Review of Higher Education, 25*(3), 241–261.

American Council on Education. (1937). *The student personnel point of view.* Washington, DC: Author.

American Council on Education. (1949*). The student personnel point of view* (rev. ed.). Washington, DC: Author.

Anaya, G., & Cole, D. G. (2001). Latino/a student achievement: Exploring the influence of student-faculty interactions on college grades. *Journal of College Student Development, 42,* 3–14.

Anderson, C. W. (1993). *Preserving the life of the mind.* Madison: University of Wisconsin Press.

Anderson, J. D. (1988). *Education of Blacks in the South, 1865–1930.* Chapel Hill: University of North Carolina.

Anderson, M. S. (2001). The complex relations between the academy and industry: Views from the literature. *The Journal of Higher Education, 72,* 226–246.

Arnone, M. (2003, January). The wannabes: More public universities are striving to squeeze into the top tier. Can states afford the dreams? *The Chronicle of Higher Education,* p. A18–20.

Association of American Colleges and Universities. (1995). *The drama of diversity and democracy: Higher education and American commitments.* Washington, DC: Author.

Astin, A. W., & Lee, C. B. T. (1972). *The invisible colleges: A profile of small private colleges with limited resources.* New York: McGraw-Hill.

Astin. H., & Antonio, A. L. (2000). Building character in college. *About Campus 5*(5), 3–7.

Averill, L. J. (1969). "Sectarian" higher education and the public interest. *Journal of Higher Education, 40,* 85–100.

Ayers, D. F. (2002). Mission priorities of community colleges in the southern United States. *Community College Review, 30*(3), 1–20.

Basinger, J. (2000, August 11). A new way of classifying colleges elates some and perturbs others. *The Chronicle of Higher Education,* pp. A31–A42.

Benitez, M. (1998). Hispanic serving institutions: Challenges and opportunities. In J. P. Merisotis & C. T. O'Brien (Eds.), *Minority-serving institutions: Distinct purposes, common goals* (pp. 57–68). San Francisco: Jossey-Bass.

Billingsley, A. (1982). Building strong faculties in black colleges. *The Journal of Negro Education, 51*(1), 4–15.

Blackhurst, A., Brandt, J., & Kalinowski, J. (1998). Effects of personal and work-related attributes on the organizational commitment and life satisfaction of women student affairs administrators. *NASPA Journal, 35,* 86–108.

Bloland, P. A. (1992). *The professionalization of student affairs staff.* Ann Arbor, MI: ERIC Clearinghouse on Counseling and Personnel Services. (ERIC Document Reproduction Service No. ED347495)

Blumhofer, E. L. (2002). *Religion, education, and the American experience: Reflections on religion and American public life.* Tuscaloosa: University of Alabama Press.

Bohr, L., Pascarella, E. T., Nora, A., & Terenzini, P. T. (1995). Do black students learn more at historically black or predominantly white colleges? *Journal of College Student Development, 36,* 75–85.

Breneman, D. W. (1990). Are we losing our liberal arts colleges? *College Board Review, 156,* 16–21, 29.

Breneman, D. W. (1994). *Liberal arts colleges: Thriving, surviving, or endangered?* Washington, DC: The Brookings Institution.

Brown v. Board of Education, 347 U.S. 483 (1954).

Brown, L. M. (1999). Creating opportunities for faculty research. *Black Issues in Higher Education, 16*(20), 34–39.

Brown, M. C., & Davis, J. E. (2001). The historically black college as social contract, social capital, and social equalizer. *Peabody Journal of Education, 76*(1), 31–49.

Brown, M. C., Donahoo, S., & Bertrand, R. D. (2001). The black college and the quest for educational opportunity. *Urban Education, 36*(5), 553–571.

Brown, S. E., Santiago, D., & Lopez, E. (2003, March/April). Latinos in higher education: Today and tomorrow. *Change, 35*(2), 40–46.

Browning, J. E. S., & Williams, J. B. (1978). History and goals of Black institutions of higher learning. In C.V. Willie & R. R. Edmonds (Eds.), *Black colleges in America: Challenge, development, survival (*pp. 68–93). New York: Teachers College Press.

Brownlee, S., & Linnon, N. (1990, October 15). Regional universities: Serving those who seek professional and occupational degrees, these schools occupy an important middle ground in higher education. *U.S. News and World Report*, 128–130.

Brubacher, J. S., & Rudy, W. (1997). *Higher education in transition: A history of colleges and universities* (4th ed). New Brunswick, NJ: Transaction Publishers.

Bullock, H. A. (1967). *A history of Negro education in the South: From 1619 to the present.* New York: Praeger.

Burhorn, J. F. (1980). *A study of decision making responsibility in small private liberal arts colleges as perceived by selected college groups.* Unpublished doctoral dissertation. Walden University.

Burns, M. A. (1982). Who leaves the student affairs field? *NASPA Journal, 20,* 9–12.

Burtchaell, J. (1998). *The dying of the light: The disengagement of colleges and universities from their Christian churches.* Grand Rapids, MI: Eerdmans.

Butler, J. (1990) *Awash in a sea of faith: Christianizing the American people.* Cambridge, MA: Harvard University Press.

Canon, H. J. (1982). Toward professionalization in student affairs. Another point of view. *Journal of College Student Personnel, 23,* 468–473.

Carnegie Foundation for the Advancement of Teaching. (2000). *The Carnegie classification of institutions of higher education.* Retrieved July 17, 2003, from http://www.carnegiefoundation.org/Classification/index.htm

Carnegie Foundation for the Advancement of Teaching. (2001). *Carnegie classification of institutions of higher education, 2000 edition.* Menlo Park, CA: Author.

Cejda, B. D., & Duemer, L. S. (2001, April). *The curriculum of liberal arts colleges: Beyond the major.* Paper presented at the Annual Meeting of the American Educational Research Association, Seattle, WA. (ERIC Document Reproduction Service No. ED451799)

Chambers, F. (1972). Histories of black colleges and universities. *The Journal of Negro History, 57*(3), 270–275.

Chan, S. S., & Burton, J. (1995). Faculty vitality in the comprehensive university: Changing context and concerns. *Research in Higher Education, 36,* 217–234.

Checkoway, B. (2001). Renewing the civic mission of the American research university. *The Journal of Higher Education, 72,* 125–147.

Chickering, A. W., & Gamson, Z. F. (1987, June). Seven principles for good practice in undergraduate education. *The Wingspread Journal, 9,* 2.

Clark, B. R. (1988, March). *The absorbing errand.* Paper presented at the meeting of the American Association of Higher Education, Washington, DC.

Clowes, D. H., & Levin, B. H. (1989). Community, technical and junior colleges: Are they leaving higher education? *Journal of Higher Education, 60,* 346–355.

Coaxum, J. (2001). The misalignment between the Carnegie classifications and black colleges. *Urban Education, 36*(5), 572–584.

Cohen, A. M. (1998). *The shaping of American higher education.* San Francisco: Jossey-Bass.

Cohen, A. M., & Brawer, F. B. (1989). *The American community college* (2nd ed.). San Francisco: Jossey-Bass.

Cohen, A. M., & Brawer, F. B. (2003). *The American community college* (4th ed.). San Francisco: Jossey-Bass.

Cohen, E. I. (1991). The changing role of research in masters'-only institutions: The cause for change. *Proceedings of the Council of Graduate Schools, USA, 31,* 53–59.

Coleman, C. D. (1960). The Christian Methodist Episcopal Church: The rationale and policies upon which support of its colleges is predicated. *Journal of Negro Education, 29,* 315–318.

Cremin, L. (1970). *American education: The colonial experience.* New York: Harper Collins.

Cross, K. P. (1971). Access and accommodation in higher education. *Research Reporter, 6*(2), 6–8.

Dalton, J. C., & Gardner, D. I. (2002). Managing change in student affairs leadership roles. In J. C. Dalton & M. McClinton, *The art and practical wisdom of student affairs leadership* (New Directions for Student Services, No. 98, pp. 37–47). San Francisco: Jossey-Bass.

Dassance, C. R. (1994). Student services. In A. M. Cohen & F. B. Brawer, *Managing community colleges: A handbook for effective practice.* San Francisco: Jossey-Bass.

Davis, R. B. (1991). Social support networks and undergraduate student academic-success-related outcomes: A comparison of black students on black and white campuses. In W. R. Allen, E. G. Epps, & N. Z. Haniff (Eds.), *College in Black and White: African American students in predominantly White and in Historically Black Public Universities* (pp. 143–160). Albany: State University Press of New York Press.

Delucchi, M. (1997). "Liberal arts" colleges and the myth of uniqueness. *Journal of Higher Education, 68,* 414–426.

Delworth, U., & Hanson, G. R. (1989). *Student services: A handbook for the profession* (2nd ed.). San Francisco: Jossey-Bass.

Deutsch, L. J., & Stanford, S. (1990). Graduate faculty appointments: Deciding who teaches in the master's degree program. *Proceedings of the Council of Graduate Schools, USA, 30,* 115–119.

Devarics, C. (2000). Hispanic-serving institutions make impressive strides. *Black Issues in Higher Education, 17*(9), 32–35.

Diener, T. (1985). Job satisfaction and college faculty in two predominately black institutions. *The Journal of Negro Education, 54*(4), 558–565.

Doucette, D. S., & Dayton, L. L. (1989). A framework for student development practices: A statement of the league for innovations in the community college. In J. C. Dalton & M. McClinton (Eds.), *The art and practical wisdom of student affairs leadership* (New Directions for Student Services, No. 98, pp. 61–70). San Francisco: Jossey-Bass.

Durbin, N. E., & Kent, L. (1989). Postsecondary education of white women in 1900. *Sociology of Education, 62,* 1–13.

Educating the largest minority group. (2003, November 28). *The Chronicle of Higher Education*, pp. B6–B9.

Educational attainment: Better than meets the eye, but large challenges remain. (2002). Pew Hispanic Fact Sheet. Retrieved June 28, 2004, from www.pewhispanic.org

Eimers, M. T., Braxton, J. M., & Bayer, A. E. (1998, November). *The implications of teaching norms for the improvement of undergraduate education in teaching-oriented colleges.* Paper presented at the annual conference of the Association for the Study of Higher Education. Miami, FL. (ERIC Document Reproduction Service No. ED427587)

Estanek, S. M. (1999). Student affairs and truth: A reading of the great books. *NASPA Journal, 36,* 278–287.

Ethington, C., & Smart, J. (1986). Persistence to graduate education. *Research in Higher Education, 24,* 287–303.

Etzkowitz, H., Webster, A., & Healey, P. (Eds.). (1998*). Capitalizing knowledge: New intersections of industry and academia.* Albany: State University of New York Press.

Evans, A. L., Evans, V., & Evans, A. M. (2002). Historically black colleges and universities (HBCUs). *Education, 123*(1), 3–16, 180.

Evans, N. J. (1988). Attrition of student affairs professionals: A review of the literature. *Journal of College Student Development, 29,* 19–24.

Fairweather, J. S. (1994). Faculty rewards: The comprehensive college and university story. *Metropolitan Universities, 5,* 54–61.

Fenske, R. H. (1989). Evolution of the student services profession. In U. Delworth & G. Hanson (Eds.), *Student services: A handbook for the profession* (2nd ed., pp. 25–56). San Francisco: Jossey-Bass.

Fields, C. D. (2000). Can HBCUs compete for Black faculty? *Black Issues in Higher Education, 17*(20), 39–41.

Fincher, C. (1989, August). *The influence of British and German universities on the historical development of American universities.* Paper presented at the Annual Forum of the European Association for Institutional Research, Trier, Germany. (ERIC Document Reproduction Service No. ED443301)

Finnegan, D. E., & Gamson, Z. F. (1996). Disciplinary adaptations to research culture in comprehensive institutions. *The Review of Higher Education, 19,* 141–177.

Freeman, K., & Thomas, G. E. (2002). Black colleges and college choice: Characteristics of students who choose HBCUs. *Review of Higher Education, 25*(3), 349–358.

Gamson, Z. (1997). Higher education and rebuilding civic life. *Change, 29,* 10–13.

Garcia, E. (2001). *Hispanic education in the United States: Raices y Alas.* Lanham, MD: Rowman & Littlefield.

Garibaldi, A. (1984). *Black colleges and universities: Challenges for the future.* New York: Praeger.

Gary, L. E. (1975). The significance of research for the survival of black colleges. *Journal of Black Studies, 6*(1), 35–34.

Geiger, R. (1985). After the emergence: Voluntary support and the building of American research universities. *History of Education Quarterly, 25,* 369–381.

Geiger, R. L. (1990). Organized research units: Their role in the development of university research. *Journal of Higher Education, 61,* 1–19.

Geiger, R. L. (2000). *The American college in the nineteenth century.* Nashville, TN: Vanderbilt University Press.

Gleazar, E. F., Jr. (1980). *The community college: Values, vision and vitality.* Washington, DC: American Association of Community and Junior Colleges.

Gloria, A. M., & Rodriguez, E. R. (2000). Counseling Latino university students: Psychosociocultural issues for consideration. *Journal of Counseling and Development, 78,* 145–154.

Goldman, B. A., & Beach, S. S. (2001). Unique and highly acclaimed. *Community College Journal, 71*(5), 46–49.

Gratz v. Bollinger, 539 U.S. 244 (2003).

Gregory, M. (2003, September 12). A liberal education is not a luxury. *The Chronicle of Higher Education,* p. B16.

Gregory, S. T. (2003). Planning for the increasing number of Latino students. *Planning for Higher Education, 31*(4), 13–19.

Grutter v. Bollinger, 539 U.S. 982 (2003).

Guthrie, D. S. (1992). Mapping the terrain of church-related colleges and universities. In D. S. Guthrie & R. L. Noftzger (Eds.), *Agendas for church-related colleges and universities* (pp. 3–18). San Francisco: Jossey-Bass.

Hackney, S. (1986). The university and its community: Past and present. *Annals of the American Academy of Political and Social Science, 488,* 135–147.

Harkavy, I. (1997). The demands of the times and the American research university. *Journal of Planning Literature, 11,* 333–336.

Harley, D. A. (2001). Desegregation at HBCUs: Removing barriers and implementing strategies. *The Negro Educational Review, 52*(4), 151–164.

Hekelman, F. P., Zyzanski, S. J., & Flocke, S. A. (1995). Successful and less-successful research performance of junior faculty. *Research in Higher Education, 36,* 235–251.

Henderson, B. B., & Kane, W. D. (1991). Caught in the middle: faculty and institutional status and quality in state comprehensive universities. *Higher Education, 22,* 339–350.

Hernandez, J. (2002). A qualitative exploration of the first-year experience of Latino college students. *NASPA Journal, 40*(1), 69–84.

Hersh, R. H. (1999) Generating ideals and transforming lives: A contemporary case for the residential liberal arts college. *Daedalus, 128*(1), 173–175.

Hickney, A. A., Cohen, E. L., & Reid-Williams, S. (1991). Changing role of research in master's programs. *Proceedings of the Council of Graduate Schools, USA, 31,* 53–59.

Hickson, M. G. (2002). What role does the race of professors have on the retention of students attending historically black colleges and universities? *Education, 123*(1), 186–189.

Higher Education Research Institute, University of California at Los Angeles. *The American freshmen: National norms for the Fall 1996.* Los Angeles: Author.

Hirt, J. B. (1992). Professionalism, power, and prestige: Ideology and practice in student affairs. *Dissertation Abstracts International, 53*(02A), 0420. (UMI No. 9220679)

Hirt, J. B. (2001). [Where are aspiring student affairs professionals trained?] Unpublished raw data.

Hispanic yearbook. (2002). McLean, VA: TIYM Publishing Company.

Hopwood v. Texas, 78 F.3d 932 (1996).

Humphries, F. S. (1995). A short history of blacks in higher education. *The Journal of Blacks in Higher Education, 6,* 57.

Hunt, T. C., & Carper, J. C. (1988). *Religious colleges and universities in America: A selected bibliography.* New York: Garland.

Hunt, T. C., & Carper, J. C. (1996). *Religious higher education in the United States: A source book.* New York: Garland.

Hurtado, S, Carter, D. F., & Spuler, A. (1996). Latino student transition to college: Assessing difficulties and factors in successful college adjustment. *Research in Higher Education, 37,* 135–157.

Jackson, C. L., & Nunn, E. F. (2003). *Historically Black colleges and universities: A reference handbook.* Santa Barbara, CA: ABC Clio.

Jackson, D. H. (2002). Attracting and retaining African American faculty at HBCUs. *Education, 123*(1), 181–185.

Jencks, C., & Riesman, D. (1968). *The academic revolution.* Garden City, NY: Doubleday.

Johnson, B. J., & Harvey, W. (2002). The socialization of black college faculty: Implications for policy and practice. *Review of Higher Education, 25*(3), 297–314.

Johnsrud, L. K., & Heck, R. H. (1998). Faculty worklife: Establishing benchmarks across groups. *Research in Higher Education, 39,* 539–555.

Justiz, M. J., Wilson, R., & Bjork, L. G. (1994). *Minorities in higher education.* Phoenix, AZ: American Council on Education.

Kamens, D. (1971). The college "charter" and college size: Effects on occupational choice and college attrition. *Sociology of Education, 44,* 270–296.

Kaplan, S. (1987, October/November). AASCU's clarion call to state colleges and universities. *Change,* 48–50.

Kasten, K. L. (1984). Tenure and merit pay as rewards for research, teaching, and service at a research university. *Journal of Higher Education, 55,* 500–514.

Katsinas, S. G. (1996). Preparing leaders for diverse institutional settings. In J. C. Palmer & S. G. Katsinas (Eds.), *Graduate and continuing education for community college leaders: What it means today* (New Directions for Community Colleges, No. 95, pp. 15–25). San Francisco: Jossey-Bass.

Keim, M. C. (1989). Two-year college faculty: A research update. *Community College Review, 17*(3) 34–43.

Kennedy, D. (1997). *Academic duty.* Cambridge, MA: Harvard University Press.

Kerlin, S. P., & Dunlap, D. M. (1993). For richer, for poorer: Faculty morale in periods of austerity and retrenchment. *Journal of Higher Education, 64,* 348–377.

Kim, M. M. (2002). Historically black vs. white institutions: Academic developments among black students. *Review of Higher Education, 25*(4), 385–407.

Kimball, B. (1986). *Orators and philosophers: A history of the idea of liberal education.* New York: Teachers College Press.

Kluge, P. F. (2003, February 28). Kamp Kenyon's legacy: Death by tinkering. *The Chronicle of Higher Education,* p. B9.

Komives, S. R., & Woodard, D. B. (2003*). Student services: A handbook for the profession* (4th ed.). San Francisco: Jossey-Bass.

Kuk, L. (2002, December 9). Character: A missing link in student affairs preparation. *NASPA NetResults.* Washington, D.C.: National Association of Student Affairs Administrators. Retrieved June 26, 2003, from http://www.naspa.org/netresults/article.cfm?ID=883

Laden, B. (1999). Two-year Hispanic-serving colleges. In B. Townsend (Ed.), *Two year colleges for women and minorities: Enabling access to the baccalaureate* (pp. 151–194). New York: Falmer.

Laden, B. V. (2001). Hispanic-serving institutions: Myths and realities. *Peabody Journal of Education, 76,* 73–92.

Lane, K. (2001). Educating a growing community. *Black Issues in Higher Education, 18*(16), 28–31.

Lang, E. M. (1999). Distinctively American: The liberal arts college. *Daedalus, 128(1),* 133–134.

Leonard, E. A. (1956). *Origins of personnel services in American higher education.* Minneapolis: University of Minnesota Press.

Lorden, L. P. (1998). Attrition in the student affairs profession. *NASPA Journal, 35,* 207–217.

Lovell, C. D., & Kosten, L. A. (2000). Skills, knowledge, and personal traits necessary for success as a student affairs administrator: A meta-analysis of thirty years of research. *NASPA Journal, 37,* 553–573.

Lucas, C. J. (1994). *American higher education.* New York: St. Martin's Griffin.

Malaney, G. D., & Shively, M. (1995). Academic and social expectations and experiences of first-year students of color. *NASPA Journal, 33,* 3–18.

Massey, W. C. (1994, October). *The public university for the twenty-first century: Beyond the land grant.* David Dodds Henry Lecture, University of Illinois, Chicago. (ERIC Document Reproduction Series No. ED401837)

McGrath, D., & Spear, M. B. (1991). *The academic crisis of the community college.* Albany: The State University of New York Press.

McMurtrie, B. (2000, October 20). Future of religious colleges is bright, say scholars and officials. *The Chronicle of Higher Education,* p. A41.

Michalak, S. J., & Robert, J. F. (1981). Research productivity and teaching effectiveness at a small liberal arts college. *Journal of Higher Education, 52,* 578–597.

Milosheff, E. (1990). Factors contributing to job satisfaction at the community college. *Community College Review, 18,* 12–22.

Mingle, J. R. (1992). *Faculty work and the cost/quality/access collision.* Denver: Education Commission of the States. (ERIC Document Reproduction No. ED356730)

Mooney, C. J. (1994, May 25). What the Lord wanted: Evangel College offers "serious Christians" an alternative to secular institutions. *The Chronicle of Higher Education,* p. A21.

Mooney, C. J. (1995, May 19). Religious revival grips students at church colleges. *The Chronicle of Higher Education,* p. A19.

National Center for Education Statistics. (1999). *National study of postsecondary faculty.* Washington, DC: U.S. Department of Education.

National Center for Education Statistics. (2000). *Integrated postsecondary education data system (IPEDS).* Washington, DC: U.S. Department of Education.

National Center for Education Statistics. (2001a). *Digest of education statistics.* Retrieved September 19, 2003, from http://nces.ed.gov/pubs2002/digest2001/tables/dt027.asp

National Center for Education Statistics. (2001b). *Institutional policies and practices: Results from the 1999 national study of postsecondary faculty, institution survey.* Washington, DC: U. S. Department of Education, Office of Educational Research and Improvement.

National Center for Education Statistics. (2002). *Digest of education statistics, 2001.* Washington, DC: U.S. Department of Education.

Naylor, N. A. (1977). The theological seminary in the configuration of American higher education: The ante-bellum years. *History of Education Quarterly, 17,* 17–30.

Nettles, M. T., Wagener, U., Millett, C. M., & Killenbeck, A. M. (1999). Student retention and progression: A special challenge for private historically Black colleges and universities. In G. H. Gaither (Ed.), *Promising practices in recruitment, remediation, and retention.* (New Directions for Higher Education, No. 108, pp. 51–67). San Francisco: Jossey-Bass.

Neubert, G. A., & Binkso, J. B. (1998). Professional development schools: The proof is in the performance. *Educational Leadership, 55,* 44–6.

Nuss, E. M. (2003). The development of student affairs. In S. R. Komives & D. B. Woodard (Eds.), *Student services: A handbook for the profession* (4th ed., pp. 65–88). San Francisco: Jossey-Bass.

O'Banion, T. (1971). *New directions in community college student personnel programs.* Washington, DC: American College Personnel Association.

O'Brien, E. M., & Zudak, C. (1998). Minority-serving institutions: An overview. In J. P. Merisotis & C. T. O'Brien (Eds.), *Minority-serving institutions: Distinct purposes, common goals* (New Directions for Higher Education, No. 102, pp. 5–15). San Francisco: Jossey-Bass.

O'Grady, J. P. (1969). Control of church-related institutions of higher learning. *Journal of Higher Education, 40,* 108–121.

Ogren, C. A. (2003). Rethinking the "nontraditional" student from a historical perspective: State normal school in the late nineteenth and early twentieth centuries. *The Journal of Higher Education, 74,* 640–664.

O'Keefe, J. M. (1997). *Catholic education at the turn of the new century.* New York: Garland.

Oklahoma Higher Education. (1998). *Oklahoma state regents for higher education student data report.* Retrieved April 1, 2003, from www.okhighered.org/student-data-report/98-99/

Olivas, M. (1997). Research on Latino college students: A theoretical framework and inquiry. In A. Darder, R. Torres, & H. Gutierrez (Eds.), *Latinos and education: A critical reader* (pp. 14–29). New York: Routledge.

Outcalt, C. L. (2002). *A profile of the community college professoriate, 1975–2000.* Unpublished doctoral dissertation, University of California, Los Angeles.

Outcalt, C. L., & Skewes-Cox, T. E. (2002). Involvement, interaction, and satisfaction: The human environment at HBCUs. *Review of Higher Education, 25(3),* 331–347.

Pace, C. R., & Connolly, M. (1999, May-June). *Where are the liberal arts?* Paper presented at the Annual Forum of the Associate for Institutional Research, Seattle, WA. (ERIC Document Reproduction Service No. ED433760)

Pascarella, E. T., & Terenzini, P. T. (1991). *How college affects students.* San Francisco: Jossey-Bass.

Pedersen, R. (1988). Small business and the early public junior college. *Community, Technical, and Junior College Journal, 59*(1), 44–46.

Perna, L. W. (2001). The contribution of historically black colleges and universities to the preparation of African Americans for faculty careers. *Research in Higher Education, 42*(3), 267–295.

Pfnister, A. O. (1984). The role of the liberal arts college: A historical overview of the debates. *Journal of Higher Education, 55,* 145–170.

Pickering, J. W., & Calliotte, J. A. (2000). *Who are we? Where do we want to go?* A report on the membership of the American College Personnel Association. Retrieved October 22, 2002, from http://www.acpa.nche.edu

Plessy v. Ferguson, 163 U.S. 537 (1896).

Presley, J. A. B., & Clery, S. B. (2001). Middle income undergraduates: Where they enroll and how they pay for their education. *Education Statistics Quarterly, 3*(3), 78–83.

Putnam, L. J. (1964). Are church-related schools in danger of disappearing? *Journal of Higher Education, 35,* 344–345.

Rand, E. W. (1956). Selection of board members in Negro church-related colleges. *Journal of Negro Education, 25,* 79–82.

Reisberg, L. (1999, March 5). Enrollments surge at Christian colleges. *The Chronicle of Higher Education,* p. A42.

Reisser, L. (2002). Self-renewal and personal development in professional life. In J. C. Dalton & M. McClinton, *The art and practical wisdom of student affairs leadership* (New Directions for Student Services, No. 98, pp. 49–59). San Francisco: Jossey-Bass.

Rentz, A. (1996). *Student affairs practice in higher education.* Springfield, IL: Charles C. Thomas.

Rentz, A. L., & Saddlemire, G. L. (1988). *Student affairs functions in higher education.* Springfield, IL: Charles C. Thomas.

Resneck Pierce, S. (2000). Change and its consequences: A case study. *Liberal Education, 86*(4), 50–55.

Reynolds, A. (1992). Charting the changes in junior faculty. *Journal of Higher Education, 63,* 637–650.

Rice, R. E. (1996). *Making a place for the new American scholar.* Washington, DC: American Association for Higher Education.

Rodriguez, A. L., Guido-DiBrito, F., Torres, V., & Talbot, D. (2000). Latina college students: Issues and challenges for the 21st century. *NASPA Journal, 37,* 511–527.

Roebuck, J. B., & Murty, K. S. (1993). *Historically Black colleges and universities: Their place in American higher education.* Westport, CT: Praeger.

Rudolph, F. (1962). *The American college and university: A history.* New York: Alfred A. Knopf.

Rudolph, F. (1977). *Curriculum: A history of the American undergraduate course of study since 1636.* San Francisco: Jossey-Bass.

Ruscio, K. P. (1987). The distinctive scholarship of the selective liberal arts college. *Journal of Higher Education, 58,* 205–222.

Saxon, D. S., & Milne, W. I. (1985). Research, graduate and professional education: Some observations and issues. In L. W. Koeplin & D. A. Wilson (Eds.*), The future of state universities* (pp. 9–24). New Brunswick, NJ: Rutgers University Press.

Schmidt, P. (2003, November 28). Academe's Hispanic future. *The Chronicle of Higher Education,* p. A8–A12.

Schnell, J. (1992). *Comparing the role of the teacher in small liberal arts colleges and large public universities.* (ERIC Document Reproduction Service No. ED 349891)

Schulte, L. E., Thompson, F. T., & Hayes, K. (2001). Undergraduate faculty and student perceptions of the ethical climate and its importance in retention. *College Student Journal, 35,* 565–76

Seidman, E. (1985). *In the words of faculty: Perspectives on improving teaching and educational quality in community colleges.* San Francisco: Jossey-Bass.

Shemky, R. L. (1967). Catholic higher education: The effect of the academic environment on the stability of the lay faculty. *Journal of Higher Education, 38,* 70–77.

Slaughter, S., & Leslie, L. L. (1997). *Academic capitalism: Politics, policies and the entrepreneurial university.* Baltimore: The Johns Hopkins University Press.

Smallwood, S. (2002, March 1). Twin setbacks hit faculty-union drives at private colleges. *The Chronicle of Higher Education,* p. A12.

Smart, J. (1986). College effects on occupational status attainment. *Research in Higher Education, 24,* 73–95.

Smart, J. (1988). College influences on graduates' income levels. *Research in Higher Education, 29,* 41–59.

Southern Education Foundation. (1995). *Redeeming the American promise.* Atlanta: Author.

Spangler, M. S., Grosz, K. S., Byrnes, N., Harlan, R., & Romero-Motlagh, O. (1991). *Caught in "upward drift": An assessment of comprehensive universities and colleges.* (ERIC Document Reproduction Service NO. ED333777)

Stahler, G. J., & Tash, W. R. (1994). Centers and institutes in the research university: Issues, problems and prospects. *Journal of Higher Education, 65,* 540–554.

Stamatakos, L. C. (1981a). Student affairs progress toward professionalism: Recommendations for action part I. *Journal of College Student Personnel, 22,* 56–61.

Stamatakos, L. C. (1981b). Student affairs progress toward professionalism: Recommendations for action part II. *Journal of College Student Personnel, 22,* 197–207.

State perspectives on higher education faculty. (2000, December). *Network News, 19,* 1–4.

Stearns, C., & Watanabe, S. (2002). *Hispanic Serving Institutions: Statistical trends from 1990 to 1999* (NCES 2002-051). Washington, DC: U.S. Department of Education, National Center for Education Statistics.

Stober, S. S. (1995). *Survival strategies for liberal arts colleges.* (ERIC Document Reproduction Service No. ED 386101)

Sydow, D. L., & Sandel, R. H. (1998). Making student retention an institutional priority. *Community College Journal of Research and Practice, 22*(7), 635–643.

Tewksbury, D. G. (1932*). The founding of American colleges and universities before the Civil War.* New York: Bureau of Publications, Teachers College, Columbia University.

Thielen, J. R. (2003). Historical overview of American higher education. In S. R. Komives & D. B. Woodard (Eds.), *Student services: A handbook for the profession* (pp. 3–22). San Francisco: Jossey-Bass.

Thiessen, E. J. (2001). *In defence of religious schools and colleges.* Montreal: McGill-Queen's University Press.

Thomas, W. (2002). The moral domain of student affairs leadership. In J. C. Dalton & M. McClinton (Eds.), *The art and practical wisdom of student affairs leadership* (New Directions for Student Services, No. 98, pp. 61–70). San Francisco: Jossey-Bass.

Thompson, C. H. (1960). The present status of the Negro private and church-related college. *Journal of Negro Education, 29,* 227–244.

Tierney, W.G. (1997). Organizational socialization in higher education. *Journal of Higher Education, 68,* 1–16.

Turrentine, C. G., & Conley, V. M. (2001). Two measures of the diversity of the labor pool for entry-level student affairs positions. *NASPA Journal, 39,* 84–102.

Urban, W., & Wagoner, J. (2000). *American education: A history* (2nd ed.). Boston: McGraw-Hill.

U.S. Census Bureau (2002). *Resident population estimates of the United States by sex, race and Hispanic origin: April 1 to July 1, 1999, with short-term projection to June 1, 2001.* Washington, DC: Author.

Van Tassell, F. (1999). Policy impact on professional development schools when faculty and administrator views conflict regarding the university reward system. *Action in Teacher Education, 21*(2), 1–7.

Vaughan, G. B. (1997). The community college's mission and milieu: Institutionalizing community-based programming. In E. A. Boone (Ed.). *Community leadership through community-based programming* (pp. 21–58). Washington DC: Community College Press.

Voorhees, R. A., & Zhou, D. (2000). Intentions and goals at the community college: Associating student perceptions and demographics. *Community College Journal of Research and Practice, 24*(3), 219–232.

Wall, H. M. (1990). *Fierce communion: Family and community in early America.* Cambridge, MA: Harvard University Press.

Wangberg, E. G. (1987, December). Encouraging research and scholarship in master's only institutions. Paper presented at the annual meeting of the Council of Graduate Schools, Washington, DC. (ERIC Document Reproduction Service No. ED292366)

Weissman, J., Bulakowski, C., & Jumisko, M. (1998). A study of White, Black, and Hispanic students' transition to a community college. *Community College Review, 26*(2), 19–42.

The White House Initiative on Educational Excellence for Hispanic Americans. (2000). *What are Hispanic serving institutions?* Washington, DC: Author.

Wilds, J. D., & Wilson, R. (1998). *Minorities in higher education: Twelfth annual status report on minorities in higher education.* Washington, DC: American Council on Education.

Williamson, E. G. (1961). *Student personnel services in colleges and universities.* New York: McGraw-Hill.

Willie, C. V., & Edmonds, R. R. (1978). *Black colleges in America: Challenge, development, survival.* New York: Teachers College Press.

Wilson, R. (2003, November 28). Wanted: Hispanic professors. *The Chronicle of Higher Education,* pp. A15–A16.

Wolfe, A. (2002, February 8). Faith and diversity in American religion. *The Chronicle of Higher Education,* p. B7.

Youn, T. I. K. (1992). The characteristics of faculty in comprehensive institutions. Boston, MA: New England Resource Center for Higher Education. (ERIC Document Reproduction Service No. ED 371691)

Youn, T. I. K., & Gamson, Z. F. (1994). Organizational responses to the labor market: A study of faculty searches in comprehensive colleges and universities. *Higher Education, 28,* 189–205.

Zirkle, P. A. (2001). From the heart of the church, the colleges, or the commentators? *Journal of Law and Education, 30,* 305.

Author Biography

Joan B. Hirt is Associate Professor of Higher Education and Student Affairs in the Department of Educational Leadership and Policy Studies at Virginia Tech. Dr. Hirt earned her B.A. in Russian Studies from Bucknell University in 1972, her M.A.Ed. in Student Personnel from the University of Maryland, College Park in 1979, and her Ph.D. in Higher Education Administration from the University of Arizona in 1992.

She spent 15 years as a student affairs professional, working in residence life, housing and dining services, and a dean of students office before becoming a faculty member in 1994. In the course of her career, Dr. Hirt served as President of the Western Association of College and University Housing Officers. She is the recipient of numerous awards including the Annuit Coeptis Emerging Professional and Annuit Coeptis Senior Professional awards conferred by the American College Personnel Association, the Outstanding Contribution to Student Affairs through Teaching Award presented by the National Association for Student Personnel Administrators Region III, and the Thomas M. Magoon Distinguished Alumni Award conferred by the Counseling and Personnel Services Department at the University of Maryland.

Dr. Hirt has authored or co-authored over 30 refereed articles, books, and monograph chapters. She has co-authored two other volumes on professional issues in student affairs. *Supervising New Professionals in Student Affairs* (2003) was written with Steve Janosik, Don Creamer, Roger Winston, Sue Saunders, and Diane Cooper. The same group published *Learning Through Supervised Practice in Student Affairs* in 2002. While her secondary research endeavors have focused on issues of diversity in higher education, her abiding interest is in issues of professionalization in student affairs.